HERMAN MELVILLE

Herman Melville

AMONG THE MAGAZINES

Graham Thompson

University of Massachusetts Press
Amherst & Boston

Printed in the United States of America

ISBN 978-1-62534-324-6 (paper); 323-9 (hardcover)

Set in Adobe Caslon Pro
Printed and bound by Maple Press, Inc.

Cover design by Sally Nichols
Cover illustration by Carl Emil Doepler, "View of the Interior of the Finishing-room," 1855.
From *The Harper Establishment; or, How the Story Books Are Made* by Jacob Abbott.

Library of Congress Cataloging-in-Publication Data

Names: Thompson, Graham, 1965–author.
Title: Herman Melville : among the magazines / Graham Thompson.
Description: Amherst : University of Massachusetts Press, 2018. Includes |
bibliographical references and index.
Identifiers: LCCN 2017020929| ISBN 9781625343246 (pbk.) | ISBN 9781625343239
(hardcover)
Subjects: LCSH: Melville, Herman, 1819–1891–Criticism and interpretation. |
Periodicals–Publishing–United States–History–19th century |
Literature publishing–United States–History–19th century.
Classification: LCC PS2387 .T46 2018 | DDC 813/.3–dc23
LC record available at https://lccn.loc.gov/201702029

British Library Cataloguing-in-Publication Data
A catalog record for this book is available from the British Library.

For Zoe

Contents

Preface

Ignorance is a great teacher. When I first wrote about Herman Melville nearly twenty years ago, I gave no thought to the original publication of a story I treated as a freestanding piece of fiction in need of interpretation. If, as part of my research, I did read somewhere that "Bartleby, the Scrivener" first appeared anonymously in the November and December 1853 issues of *Putnam's Monthly Magazine,* then that information evidently went in one eye and out the other. I wasn't alone. Between the composition of "The Happy Failure" and "The Fiddler" in the summer of 1853 and the publication of *The Piazza Tales* in May 1856, Herman Melville published seven pieces in *Harper's New Monthly Magazine* and seven—three in serial form—in *Putnam's,* which also rejected "The Two Temples" and serialized *Israel Potter. Harper's* and *Putnam's,* however, attract little more attention in the vast expanse of Melville criticism than an object to which *Putnam's* compared itself in its first editorial of January 1853: a speck of "star-dust" in "the celestial dairy" of America.

Eventually, after more than ten years, the light from that speck of star-dust crossed the galaxy to land on my eye. The more I noticed its gleam, no amount of blinking would wipe it away. Melville worked exclusively as a magazine writer between the completion of his lost novel, *The Isle of the Cross,* in 1853 and the publication of his final novel, *The Confidence-Man,* in 1857. He earned more money from magazine writing in these few years than from the combined sales during his lifetime of *Moby-Dick, Pierre,* and *The Confidence-Man.* The circulation of *Harper's* reached two hundred thousand per issue at its peak, which meant Melville's writing reached a broader audience than ever before. Even the less popular *Putnam's* sold many times more copies per issue than did Melville's novels. Could these simple facts affect our understanding of "Bartleby" and Melville's other stories? Were there new ways to understand Melville and the work he published in *Harper's* and *Putnam's* if we reinstated their ties to 1850s periodical publishing? Were there more intricate stories to tell about Melville's own magazine storytelling? This book is an attempt to overcome my own ignorance and to answer these questions. In short, its response is an emphatic "yes."

Herman Melville: Among the Magazines is the first book to reconnect Melville to a cultural form that attained new significance in the nineteenth century. *Putnam's* and *Harper's* were only two of thousands of magazines that lit up America. The number of weekly and monthly titles grew from a handful in 1800 to over three and a half thousand by the century's end. Many more came and went along the way. A feature of literary life for several decades, magazines and periodicals grew in number from the 1830s and 1840s onward because of the development of a print industry taking advantage of mechanical advances in papermaking and printing, faster transportation networks, healthy literacy rates, and expanding and diversifying demand from educated urban consumers. Once established, the momentum of magazine culture was unstoppable. Multi-authored, serially published, and collaboratively produced, the magazine form bequeathed mass culture to America after the Civil War. Like many other writers, Melville was swept up in the surf of this magazine mania. Writing the book I discovered a new Melville "embedded" in the forgotten materials, editors, writers, and literary traditions of the magazine world.

I also found an author who responded to magazine writing with confidence rather than skepticism or anxiety. Melville's work for *Putnam's* and *Harper's* shows that he extended his fascination with the paper world on which he wrote and on which industrialized print culture relied; writing for magazines ratified Melville's belief that authorship was a material as much as an intellectual activity and reaffirmed his sense of himself as a writer after the commercial failures of *Moby-Dick* and *Pierre.* To think of Melville as a downwardly mobile writer forced to grub along in an inferior literary sphere is to misunderstand his faith in his own art and the significance of magazines to the cultural habits of literate Americans. Melville's writerly confidence is evident in the way he responded both pragmatically and with dazzling displays of innovation to the conventions of magazine publishing, the aesthetic and intellectual preferences of editors, and the staple genres of magazine content. Ranging across these genres as he wrote for *Harper's* and *Putnam's,* Melville succeeded where many other writers in the 1850s failed: he reinvented the magazine sketch and tale traditions in ways that helped create the modern short story.

I prefer to tell the story of this literary achievement rather than read Melville's magazine writing symptomatically for broader cultural, historical, or political diagnosis. In part, this is because the results of such diagnoses are already numerous and powerful. But there are two others reasons. First, concentrating on his literary achievements helps us better see Melville's magazine years as a transitional phase in a long and varied career, one in which he was not always a writer, did not always have ambitions to be a writer, professional or otherwise, and would not always be a writer for whom making a living from writing was a primary concern. Second, that speck of star-dust leads the eye away from readers and their judgments to writers and their actions; from the complexities of various aspects of American history as they emerge in Melville's representation of them to the contingencies of magazine publication. As much as they are literary narratives subject to interpretation following publication, Melville's stories are objects that narrate their own journey to magazine publication. By reading Melville's writing as magazine writing, I concentrate on the sequence that connected thinking, writing, and magazine publication and attend to the practicalities of writing that existed before the cycle of distribution, circulation, and reading was set in train.

I am grateful to the many people who helped turn up the dimmer switch on the narrow beam of light with which *Among the Magazines* began. The British Academy and the University of Nottingham provided invaluable financial support. For their patience and direction, I thank the archivists and librarians at the Houghton Library, Harvard; the Department of Rare Books and Special Collections at Princeton University Library; and the Morgan Library & Museum in New York City. Although this book spends little time on nineteenth-century readers, it had some careful readers of its own. And I am grateful to many other interlocutors who provided advice, stimulation, mentorship, and support. So my thanks to Hester Blum, John Fagg, Paul Giles, Leon Jackson, Richard King, Bob Levine, Katie McGettigan, Pete Messent, Dave Murray, Judie Newman,

Matthew Pethers, John Stauffer, Anthea Trodd, Robin Vandome, Sara Wood, and Brian Yothers. For taking up my original proposal and persevering with me, great thanks to Brian Halley. For the keenest of eyes, thank you to Mary Bellino. I take responsibility, of course, for any botches.

Zoe Trodd deserves a paragraph of her own. This book only flourished in her ambit. The year in which much of it was written was also a year that changed my life in ways I hadn't believed possible. The two events—book and life—now seem inseparable. Like us. Whatever qualities I now see in this book I know are there because of Zoe's help. You are a dream from which I hope never to awake.

Part of chapter 1 appeared in "The 'Plain Facts' of Fine Paper in 'The Paradise of Bachelors and the Tartarus of Maids,'" *American Literature* 84.3 (2012): 505–32. It is republished by permission of Duke University Press. Other parts of the book appeared in "Bartleby and the Magazine Fiction," in *The New Cambridge Companion to Herman Melville,* ed. Robert Levine (New York: Cambridge University Press), 99–112, and are reprinted with permission.

Abbreviations

The following volumes of *The Writings of Herman Melville* (Evanston and Chicago: Northwestern University Press and the Newberry Library) are abbreviated in the text and notes:

C *Correspondence,* ed. Lynn Horth (1993).

IP *Israel Potter: His Fifty Years of Exile,* ed. Harrison Hayford, Hershel Parker, and G. Thomas Tanselle (1982).

J *Journals,* ed. Howard C. Horsford with Lynn Horth (1989).

MD *Moby-Dick; or, The Whale,* ed. Harrison Hayford, Hershel Parker, and G. Thomas Tanselle (1988).

P *Pierre; or, The Ambiguities,* ed. Harrison Hayford, Hershel Parker, and G. Thomas Tanselle (1971).

PT *The Piazza Tales and Other Prose Pieces, 1839–1860,* ed. Harrison Hayford, Alma A. MacDougall, and G. Thomas Tanselle (1987).

PP *Published Poems,* ed. Robert C. Ryan, Harrison Hayford, Alma MacDougall Reising, and G. Thomas Tanselle (2009).

T *Typee: A Peep at Polynesian Life,* ed. Harrison Hayford, Hershel Parker, and G. Thomas Tanselle (1968).

WJ *White-Jacket, or The World in a Man-of-War,* ed. Harrison Hayford, Hershel Parker, and G. Thomas Tanselle (1970).

HERMAN MELVILLE

Introduction

Early on Saturday, January 11, 1851, Herman Melville headed out into the snowy landscape typical of a western Massachusetts winter with his wife, Elizabeth, his mother, Maria, and his sister Frances. Pulled by their horse, Charlie, the family traveled by sleigh several miles northeast through the Berkshire Hills. Melville was by all accounts an energetic sleigh driver. He regularly entertained guests and relations with afternoon rides to pick up letters from the local post office and on circuits of Arrowhead farm; ten days earlier he had collected his wife by sleigh from the train depot when she returned from her Thanksgiving and Christmas trip to Boston. The destination of this Saturday excursion was Dalton, a small town on the east branch of the Housatonic River, whose waters joined the west and southwest branches just north of Melville's Arrowhead home in Pittsfield. The family did not return home until nearly six in the evening. But the trip was not just an opportunity for Melville to spend time driving through picturesque winter scenes shaped by the frozen form of water; he was drawn to Dalton because of what happened there to water's liquid form.

Located at a point where the Housatonic falls from the hills and picks up speed, the town was perfectly suited to water-powered mill industry. Dalton benefited from one further advantage: a substratum of quartz beneath the surrounding hills that produced the purified water supply prized by manufacturers of durable, high-quality paper. Dalton's population in 1850 was just over one thousand; when Melville and his family visited they would have found five working paper mills, and another opened later in the year. In January 1851, Melville was in the middle of writing *Moby-Dick* (1851). Although no original manuscript survives, he likely wrote the later parts of his great novel of the watery ocean on distilled Housatonic water given substance by the linen rags with which Dalton manufacturers combined it to make paper.

The trip to Dalton was part of Melville's working week. He acquired the physical material on which to write and he would make papermaking his theme in the second half of "The Paradise of Bachelors and the Tartarus of Maids," a story published four years later in *Harper's New Monthly Magazine.* Some weeks after the trip, Melville wrote to the New York editor and publisher Evert Duyckinck on paper embossed with a papermaker's mark: "CARSON'S DALTON MS." Beside the stamp Melville annotated the words: "—about 5 miles from here, North East. I went there & got a sleigh-load of this paper. A great neighborhood for authors, you see, is Pittsfield" (*C* 179). The Berkshire Hills were the home or summer home of several other writers familiar to Melville during this period: Nathaniel Hawthorne, William Cullen Bryant, Oliver Wendell Holmes, Fanny Kemble, Henry Wadsworth Longfellow, and Catharine Maria Sedgwick.[1] Rather than this writerly network, however, the annotation on the letter to Duyckinck—no doubt also intended to puncture Duyckinck's metropolitan sense of superiority—suggests that more important to Melville's understanding of what constituted a "great neighborhood for authors" was his place in the heart of the Berkshire County papermaking industry.

Melville's proximity to the papermaking industry illustrates that as much as writing relies on an author's cerebral and imaginative faculties, it also relies on the material and practical endeavor of authors in a publishing system. Acquiring paper was only the first in a sequence of events that became increasingly pressing for Melville after his visit to Dalton. While he wrote new sections of *Moby-Dick* in his notoriously illegible handwriting, his sisters transcribed and made fair copy of what he had written. Melville also prepared *Moby-Dick* for publication like no other of his novels. He finished writing the book without the offer of a contract; Harper & Brothers, publisher of his four previous novels, turned down Melville's request for an advance on the grounds that he remained in debt to them for nearly $700 following poor sales of *Mardi* (1849) and weaker sales for *Redburn* (1849) and *White-Jacket* (1850) than expected of the author of *Typee* (1846) and *Omoo* (1847). Melville only finalized a contract with Harper once he had himself engaged a printer—Robert Craighead of New York, printer of *Typee*—to set the type and produce printing plates for the novel; Harper then paid for and used these plates. During the summer of 1851, between Pittsfield and temporary sojourns in the dust and heat of New York City organizing printing and contractual arrangements, Melville finished writing *Moby-Dick* while Craighead worked simultaneously on the typesetting; Melville rather than the publisher took responsibility for editing and proofing (*MD* 660–64).[2]

For all books, being read is the denouement to a much longer story of creation and distribution that in the nineteenth century began with rags in a paper mill and ended with the postal service, the bookseller, and the distribution agent. And being read, as Leah Price has argued of Victorian Britain, was just one of many uses to which books were put.[3] One part of bringing a book to publication is writing its literary content; the copy of *Moby-Dick* that readers held in their hands in 1851 was also the result of Melville's idiosyncratic involvement in its publishing journey. This book takes up the significance of a different kind of publishing journey during the years from 1853 to 1856, when Melville's writing appeared first in magazine rather than book form. Spared the rigors imposed by *Moby-Dick,* when he wrote for magazines Melville nevertheless faced new writing and publishing practices and new relationships that shaped the next phase of his writing career.

My primary aim, then, is to fathom Melville's magazine writing by doing better justice to the cultural form in which it first appeared. Melville published some of his most widely read and admired work—"Bartleby, the Scrivener" and "Benito Cereno," for instance—during this period. Magazines were not merely the containers of his work. They mediated and shaped Melville's literary ambitions, and the stories were print objects with specific publishing histories; Melville had to engage with magazine publishers, editors, and conventions if he wanted to see his writing in print and receive payment. In short, magazines presented Melville with new challenges. This book examines his literary response.

Entering the Magazine Machine

Melville would have been unusual among nineteenth-century writers had he not written for magazines, but it was not inevitable that he became a magazine writer. His reluctance to commit himself to the periodical form is evident on two occasions in 1850 and 1851. The first provides only circumstantial evidence but suggests pragmatic thoughts were already exercising him. On August 10, 1850, Melville's father-in-law, Lemuel Shaw, received a letter from the editor of the popular magazine *Godey's Lady's Book* asking for Melville's current address. At the back of the January 1851 issue of *Godey's* an advertisement appeared describing the delights awaiting readers during the following year. Beneath a headline proclaiming "THE LADY'S BOOK FOR 1851 SHALL EXCEED EVERY OTHER MAGAZINE" was a three-column list of writers familiar to the magazine's readers, together with "some writers of great celebrity, whose names have not yet appeared in the 'Book.'" The penultimate name in the third column was Herman Melville, just above "Nathl. Hawthorn."[4] Presuming Shaw passed along Melville's address and Melville replied positively to *Godey's* request, he was clearly thinking of supplementing his income with magazine work. There is, however, no evidence that Melville ever broke away from writing *Moby-Dick* to submit contributions to the magazine.

The second occasion is the letter to Duyckinck pointing out what "a great neighborhood for authors, you see, is Pittsfield." Melville's purpose in this letter was primarily to refuse Duyckinck's request that he send a contribution—"A dash of salt spray"—and a daguerreotype of himself for *Holden's Dollar Magazine,* a new publication Duyckinck was due to begin editing with his brother, George, in April 1851. The terms of Melville's rejection of the daguerreotype are well known: as "almost everybody is having his 'mug' engraved nowadays . . . to see one's 'mug' in a magazine, is presumptive evidence that he's a nobody. . . . I respectfully decline being oblivionated by a Daguerreotype." The written contribution Melville refused by emphasizing that his Berkshire County residence had removed him from the literary culture of New York City and the persona of the famous young writer of sea fiction that Duyckinck was asking him to reprise: "Where am I to get salt spray here in inland Pittsfield? I shall have to import it from foreign parts. All I now have to do with salt, is when I salt my horse & cow." Neither did Melville want distractions, even the distraction of "so small a thing" as writing for a magazine, that would take him away from the writing of *Moby-Dick*: "I am not in the humor to write the kind of thing you need," he wrote Duyckinck (*C* 179–80). By 1853, after the failures of *Moby-Dick* and *Pierre* (1852) and the rejection by Harper & Brothers of the now lost novel *The Isle of the Cross,* Melville could not afford to do without such distractions.

The magazine environment of the 1850s was febrile. An average of 150 magazines were founded each year of the decade, and so Melville was soon handed the opportunity to be a magazine writer again in October 1852, when he received a letter from the publisher of his first novel.[5] George Palmer Putnam was planning "an original periodical of a character different from any now in existence" and wanted "to have the best talent of the country to aid us in the undertaking." Putnam was not singling out Melville. He sent the stock letter to dozens of other American writers, including Emerson, Hawthorne, Longfellow, Thoreau, and Cooper. To achieve his ambitions for the magazine, Putnam made it clear that as "gratuitous contributions ought not to be relied on, even though they could be, we expect to pay as liberally as the nature of the work will allow for all articles that we accept."[6] Melville did not respond to Putnam's call until the following summer, by which point he had also reached agreement with the Harper firm to write for their magazine. *Harper's New Monthly* first appeared in June 1850, publishing largely reprinted and imported material, but soon started to include more native content as competing magazines such as *Godey's* and *Putnam's* advertised the American pedigree of their writers. The competition in books between Melville's two publishers now moved into the world of magazines. The deal Melville reached with Harper was that any payment for his magazine writing would not be set against the debts accrued by his novels. At this point Melville again started to earn money from his writing. Now, though, he was a magazine writer.

The arrival of *Harper's* and *Putnam's* indicates how the magazine market diversified after the 1840s. Already successful book publishers, the owners of these new entrants to the magazine world brought with them innovative methods and standards to service the stratifying taste cultures evident particularly among growing numbers of urban consumers. Magazine publishing entered a new phase of development at precisely this point. Meredith McGill ends her study of "the culture of reprinting" in the year Melville published his first story in *Putnam's.* This magazine, McGill argues, with its emphasis on indigenous content, marked a decisive shift away from the "exuberant understanding of culture as iteration and not origination" that marked the 1830s and '40s, when the unauthorized reprinting of foreign literature—in books and magazines—was at its peak.[7] How, then, does this book navigate the new magazine terrain of which Melville was now part?

This terrain is available to us largely thanks to the enormous array of digitization projects in the late 1990s and 2000s that made nineteenth-century magazines more easily accessible.[8] One aim of this book is to counterbalance an unintended consequence of digitization: the consolidation of the critic as a vicarious reader. The raison d'être of digitization is reading, and digitization relies on making available facsimile pages of magazines as they first appeared. But digitization also instigates particular kinds of critical reading. Because the sheer volume of material prohibits command over magazine content, critics have better explored the cultural work magazine consumption performed rather than the material history or significance of specific magazine pieces or magazine writers. Consequently, we know how magazines mediated nineteenth-century ideas and serviced an increasingly important middle class eager to consume its own image in the pages of magazines.[9] By prioritizing the readers who consumed magazines, and the social and cultural contexts, networks, and media histories of which readers and magazines were part, what we know above all else are the ideological habitats of reading communities, which magazines did not simply cater to but helped create. This work is clearly important and enlivens any discussion of nineteenth-century literature and culture. But it is not the history of magazines. In training the critical eye on reading, digitization leaves in the dark a world less easily preserved but without which Melville's magazine writing would never even have reached its readers.[10]

As a way of starting to make that world visible, consider this example. To achieve his ambitions for what would become *Putnam's Monthly,* Putnam inspired contributions from the recipients of his stock letter by appealing to the yardstick of quality. "The facilities connected with an established publishing business," he claimed, "will enable us to place the work at once on a high footing."[11] The "facilities" Putnam had in mind were the materials, personnel, and practices he could bring into alignment: high-quality paper, on which he insisted; fresh type set by John Trow, a leading New York printer and renowned early adopter of new technology; an editorial team of experienced journalists and writers—Charles Frederick Briggs,

George William Curtis, and Parke Godwin; a stable of artists and engravers Putnam had been employing since the 1840s; and a subscription list of distinction bought from the owners of the defunct *Whig Review*. For Putnam, the quality of his magazine would be guaranteed not only by content; the object that reached the hands of his reader should be equally distinguished. Still relatively little is known about how this sequence of managed magazine materiality accommodated Melville or how writing for magazines shaped his work. The same is true of Hawthorne. Poe is slightly better served, as are Stowe, Henry James, and other important popular nineteenth-century writers such as E. D. E. N. Southworth and Fanny Fern. But even in these instances, the tendency is for magazine publication to play an ancillary role to the broader historical and ideological contexts in whose shadow material publication history can seem antiquarian by comparison.[12]

In contrast, this book focuses on writing rather than reading. Other than the magazine editors who read Melville's work, the nineteenth-century readers of *Harper's* and *Putnam's* remain largely opaque. By taking a writer's-eye view of magazine publishing, Melville's place within it, and his exploration of its limits and possibilities, I take up the story from McGill's endpoint and ask how Melville responded to the demand for literary origination. The answers this book provides, particularly in chapter 5, supplement McGill's work by showing that iteration and origination were two ends of a spectrum whose intermediate points Melville often occupied. Melville offered plenty of origination. He also relied on a version of the reprinting ethos for "Bartleby," which had very clear origins in the first chapter of James Maitland's *A Lawyer's Story* (1853). And Melville "reprinted" the forgotten narratives on which he based *Israel Potter* and "Benito Cereno" but edited them so thoroughly that they passed as original works.

By looking out from the latticework of magazine publishing from a writer's-eye view, this book asks: What did it mean to be a magazine writer in the 1850s? What did it require of an author, especially an author like Melville who turned to magazines after writing novels? How did Melville understand, anticipate, and adjust to the magazine form and where is the evidence in the work he published? Under what circumstances did editors judge and publish his work? In short, what is the ante-consumption history of Melville's magazine writing?

The Embedded Author

I use the concept of "embedded authorship" to help answer these questions. My understanding of this concept forms at the confluence of recent approaches to authorship in nineteenth-century America and a well-established critical tradition that has long grappled with spatial metaphors to understand Melville's place in literary and cultural history. From Lewis Mumford's depiction of him standing "alone in a desert" to William Spanos's description of the "exilic silence" of his later work, Melville exists as a writer in isolation. In Nina Baym's Möbius strip–like formulation, Melville occupies the position of an insider who becomes an outsider to offer "consensus criticism of the consensus," while for Samuel Otter, Melville has "an inside sense of the power of ideology, its satisfactions and its incarcerations." In his short fiction, Marvin Fisher argues, Melville chooses "to *go under* as a literary strategy, to become our first major underground writer." For William Dillingham, this fiction is where "an unfolding . . . takes place on the second plane submerged beneath layers of inoffensive wit, congenial reminiscing, and Irvingesque worldly maturity."[13]

Neither does Melville sit comfortably in place in the mid-nineteenth century. The title of Fisher's first chapter, "Portrait of the Artist in America," suggests Melville's Joycean, proto-modernist qualities; Mumford describes Melville as "a modernist before his time"; while for Spanos the later work is not only "proleptic of the poststructuralist or postmodern occasion" but of "proleptic import for the contemporary occasion."[14] Isolated, exiled, outside, inside, under, beneath, and out of sequence: the spaces Melville occupies see him dislocated from the more ordinary and everyday spaces of nineteenth-century America. This books reorients Melville's work in a slightly different way: by embedding rather than dislocating. Melville and his writing were recovered in the twentieth century and pushed above the surrounding terrain in the topography of American literary culture; my aim is to press the writer and his writing back, so they share the same contour lines with, and nestle more fittingly against, the practicalities of the writing and publishing life in which they were once grounded.

Embedded authorship takes its lexical cue from Leon Jackson's study of literary markets and society in nineteenth-century America, but repurposes embeddedness to suit my concern with the material creation of magazines. Jackson's work is important because it drills down into the specificities of authorship to question long-standing assumptions about literary production and circulation. Primarily, it undercuts the idea that gradual and inevitable professionalization in a singular marketplace was the distinctive transformation of nineteenth-century authorship. Jackson shows that authors existed in multiple economies where the circulation of books—through trade, as gifts, or in other forms of exchange—helped consolidate "social bonds" to the extent that "webs of connection . . . were no less important a part of a transaction than any money that might have changed hands." The more important story of the nineteenth century, he argues, is how those webs dissolved and lost significance as literary exchange became more impersonal. As cash and contracts assumed greater significance, social bonds gave way to "various mediatory individuals and agencies who stood between an author and his or her readers." What distinguished the first half of the nineteenth century, Jackson concludes, was the "social disembedding" of authorial activity.[15]

The speed and reach of this disembedding was variable. Francesca Sawaya, for instance, outlines the persistence of philanthropy and patronage to literary activity for writers including Mark Twain, William Dean Howells, Henry James, Charles Chesnutt, and Theodore Dreiser into the twentieth century.[16] But for Melville the case is clearer. In his preference for the Berkshire County papermaking industry over the region's network of writers one can see "social disembedding" in action. Following in the wake of his removal to Pittsfield from New York City, Melville distanced himself from the bonds established through his publishers and the appearance and success of his early work. Although he remained on personable terms with Duyckinck, even after a lukewarm review of *Moby-Dick* in *The Literary World,* Melville left behind potentially significant social affiliations that could have supported his future career.

Jackson's model is by far the best available for understanding the changing complexion of literary markets in the nineteenth century. But it says more about the economies in which authorship operated than authorship itself. By drawing on the work of the economic anthropologist Karl Polanyi, Jackson takes a structural approach in which authorship moves to the rhythms of economic and social forces. Ultimately, economies always determine authorship: if an economy is embedded, literary activity serves the function of cementing social bonds; if an economy is disembedded, literary activity becomes a financial or contractual practice. Jackson's transactional approach to authorship also means that exchange is his primary focus rather than the composition of literary objects. But authorship can precede the exchange, or even the potential exchange, of a literary object. If a literary object is an effect, exchange is not its only cause. And exchange certainly does not predictably determine the form and content, the shape and nature, of a literary object.

The changes Jackson describes as social disembedding had practical consequences for writers who needed to adjust their bearings to the altered dynamics of book and magazine publishing. As a result of his removal to Pittsfield and his decision to write for magazines in the wake of *Pierre,* Melville had to establish new working relationships with those other "mediatory individuals and agencies"—papermakers, typesetters, printers, magazines, editors, and publishers—who managed the sequence of events that turned rags and water into books and magazines in a depersonalizing environment. While no longer serving the social purpose of an earlier moment, neither were these working relationships straightforwardly economic or marketized. Nor were they just the context in which writers were situated. Instead, these relationships were part of a chain of material creation that included writers—in addition to many other actors and events—and to which writers improvised pragmatic responses. When I say that Melville was embedded in these material relations, then, I use embeddedness not in the strictly socioanthropological sense that Jackson uses it, but metaphorically to indicate spatial connection to that chain of material creation.

An author's embeddedness might be deep or shallow. Buying paper and transporting it home from a mill on a sleigh is a deeper form of embeddedness than Thomas Carlyle's employment of a stationery manufacturer, Parkins & Gotto, to service his paper needs. Embeddedness may also be strong or weak. Melville never shared as supportive a relationship with any of his publishers as Hawthorne shared with William Ticknor. Instead, his relationship with Putnam and the Harpers was pragmatic and businesslike on all sides. Embeddedness can be close or distant. Poe was so beset by the business of magazine publishing that he was editing magazines in which his tales and poems were also appearing. Melville remained in Pittsfield throughout his magazine-writing career and worked to no schedule except his own. So while Melville probably had a heightened understanding of the interaction of a writer with the physical materials of writing after his visit to Dalton, he lacked—and showed no signs of wanting to cultivate—the editorial guidance a Ticknor might have provided to turn his career in a different direction. Unlike Poe, Melville never got so close to magazines that he became an editor, but, as I show in chapter 5, editing was sufficiently important for him to assume the role of editor when he customized the real-life events that inspired *Israel Potter* and "Benito Cereno."

A writer's embeddedness can also change over time. Writers can move from being suppliers of content to editors of content. Charles Frederick Briggs and George William Curtis, two characters who reappear in more detail later in this book, were both editors of *Putnam's*. But Briggs first had ambitions as a novelist and achieved some success in the 1840s; Curtis first wrote travel narratives and social satires. Curtis, in particular, remained reluctant to become a full-time paid editor. But the changing landscape of publishing saw both of them making their livings primarily through editing in the 1850s. Their embeddedness developed unpredictably, and they found themselves in unexpected roles that shaped their future careers. In this transition it is also possible to see how embeddedness is bidirectional. Writers and authors respond to the changing nature of the publishing environment in ways that then allow them to shape the nature of literary activity in that environment. While he was acting as gatekeeper at *Putnam's* and defining its reputation, Curtis was also writing a regular column for *Harper's*.

Like the Housatonic River picking up tributaries on its journey toward the ocean, so other processes—transcribing, editing, printing—supplement the journey of writing toward publication that in Melville's case began with purchasing the paper on which to write. Embedded authorship emphasizes that although an author's stories are subject to interpretation following publication, they are also material objects that witness the circumstances and processes by which they come to publication. Neither the complexion nor the coordination of this preconsumption process are yet fully understood in the case of Melville's magazine writing. But magazines were not just the symptom of a mass culture whose momentum spilled them across the streets, parlors, and railway carriages of the United States; magazines were the material objects and the cultural form—multi-authored, collaboratively produced, serially published—whose capacity to organize the various specialized elements of production bequeathed mass culture to America in the late nineteenth century.

By prioritizing the magazine, I develop my concept of embedded authorship in three directions pertinent to Melville. First of all, by their nature magazine contributions required a different relationship between author and publisher than did a novel. For Melville there was certainly none of the protracted contractual negotiation at which he had shown himself to be increasingly inept, even with his lawyer-brother Allan acting as attorney. If the coming to publication of *Moby-Dick* was unusual, when negotiating over *Pierre* Melville just made a bad deal. He received royalties of twenty-five cents per copy, but only after sales reached the 1,190 necessary for Harper to recoup its costs. A paltry 233 copies qualified for the royalty in the first year, nowhere near enough to clear Melville's exiting debt to his publisher. Fire destroyed unsold copies when the Harper warehouse burned down in December 1853 and, despite a short reprint run in 1855, Melville did not receive a single cent on the book. With *The Isle of the Cross* he never got as far as a contract.

Writing for magazines removed Melville from the hands of publishers and into the hands of editors whose priority was getting the next month's issue ready for print. At *Harper's* Melville's work passed through the hands of Henry Raymond, while at *Putnam's* Charles Frederick Briggs and George William Curtis were the key intermediaries. Each issue of *Harper's* and *Putnam's* contained at least fifteen to twenty different sections—sometimes more—comprising stories, essays, sketches, reviews, and various editorial pieces. Magazines were exercises in collaboration; to stand a chance of succeeding in a competitive market, print and production processes needed efficient management. Melville was now one among many authors of these magazines. To keep things straightforward writers were paid by the page. Rates varied from writer to writer, but Melville received the relatively high amount of five dollars. As long as his stories were accepted, he was paid. From his magazine fiction during these years, Melville earned $1,329.50, or an average of almost $450 per year. This exceeded his lifetime earnings from both *Moby-Dick* and *Pierre* (*PT* 494).[17] As a magazine writer, then, Melville was embedded in new kinds of relationships with editors and publishers, where the stakes of each transaction were lower but, when combined, far more rewarding.

The fiction Melville wrote for *Harper's* and *Putnam's* was also embedded literally in the magazines themselves. With the exception of "The Encantadas," which appeared under the pseudonym Salvator R. Tarnmoor, *Harper's* and *Putnam's* published all of Melville's fiction anonymously. Without the imprimatur of his name and beyond the bounds of his reputation, Melville's magazine writing rubbed shoulders with all manner of prosaic and exotic company typical of the miscellaneous nature of magazines. Neither did Melville have any control over when his stories appeared in *Harper's* and *Putnam's*; sometimes they were published several months after submission and payment. Together with the contingencies of location and juxtaposition, this meant magazines embedded Melville's anonymous authorship between their covers in a way that did little to distinguish writers and instead sacrificed them for the sake of the magazine's identity.

Finally, to work as magazine fiction, Melville's writing needed to embed itself within the forms, genres, and conventions in which magazines traded. Melville was familiar with the form and content of magazines. He subscribed to *The Literary World* (until early 1852) and to *Harper's,* and even in his famous letter to Hawthorne complaining that "dollars damn me" he mentions having read Hawthorne's "The Unpardonable Sin" in, appropriately enough, *Dollar Magazine.* Magazines were not a mystery to Melville; he understood their conventions in the same way he understood the conventions of the sea fiction and travel narratives he embraced so successfully in his early books. Although he explored the genre of historical fiction in *Israel Potter* and "Benito Cereno," the modes in which Melville worked were principally the sketch and the tale, or what Melville would help become the short story. When critics uproot Melville's stories, shake them free of the magazines in which they first appeared, and examine them in the clear light of the laboratory rather than the woody shade of the planted border, too often they develop characteristics thought to be evidence of some new species. But the originality and innovation of Melville's stories only becomes apparent when they are set against their magazine companions. Reading Melville's work as magazine fiction means recognizing its embeddedness in the generic conventions of magazine writing.

Melville's Magazine Legacy

Embedding Melville in the magazine world also affords the opportunity to return anew to a conundrum often posed of him: Why did he fall into obscurity and why was he not understood by his contemporaries to be the important writer he is considered today? One further aim of this book is to suggest new ways to think about this puzzle. After *Typee,* Melville wrote seven novels, including *The Isle of the Cross,* plus all of the magazine pieces; he published his final novel, *The Confidence-Man,* in 1857. *Moby-Dick* may have disappointed readers of Melville's earlier work, while *Pierre* baffled and angered them, but the possibility was not lost that Melville would again write something to satisfy a book-buying audience. Neither were reviews of *The Confidence-Man* disastrous compared to *Pierre,* especially in Britain; they were, though, noticeably shorter and fewer in number. Even the good reviews looked back fondly to *Typee* and *Omoo* as they overestimated the capacity of Melville's reputation to sell books; the bad reviews contrasted Melville's Mississippi masquerade with the earlier work even more starkly.[18] In the space of ten years Melville found an audience only to lose it. The literary world in which he wrote quickly used up the accelerant of his early work; he burned brightly but no back-up was in place to help him preserve fuel.

The magazine years, then, are the fulcrum on which the beam of Melville's reputation and success balances. Three years before his death in 1891, Melville published a collection of poems, *John Marr and Other Sailors,* for which only one newspaper notice survives. The reviewer reminds his readers that "the reputation of no American writer stood higher forty years ago than that of Herman Melville" before judging that "his verse is marked by the same untrained imagination which distinguishes his prose."[19] Yet the magazine years also interrupt this declension narrative. The subscription and readership numbers of *Harper's* and *Putnam's* mean Melville was more widely read than ever. Unfortunately, given that Melville's contributions appeared anonymously, most readers were unaware who they were reading. The magazine form supporting Melville's writing career at the healthy rate of five dollars a page simultaneously concealed his identity to the readers who might become buyers of his books.

Of course, other factors contributed to Melville's failure to recover an audience, not least his determination to experiment; and *Israel Potter* and

The Piazza Tales were made available to readers in book form, the latter albeit with a publisher, Dix & Edwards—owner of *Putnam's* from March 1855 and publisher of *The Confidence-Man*—that went out of business in August 1857. The important point is that when *The Confidence-Man* was published Melville was more widely read than he had ever been. After complaining to Hawthorne that "dollars damn me!" Melville also wrote: "What I feel most moved to write, that is banned—it will not pay. Yet, altogether, write the *other* way I cannot" (*C* 191). Written while he was finishing *Moby-Dick,* this comment has come to stand as a convenient shorthand identifying Melville's dissatisfaction with the demands of the literary market. But the comment is better understood in the context of the completion of that large and difficult novel. When it came to writing for magazines, Melville proved that he could undoubtedly "write the *other* way."

Paying attention to Melville's embeddedness in magazine forms and publishing helps us reassess his place in the literary culture of the 1850s and the criteria by which we should judge his reputation and success. Rather than an addendum to a once promising career, the magazine years saw Melville's writing flourish in new, imaginative, and popular ways. Looking at its reception cannot measure the success of this writing. Beyond brief appraisals in the letters of a small literary circle who knew of Melville's authorship, no records exist of what most readers thought, and magazines, apart from brief newspaper notices commenting on the content of new issues, were not reviewed like books. That Melville's magazine enterprise was temporary, only adequately rather than richly rewarded, and did not lead to commercially successful books was the fault of neither Melville nor the reading public, nor even his publishers. The assumption these effects should follow results from an anachronistic understanding of a literary world more fluid, less professionalized, and less secure than what developed in the twentieth century.

In emphasizing the idiosyncratic nature of Melville's experience of magazine writing, I share Trish Loughran's view of the print world. While industrial changes affecting the production and circulation of print after the 1820s may have eventually centralized literary production, they also produced "simultaneous experiences of *dis*integration and national fragmentation" whose material evidence often evades retrospective impulses to flatten and unify national development.[20] Melville's experience is instructive, but if it was typical of anything at all about magazine publishing in the 1850s, dropping in and dropping out of the magazine world as Melville did was typical only of the discontinuity that plagued magazines. Some, like *Putnam's,* dazzled but were snuffed out relatively quickly because they were not financially viable; many others were damp squibs that lasted only a single issue; only the lucky ones like *Harper's* perfected a formula that enabled them to burn brightly and continuously over many decades. As magazines came and went, so did opportunities for writers.

Renewed interest and appreciation of the poetry Melville turned to writing in the 1860s helps cast the magazine years as a transitional phase in a long and varied writing career.[21] Melville, like any other author trying to earn money by writing, was never entirely outside a market economy, since one's reputation commodifies the possibilities of one's future publishability. But it is a mistake to think that the desire to write, or the necessity of doing so, is always oriented to, or determined by, an economic market. In 1847, after the publication of *Typee* but before the publication of *Omoo,* Melville was engaged to Elizabeth and spent time in Washington with his brother Allan looking for a political appointment to ease the financial transition into marriage. Before he began writing magazine fiction in 1853 there was some prospect he might be appointed U.S. consul to the Sandwich Islands. In 1866, at the age of forty-seven, he took up employment as a New York customs officer. Writing was only one among several ways by which Melville earned, or thought of earning, a living; his commercial success and failure was contingent on an admixture of impulses and events sometimes within but often beyond his control given the volatile publishing culture of nineteenth-century America.

This book, then, cares little for narratives of obscurity and decline. The apocryphal story that Herman Melville became Henry Melville in a *New York Times* obituary is an invention of the twentieth century.[22] O. G. Hillard was responsible for the obituary, which appeared a week after the author's death. For Hershel Parker, Hillard's claim that Melville was the equal only of James Russell Lowell—the poet, editor of the *Atlantic Monthly,* and politician who died six weeks before Melville—does not do justice to Melville's greatness. But Melville's greatness as a writer belongs to the twentieth century as well. Hillard makes the more compelling point that one chooses obscurity as much as one falls into it and that Melville was "contented to be forgotten." He also offers the tantalizing prospect that had Melville, like Lowell, "been offered the editorship of some magazine, he would probably have accepted the position and filled it well."[23] Unfortunately, literary history is full of what ifs. The book preface to *Israel Potter* imagines a letter from an editor "To His Highness the Bunker-Hill Monument," but Melville never did sit formally at the editor's table. For several years in the mid-1850s, however, he was squarely part of the magazine world, far away from the twentieth-century inventions that bequeath him to contemporary readers.

The Art of Paid Labor

My final aim is to provide answers to the questions that follow from taking a writer's-eye view of Melville's embeddedness in the world of magazine publishing: What qualities does a writer bring to the composition of a text that make it suitable for magazine publication? What makes that text memorable rather than forgettable? What qualities account for the longevity of "Bartleby" and some of Melville's other magazine writing, especially given the ordinariness of their first existence? To answer these questions, I retain a faith in the writer, the text, and textuality that is sometimes at odds with the rewriting of America's literary and print history over the last fifteen years. This faith is prompted by a conviction that historically inflected criticism does not always provide the appropriate tools for understanding the form of literary texts; and certainly, that it offers little help when we try to decide what enables texts to endure the passage of time.

The most significant books to change our understanding of nineteenth-century literature and print culture challenge prevailing, often long-standing accounts of the period by revealing the significance of localized and plural print experiences. They are models of scholarship based on extensive archival research; all vividly explore the complex circumstances that produced and circulated print. They all have a commitment to get the history right. Jackson, for instance, aims for "a more historical and nuanced analysis than the professionalization model can provide." McGill wants to "reach back through the foundational anxieties of literary nationalism to uncover a literature defined by its exuberant understanding of culture as iteration and not origination." One criticism of this work, however, is that trying to get history right also risks sealing it in a time capsule. Reconstructing writers and texts so rigorously in the context of their contemporaneous publication, reprinting, and circulation risks becoming what Jonathan Dollimore has described as "a contextualizing which is also, and more fundamentally a containment."[24] The historicist impulse can sever the arteries of literary history; because it asks different questions, it cannot entirely explain why, for instance, Melville's stories still have a heartbeat all these years later.

The literary history of nineteenth-century print has tended, then, to prioritize history over the literary. Every literary occasion is historically situated, but it is a critical choice to repeatedly make historical situatedness the ground for literary analysis. Questions about authorial creativity and transhistorical literary value are largely deferred—or dismissed—in cultural histories that focus on the circumstances in which texts existed and circulated. The wiring of context to text bypasses the material and practical activities of writerly creation and imagination. In a fascinating account of writers and their mentors in the nineteenth century, for instance, David Dowling starts with a disclaimer: "Authorship . . . functions in this book as a component of publishing history, which I treat as socially driven, diverse, and dependent on the economies of circulation in the literary market, a perspective that dismantles the myth of the autonomous romantic artist."[25] There are subtler understandings of authorship. McGill offers a much more granular sense of how Poe and Hawthorne balanced creative and industry imperatives. But the options of romantic authorship or an authorship reduced to "a component of publishing history" are altogether too limiting. As history dominates in the contingencies of literary and print studies, it risks relegating the writer to mere functionary rather than just dismantling the myth of the romantic artist.

I aim for a different understanding of authorship. An imaginative writer like Melville certainly operated in a commercializing media system. How he interacted with that system, and the results of that interaction, were still affected by decisions and choices Melville made. And whether we consider him an artist, an author, or just a plain writer writing copy, the best evidence to help answer questions about Melville's magazine writing is still often to be found in the writing itself, especially when the biographical trail goes cold during the mid-1850s or the magazine archives prove no help. If we make the critical choice to tip the balance back in favor of the literary over the historical, we do not have to abandon the magazine world in which Melville's stories first appeared. We can ask how our understanding of Melville's authorship changes when we press his writing back between the leaves of the magazines in which it was published. And we can do so without allowing magazine publication to delimit the possible answers. Writing can be paid labor that tells more than the story of its own dependencies.

Acknowledging and engaging the internal, formal qualities of Melville's stories is part of my project here. These are not old-fashioned concerns—though they may sometimes be considered unfashionable—but concerns that persist.[26] The critical reflex that regarded timelessness as a marker of literary value is a cliché long since banished; the historicist or ideological reflex that replaced it risks becoming its own cliché. But one notable development paralleling the turn to print history in American literary studies since the early 2000s is the return to the text as a formal object, whether this is under the guise of new formalism, surface reading, object-oriented ontology, or a post-critique method that in the face of "the tsunami of context-based criticism," Rita Felski argues, should adopt instead "a greater receptivity to the multifarious and many-shaded moods of texts."[27]

The following chapters pay due diligence to the historicizing impetuses of important reappraisals of nineteenth-century print, but they are also driven by an underlying sense that the internal or formal "moods" of some of Melville's stories have qualities that elude even the most sophisticated and nuanced reconstruction of historical context. One does not have to believe in the old kind of eternal or universal values to believe that textual durability might have internal as well as external causes. Print history can answer intractable questions about textual publication, reception, and reputation; it helps less when one tries to understand the imaginative acts of authorial creation that bring texts into existence in the first place. Other actors in publishing networks have valuable specialist skills that the cycle of print should integrate. But unlike the work of the many typesetters, printers, and editors involved in the print world, a writer's output is also much more portable and potentially more transferrable, recyclable, and long-lasting.

Bringing together the material and the textual, each of the following chapters identifies how Melville was embedded in nineteenth-century magazine culture and the impact of this embeddedness on his writing's formal qualities. Chapter 1 takes up the significance of Melville's trip to buy paper in Dalton. Distinguishing between an economy of paper and an economy of print publishing to which paper is only sometimes connected, in this chapter I argue two things: that Melville had a detailed knowledge of paper and papermaking; and that when paper appears in his magazine writing it does so to reaffirm Melville's own sense of himself as a writer, not to mark his alienation from an industrializing print marketplace. In both "Bartleby" and "The Paradise of Bachelors and the Tartarus of Maids" he returned to paper for his subject matter; he showed that for all the agonies and struggles it may have caused him, it remained the material in which he placed his trust.

Chapter 2 explores the genre conventions of magazine writing in which Melville's work sat. In the 1850s he was plying his trade in magazines that were miscellaneous collections of sketches, tales, and essays, and where nobody yet used the term "short story." This chapter examines how Melville ranged across genres in his magazine work, treading a fine line between conforming to and breaking away from magazine conventions; I argue that in doing so Melville accomplished what many other writers in the 1850s failed to do: reinvent the magazine sketch and tale traditions in ways that create the modern short story. From his embeddedness within the demands of genre, Melville burst his way out of its confines.

In chapter 3 I turn to Melville's editors at *Putnam's Monthly Magazine,* Charles Frederick Briggs and George William Curtis, who were responsible for rejecting and accepting Melville's work. Curtis also worked for *Harper's* at the same time. It was their judgments that turned Melville's stories into magazine writing. Together with the turbulent history of *Putnam's,* this chapter looks at the literary and editorial, intellectual, and aesthetic judgments Briggs and Curtis brought to Melville's work. By capturing the texture of the literary history that ensnared Melville, I show that Briggs and Curtis's editorial judgment embedded Melville's writing in micro-contexts not always in harmony with the ideological macro-contexts critics now use to read the magazine pieces.

Chapter 4 concentrates on magazine paratexts. Each piece of Melville's anonymous and pseudonymous magazine writing was embedded among dozens of other articles and illustrations. Magazines were a rag-bag in which the ordinary sat beside the virtuoso, the original next to the reprinted, and the forgettable beside the enduring. Melville's stories were not read in isolation as they now are; they were read in the shadow of the material alongside which they were printed and published. While it is impossible to recreate the 1850s experience of reading a magazine, reading the issues of *Harper's* and *Putnam's* magazines in which Melville's writing appeared enables his stories and the magazines themselves to come to life in unexpected ways.

Finally, chapter 5 places the magazine writing into the longer context of a career in which Melville habitually relied on other literary sources. The magazine writing was different in one significant respect: rather than supplementing his own work with sources, Melville for the first time took existing, though long forgotten, sources and turned them into new stories. With "Benito Cereno" and *Israel Potter,* Melville embedded his magazine writing ever more in the prosaic terrain of his literary culture; Melville also now turned himself for the first time into an editor whose job was to alter the work of other authors for the pages of *Putnam's.* Melville brilliantly upcycled these sources; he took discarded material and reused it to create narratives of much better quality than the originals, most spectacularly in "Benito Cereno," where his editorial eye turned a routine sea captain's narrative into the prototype for the American thriller.

On November 17, 1851, ten months after the family trip to buy paper from Carson's mill in Dalton, Melville wrote a long letter to Hawthorne, who was soon to move from the town of Lenox—a seven-mile journey from Arrowhead—to West Newton, a village outside Boston, some 130 miles away. Just a few days earlier, Melville celebrated the publication of *Moby-Dick* by going with Hawthorne for dinner at the Little Red Inn in Lenox. Now Melville was replying to the lost letter in which Hawthorne offered his assessment of the book Melville dedicated to him. From Melville's response and what Hawthorne said to others about *Moby-Dick*—"What a book Melville has written!" he wrote Evert Duyckinck—the letter was obviously flattering. Melville describes it as "joy-giving and exultation-breeding" and expressed his gratitude in several moments of affection that testify to the close relationship between the two men: "By what right do you drink from my flagon of life? And when I put it to my lips—lo, they are yours and not mine. I feel the Godhead is broken up like bread at the Supper, and that we are the pieces. Hence this infinite fraternity of feeling" (*C* 212). If the letter consummates a friendship begun when Melville relocated to Pittsfield, the tone suggests a fond farewell to a dear companion. While Melville and Hawthorne would remain in touch, their letters became less frequent and their time in each other's company rare. The "great neighborhood for authors" would soon lose its most distinguished resident; Melville would lose a mentor and fellow traveler; and the wider social network of writers, whose Berkshire County enclave Melville in January declared less important than the local papermaking industry, would soon reject the novel Hawthorne so admired.

Melville consoles and reaffirms himself at such an occasion of heightened emotion and impending loss, by expressing his thoughts in the language of paper and the materiality of writing. When he disregards Hawthorne's praise as mere appreciation, he does so because "not one man in five cycles, who is wise, will expect appreciative recognition" and thus "we pigmies must be content to have our paper allegories but ill comprehended" (*C* 212). The passage of time and the experience of continual change, he tells Hawthorne, are marked in the act of his writing the letter because "the very fingers that now guide this pen are not precisely the same that took it up and put it on this paper." Finally, in the first of two postscripts to a letter he admits he cannot stop writing, Melville fantasizes about what he would do if Magians made up the world: "I should have a paper-mill established at one end of the house, and so have an endless riband of foolscap rolling in upon my desk; and upon that endless riband I should write a thousand—a million—billion thoughts" (*C* 213).

A riband of foolscap may be a contradiction in terms—foolscap is a size of cut paper—but the phrase better conveys than would, say, a "riband of paper," the point Melville is making: that foolscap, produced either by hand or by the cutting of machine-made paper he observed at the Old Berkshire Mill in Dalton, is paper on which one writes, not on which one is published or circulated. In this fantasy of continuous thought and of writing unburdened by the breaks necessitated by sheets of paper, and prior to the act of readerly consumption, Melville imagines himself embedded in the workings of the papermaking machine, setting down his thoughts in words at one end of the process while at the other end in the mill beyond his house the papermakers feed and tend the machine. This book indulges Melville's fantasy: first by imagining what sort of work a writer produces who dreams of being the consumer of a private supply of paper; second by following the words on the spooling riband of foolscap accumulating on Melville's writing desk and study floor as they pass through the hands of editors, printers, and publishers into the pages of magazines; and finally by attending to at least some of the thousand, million, billion thoughts that came to him while he was embedded in the process of writing for those magazines.

1

The "Plain Facts" of Paper

More than two and a half thousand new magazines rolled off the printing presses in the United States in the quarter of a century after 1825. Survival rates were improving, but attrition was still high; many lasted no longer than a few issues.[1] In addition to their subject matter, magazines needed distinctive physical features to stand out in such a crowded market. Rounding up the contents of quality monthlies published in April 1855, the *New York Times* reported, "We like the April number of the Knickerbocker perhaps most of all because the 'Editor's Table' is not only capital—as it always is—but also is presented in clean type, of good Christian size." After relating the details of an eye infection regularly induced in one of the magazine's readers by an earlier, less satisfactory typeface, the *Times* article gives only five lines to the *Knickerbocker*'s content. Of the features in *Harper's New Monthly Magazine,* the illustrated pieces are brought first to the reader's attention, while nonillustrated material, or "Other papers of interest," are subordinated to the second tier. Missing altogether from the listing for the *Harper's* April issue, however, was an anonymously published short story whose plot seemed clearly to link the material form of the magazine to writers the *Times* considered responsible for the articles in the April issue of *Putnam's Monthly Magazine*: "Most of these one would judge to be written by gentlemen of taste and leisure—dreamy men, who go out occasionally to see life, not who are daily in contact with life's hard realities."[2] The missing story was Melville's "The Paradise of Bachelors and the Tartarus of Maids."

This omission looks like a failure to connect what seem obviously connected: the "dreamy men" whose writing appears in *Putnam's*; the gentlemen in the first part of Melville's story who inhabit "the quiet cloisters" of the "dreamy Paradise of Bachelors" (*PT* 316); and the papermaking described in the second part of the story. But making this connection relies on conjoining two material economies the *Times* saw no reason to conjoin: the economy of paper and the economy of print. In this chapter I follow the lead set by the *Times* and peel apart paper and print to argue that paper has a life before it becomes commercial print culture and that we should distinguish the paper on which writers set down their words from the paper on which commercial print culture circulates. Critics assume that Melville's literary career is an index of the state of authorship in the mid-nineteenth-century literary marketplace because they continually mistake these two economies for one another. Paper is not only print.

The chapter proceeds with two key arguments in mind. First, I show that Melville displays a much more specific and sophisticated interest in paper, its manufacture, and its uses than critics have so far recognized. Second, I argue that "Bartleby, the Scrivener" and "The Paradise of Bachelors and the Tartarus of Maids" are better read as Melville's engagement with the materials on which, and with which, they were written than as allegories of authorship in a mechanizing age. For Jacques Derrida, paper has a history "that is brief but complex" and from which we may now be retreating.[3] Any accounting of its archive would benefit from turning to Melville's writing, the better to understand the plain facts of paper before its journey through the cycle of publication, distribution, and circulation in a print economy.[4] In broader terms, Melville's treatment of paper suggests the limits of commercial print culture's power over the imaginative writer. The magazine market that paid Melville did not necessarily dictate the shape, nature, and form of the writing for which it paid; in the chess game that was publishing, Melville could still make his own moves.

Melville in the "Multitudinous and Mystical" Industry of Paper

The print industry in which Melville was embedded thrived in the mid-nineteenth century thanks to the hardware of the machine age. Manufacturers, typesetters, and printers drummed out the rhythms of print production on the toughest materials available to them; metal and wood clattered and scraped in concert to fill marketplaces with a chorus of printed forms. Yet the material in which this industry put most faith was altogether more fragile. Today paper gives way to pixels, but in the nineteenth century no alternative existed to a medium whose preeminence technology ensured by finding new ways to make it, print on it, and circulate it. No matter that paper was susceptible to fire, water, and other forms of ill treatment; print prospered and diversified during this period because of an unflagging belief in paper's legitimacy and inevitability. This faith extended beyond the publishing world. Both narrators in Melville's "Bartleby" and "The Paradise of Bachelors and the Tartarus of Maids" are businessmen who trust paper. The lawyer in the first story uses paper to ratify contracts and agreements; for the seedsman in the second story, paper is the best medium for safely distributing economic goods.

To the writers who supplied print content, paper did not always offer the same guarantees. Thomas Carlyle was notoriously pessimistic about the chaos he thought resulted from a proliferation of paper, both in "the paper age" leading up to the French Revolution and in his own contemporary Britain. More generally, commercial literary culture produced and distributed paper containers whose content must still navigate the vagaries of readerly consumption. The print industry can be a writer's willing emissary, but it cannot always ensure a favorable or even a diplomatic reception. The point when a piece of print meets a reader therefore duplicates the beginning of the writing process. When others read one's work they see what the writer sees first: that paper is a medium that does not reliably ensure the safe transmission of thought from abstract to physical form. Paper is often the incontrovertible evidence that finds a writer guilty of imperfection and failure. In the nineteenth century, an expanding print readership constantly demanding content passed harsh sentence on the convicted. In these circumstances, a writer's interaction with paper might result in agonizing struggle, not reliable communication.

The inverted climax of Melville's career appears to exemplify just such a struggle after the public failures of *Moby-Dick* and especially *Pierre*. "Bartleby" was the first of Melville's magazine pieces to make it into print; in retrospect the pitiable refusenik copyist appears a symptom of Melville's prevailing malaise and seer of his literary future. Forced to write magazine pieces because he would not or could not write the novels readers wanted, Melville was destined to a writing life after the 1850s largely without readers. What lay ahead for him was not the Tombs but the space

Bartleby eventually leaves behind: the office in which Melville performed his duties for the New York customs authorities.

"Bartleby" may even represent a judgment on long-standing agonies. So palpable was Melville's struggle to transfer his thoughts to paper from early in his writing career, Elizabeth Renker has argued, that he "chronically experienced the page as an obscuring, frustrating, resistant force against whose powers of blankness he battled as he wrote." Marriage only exacerbated Melville's predicament. There he found himself entangled in a fractious domestic writing environment, working alongside his wife and sisters as they copied and transcribed his work in the cramped space of Arrowhead. Renker argues that he transferred the frustration of his physical struggle to write on paper into violence against both the paper and the women, especially his wife. Paper and women are interchangeable in Melville's work because of a "metonymic chain associating writing with misery, women with misery, and women with writing."[5] Melville's was the grimmest of struggles.

The biographical record, however, offers little support for this line of thinking. In the fullest account of Melville's life between the publication of *Pierre* and the writing of "Bartleby" in the summer of 1853, Hershel Parker cites, but does not countenance, the opinion about this period given by his wife, Elizabeth, ten years after Melville's death. Rather than turning him into a recluse, battered by reviewers, Elizabeth claimed of the reception of *Pierre*: "In fact it was a subject of joke with him, declaring that it was but just, and I know that however it might have affected his literary reputation, it concerned him personally but very little."[6] Reviews of *Pierre* appeared first at the end of July 1852 and continued over the next few months. Almost universally bad, they were not so bad that Melville contemplated giving up writing. Instead, he immediately returned to his paper and started writing a new novel based on a true story told to him on Nantucket in July by John Clifford, the state's attorney general and an acquaintance of Melville's father-in-law, Judge Lemuel Shaw. This story of a shipwrecked sailor and the woman he marries and then deserts before marrying bigamously elsewhere and returning to his first wife many years later became *The Isle of the Cross*. Melville discussed the story with Hawthorne and thought his friend might want to work it into fictional form; after a visit to Hawthorne in Concord in December 1852, Melville decided to write the story himself and did so through the winter and spring, finishing a draft in April 1853. Whatever brickbats Melville withstood following *Pierre,* he clearly still had enough faith in his own talent not to think his literary life a hopeless one.

Nor does the evidence about Melville's life during this period substantiate some of the speculative claims Parker makes about the writer's state of mind. Melville appears only to commit a series of minor social faux pas: he failed to write to his brother Tom; he snubbed Alfred Billings Street—an acquaintance of Melville's uncle Peter—who had read a poem at the Pittsfield Young Ladies' Institute anniversary celebration; and, to his mother's disappointment, Melville missed the chance to enhance his local reputation by not contributing to a book on Berkshire County edited by Geoffrey Greylock. Parker concludes, "Peter had been humiliated, Maria was exasperated: the front the family had put up was beginning to crack." The suggestion that the "family was near hysteria" is hyperbole and says more about his family than about Melville.[7]

His mother's concerns that Herman was endangering his health by writing a new novel were understandable given that she had already lost her husband and first son, Gansevoort, prematurely. Her desire to stop Melville from writing and instead secure paid work led to discussions about a foreign consulship, a situation Parker raises to the level of "crisis" by adding to his problems the secret loan Melville had taken from Tertullus Stewart and for which Arrowhead was collateral: "During all of the discussions," Parker suggests, "the secret loan loomed large in Melville's own mind: if he went abroad would Stewart seize Arrowhead from under the family he had left there?"[8] The loan had so far not loomed large enough for Melville to keep up with payments, and how exactly Stewart would seize Arrowhead is not clear. Such action would have to be taken legally; Melville's being abroad was no grounds for circumventing the law. And given that his wife's family had bailed out Melville before, if the loan became public knowledge no doubt Judge Shaw would bail him out again rather than see his daughter put out on the street.

Against these problems, other events were as likely to give Melville comfort. Elizabeth gave birth to their third child; he visited friends and family in Manhattan, Boston, and New Rochelle; was himself visited by his old *Acushnet* shipmate Henry Hubbard; and he saw his family's financial situation improve immeasurably on May 31, 1853, when Judge Shaw made a new will leaving Elizabeth one-fifth of his estate, writing off the money he had lent Melville as advances against this share, and turned over Elizabeth's wedding fund of $3,000 to Benjamin Curtis for investment. Harper & Brothers rejected *The Isle of the Cross* in June, but Parker's claim that in the early summer of 1853 "Melville was about as beaten as a man can be" is substantiated neither by his subsequent claim that "Melville picked himself up stoutly" rather than reacting with his "characteristic recklessness" after the rejection, nor by his claim that when he started writing magazine fiction in the summer—almost immediately after Harper rejected the new novel—"Melville achieved a remarkable amount of intermittent work, relishing the new literary form which allowed him to throw his energies into a piece for a few days then put it behind him."[9] Somehow, and it is not clear how, the beaten man resurrected himself.

Biography can be correct in fact and still wrong in spirit. What, in retrospect, looks like lurching between fair skies and storms might have been experienced as the steady buffeting of life's minor headwinds. Melville's literary reputation was certainly depleted after *Pierre,* but he remained a substantial enough figure for *Putnam's* to devote an essay to him in the magazine's second issue of February 1853. Fitz-James O'Brien quotes in admiration long passages from *Omoo* and *White-Jacket.* While conceding that Melville "totters on the edge of a precipice, over which all his hard-earned fame may tumble," he concludes that Melville may yet "make a notch on the American pine."[10] But imagine that a distance lies between what others want to make of you as a writer and what one wants to make of oneself. Imagine that Melville's wife was right and that the fate of *Pierre* concerned her husband "personally but very little"; that instead of falling over the precipice because of his stubborn refusal to change direction, Melville turned and took another path leading him away from the dangers of fame; that he continued to write—magazine fiction, *The Confidence-Man,* poetry, *Billy Budd*—for reasons other than making his "notch."

Melville's magazine writing tells a different story about his paper life. Paper was already a source of pleasure for Melville before he wrote for *Harper's* and *Putnam's.* He liked it well enough that he could boast to Duyckinck about living in a neighborhood renowned for papermaking; he considered paper a suitable object for gifts he gave his family; and he sought out the finest paper on which to reply to Sophia Hawthorne after she wrote him praising parts of *Moby-Dick* (*C* 218). To be sure, writers struggle. But struggle was not a condition of Melville's being; it was an occupational hazard shared by all writers and by many other tradespeople and professionals who translated between abstract and material realms. A writer tries to match thought to writing in the same way an engineer tries to perfect a papermaking machine from a set of drawings, or a bookkeeper tries to match a set of accounts to a publisher's trading activity. Neither side in these scenarios easily corresponds to the other; the very nature of the job is to effect a compromise, and compromises are rarely perfect. Frustration is the everyday consciousness of work that engineers, accountants, and writers soon learn to live with. What one also accumulates in the course of this everyday activity is an understanding and respect for the materials of one's trade, including their strengths and limitations; these are the materials one does not give up on out of frustration but to which one keeps returning, day after day. Materials are friends and colleagues to a writer, not enemies. Paper is the site where writers imagine, create, and—however imperfectly—overcome their struggles. An embedded author like Melville is one in whose writing echo the labors of working with paper.

Writing about paper in his magazine stories, Melville shows himself a generous and thoughtful custodian of the material that had withstood the clanging and whirring metallic rollers, presses, and cutters to arrive on his desk and in his hands. The composure, articulacy, and curiosity of his narrators in "Bartleby" and "The Paradise of Bachelors and the Tartarus of Maids" are examples of subtle creativity rather than frustration and struggle. Rather than symptoms of Melville's supposedly abject writing life, both participate in a dialogue with the economy of paper and their own material production more audibly than they speak the agonies of the economy of print. His trip to Dalton shows that Melville took paper seriously in its own right. The intention here is not to silence Melville's wider commentary but rather to press one's ear closely to the page—to listen more carefully to the writing amid the hubbub of the loud and noisy print culture of the machine age. The art of listening is sometimes to want no more of stories than what the stories themselves first want to achieve; heightening the stakes of interpretation does not necessarily heighten the returns.

Exactly which mill Melville visited on his family outing to Dalton has been the source of some confusion. Harrison Elliott first pointed to the

Defiance Mill, but although David Carson did build this mill with Joseph Chamberlin in 1823, sole ownership passed to Henry Chamberlin in 1840.[11] Jay Leyda, followed by Marvin Fisher, Philip Young, and later Hershel Parker, identified the Old Red Mill as Melville's destination.[12] Once again, although Carson had been connected to this mill since its origin in 1809, he quickly sold his interest to Zenas Crane, who became sole owner of the mill in 1826. By the time Melville visited in 1851, Crane's sons owned and ran the Old Red Mill. The only mill in Dalton to which Carson was connected by 1851 was the Old Berkshire Mill, which had passed into the hands of his sons following his retirement in 1849.[13] From the descriptions of the paper made at the mill in "The Paradise of Bachelors and the Tartarus of Maids," the paper historian A. J. Valente concludes that "the most likely possibility would be the Berkshire Mill in Dalton."[14] By the time Melville wrote the story, Carson had moved to Pittsfield, where he became president of Pittsfield Bank when it was chartered in 1853, a position he maintained until his death in 1858.

There is no evidence that Melville had any financial dealings with Carson, but we do know from a letter Augusta Melville sent to her sister Helen in December 1850 that the town of Lee and not Dalton was originally planned as the destination for the "expedition . . . to get a supply of paper at the manufactory."[15] Outside of Dalton, Berkshire County more generally was an important paper-producing area of the country and by 1857 housed a total of forty-three mills. Lee, a dozen miles south of Pittsfield, produced more paper than any other town in the United States in 1840.[16] What distinguished the mills in Lee was their production of lower-quality paper, which was sold for the purpose of printing books and newspapers, including two of the largest circulating in the 1840s: Horace Greeley's *New York Tribune* and James Gordon Bennett's *New York Herald.* The demand for paper of this kind fueled a mill-building boom in Lee in the 1830s and 1840s. The mills in Dalton, while also increasingly servicing the New York City market, produced the higher-quality cut, ruled, and stamped paper for the purposes Melville lists in "The Paradise of Bachelors and the Tartarus of Maids." Although Cupid, who guides the narrator through the factory, makes a distinction between the foolscap being manufactured by the machine at the time of the narrator's visit and the "cream-laid and royal sheets" that represent, he says, their "finer work" (*PT* 333), the stationery being produced in the mill was still of much finer quality than that produced elsewhere. It was the paper Melville gave as gifts to his family after visiting Dalton in January 1851.

Why the destination of Melville's family outing changed from Lee to Dalton is not a matter of record. The fact that Melville had a choice, however, and that he opted for the fine paper of Dalton, embeds him in the contingencies of the local economies of paper that were facilitating the expansion of print more generally, but of which books, periodicals, and newspapers were only one part. The distinction between papermaking districts indicates the kind of concentration and specialization one would expect to find in a maturing papermaking industry, but it also demands a reassessment of Melville's interest in and attitude toward the paper economy. As Christina Lupton writes, "The more simply we think of ourselves returning to the page, the more assuredly we lay the grounds for new theoretical ventures by which to find, in our simplest references to paper, new proof that it was never simply there."[17] The contingencies of a paper economy offer a way of revisiting "Bartleby" and "The Paradise of Bachelors and the Tartarus of Maids" in order to focus attention on the plain facts of paper and papermaking in the story.

The means by which paper was "never simply there" were more apparent than ever as increased demand saw the introduction of new technologies at the beginning of the nineteenth century. For Kevin McLaughlin, the mechanized production of paper after the eighteenth century created an ideological paradox. While paper was increasingly the means for the dissemination of knowledge and information, it was also a medium marked by ephemerality, given that the chemical additives used in modern manufacturing hastened paper's decomposition. Literally losing its material support or substance, the paper of mass mediacy, he argues, "exceed[s] the limits of the classic concept of the work as self-contained substance."[18] As I noted earlier, the booming print industry maintained its faith in the integrity of paper despite these changes in production methods. And "The Paradise of Bachelors and the Tartarus of Maids" offers a way of modifying this argument about mass mediacy in an American context, since what differentiated the paper Melville bought in Dalton was its comparative strength, substantiveness, and longevity. The purified water from the Housatonic gave Dalton paper precisely these advantages.

While the first part of Melville's diptych, by way of contrast, and the second part more directly, offer a vision of industrial mechanization, the makers of fine paper were notably discriminating in their adoption of new technology. They were certainly quick to take up the papermaking machine—costing "twelve thousand dollars only last autumn," which Cupid shows Melville's narrator and which Melville would have seen in action in Dalton (*PT* 331)—since, once engineers solved initial teething problems, this was the one piece of technology guaranteed to dramatically increase production without unduly compromising quality.

There were two kinds of paper machines in operation during this period, the Fourdrinier and the cylinder, both of which were continually being modified and improved. Valente claims that Melville would have seen a cylinder machine in the Old Berkshire Mill, as a machine of this sort was installed in 1832. Daniel Pidgeon, writing in 1884, gave 1831 as the approximate date of the arrival of a cylinder machine at the mill, "to be followed, twenty years later, by the Fourdrinier apparatus." This would put the arrival of the Fourdrinier very close to the date of Melville's visit. According to *The History of Berkshire County, Massachusetts,* however, a Fourdrinier was "placed in the Old Berkshire Mill in 1850."[19] Given that the machine in Melville's story has only recently been installed, and taking into account Judith McGaw's argument that fine-paper makers switched from cylinder machines to Fourdriniers during the 1840s because they made superior-quality paper, it is probable that Melville saw a Fourdrinier in action. The cost of the machine in the story also suggests a Fourdrinier; they were generally more expensive than cylinder machines. If Melville did visit the Old Red Mill, he would certainly have seen a Fourdrinier in operation; Zenas Crane & Sons installed the first Fourdrinier in Berkshire County in this mill in 1843.[20] Given the proximity of the mills in Dalton, it is not inconceivable that Melville visited more than one mill.

The principal change that machines facilitated was the production of paper in long, continuous pieces. Handmade paper could only be produced in sheets, and the process involved three key operatives: the vatman, who formed the sheet by dipping a wooden-framed mesh into a vat of beaten water and cloth rags; the coucher, who transferred the sheet of pulp from the mold to a felt-covered board for initial drying; and the layboy, who separated the paper from the felt for further drying and finishing. Fourdrinier and cylinder machines incorporated all three processes into a combination of moving mesh and rollers. Pulp was added to a "headbox" at one end—the wet end—and paper emerged at the dry end for cutting.

The machines were imposing in stature. Rolled out before him "like some long Eastern manuscript," the narrator of Melville's story says, "lay stretched one continuous length of iron framework—multitudinous and mystical, with all sorts of rollers, wheels, and cylinders, in slowly-measured and unceasing motion" (*PT* 331). That the machine itself reminds him of a paper manuscript, and an ancient one that has withstood the test of time, suggests the narrator is watching not a flimsy or perishable product forming before him. When he asks his guide, Cupid, if the "thin cobweb" of pulp ever breaks, Cupid replies that "it never is known to tear a hair's point" (*PT* 333). The strength and durability of paper was paramount to Dalton papermakers. The customers for Crane & Company's banknote paper, for instance, "repeatedly specified Fourdrinier paper."[21] The quality of this paper, together with the innovation in 1844 of silk threads to prevent counterfeiting or altering the denomination meant that Crane's was soon supplying banks in Boston and New York. By 1879 it was the sole supplier of paper for official U.S. government currency and remains so today.

But Dalton papermakers were much more reluctant to utilize the kinds of chemicals or new technologies that might affect the quality of the paper they produced. When Melville's narrator stops briefly in the mill's rag room, for example, he observes girls standing before rag-cutting blades that are "immovably fixed," sharpened by hand, and across which "the girls forever dragged long strips of rags, washed white, picked from baskets at one side; thus ripping asunder every seam, and converting the tatters almost into lint" (*PT* 329). While the narrator makes much of the way the girls face the upturned blades, comparing them to condemned state prisoners being led to their doom by an officer whose sword would face in that same direction, it is the hand-cutting process and the washed rather than bleached rags the girls are shredding that indicate the narrator is in a fine-paper mill. Mechanical rag cutters could not open seams as deftly as hand cutters, and neither could they remove the buttons the narrator notices "are all dropped off" from the old shirts and that he imagines may have come from the bachelors in the first part of the story (*PT* 330). David Carson himself questioned the effectiveness of rag-cutting machines when asking another mill owner "whether the machine cleans [the rags] as well as formerly when they were dressed by girls."[22] The vision of industrial labor shaping Melville's story at this point draws on residual papermaking techniques that survive the advent of faster, mechanized processes.

Fine-paper makers also continued to use wooden rather than iron stock beaters and were cautious about introducing mechanical dryers and bleach boilers. They were also conscious of running their machines at the right speed to maintain paper quality. While Aaron Winter is only the latest critic to note that the nine-minute cycle of the pulp machine in "Paradise" suggests the nine-month period of the human gestation cycle, such a reading would privilege the symbolic unity of the story over its sensitivity to the papermaking process.[23] When he is standing before the machine with Cupid, the narrator watches the pulp pour onto a "wide, sloping board" and listens and watches as Cupid takes him through the stages of the process by which the pulp is turned from a "thin and quivering" state into something resembling first "mere dragon-fly wing" and then, after passing over and between various cylinders, something that looks like paper (*PT* 331). That Melville's narrator uses "stuff" as the collective noun for the "white, wet, woolly-looking" pulp signals a more general familiarity with papermaking vocabulary, since pulp was stored in a "stuffchest" before it entered the headbox of the papermaking machine, but he seems much less familiar with the details of the fine-papermaking process on a machine. The narrator is "amazed at the elongation, interminable convolutions, and deliberate slowness of the machine," although Cupid reveals that the process takes only nine minutes, a fact he goes on to demonstrate (*PT* 332).

The word "deliberate" is meaningful here in both of its primary connotations. While the "interminable" process may appear to the narrator to be a sign of carefulness, the "slowness" may also be intentional. Fine-paper makers like those in Dalton, according to Judith McGaw, "exhibited conservatism by running their machines more slowly" than newspaper and other lower-quality paper mills in order to ensure the strength and quality of the paper they were producing. By 1887, paper machines were capable of running at 250 feet per minute.[24] Even given the fact that Melville visited the mill in Dalton over thirty years earlier, when speeds might have only been half this figure or less, the nine minutes it takes for Cupid's name to pass from pulp to cut foolscap is indeed a long time, as the narrator points out. Cupid, however, understands this to be the cycle required for fine-paper making, and the "patronizing air" the narrator senses in his guide suggests the importance of a knowledge about specialized machinery, carefully tuned to the production of fine paper, in an industry that constantly had to balance the demands of quality against scale and speed of output (*PT* 332). This sector understood the importance of managed, rather than indiscriminate, innovation in the production process, an awareness evident in the slowness of the machine and the presence of stamping and ruling machines deployed in fine-paper mills producing stationery.

As the observer of this process, the seedsman also repays further attention. With a business that stretched "through all the Eastern and Northern areas, and even fell into the far soil of Missouri and the Carolinas," he is using envelopes at the rate of "several hundreds of thousands in a year" (*PT* 324, 325). His primary purpose for visiting the mill is to purchase paper directly from the manufacturer rather than the wholesaler. He explains that once folded, filled with seed, stamped, and "superscribed with the nature of the seeds contained," these envelopes "assume not a little the appearance of business-letters ready for the mail" (*PT* 324–25). The scale, reach, and manner of his business locate him at the heart of a paper network facilitated by a series of changes not only to the manufacture of paper in the mid-nineteenth century, but also in postal legislation, which in turn provided the impetus for the growth of a culture of letters outside business and demand for ever-increasing quantities of paper.

A slew of postal acts in the late 1840s and early 1850s completely altered the postal terrain. The number of post offices and designated post roads increased rapidly; flat rates brought down the prohibitive cost of sending a letter, which was often higher than for sending newspapers and commercial items; and the principle of prepayment was introduced, in the form of postage stamps or prepaid envelopes, although this was not mandatory until 1855.[25] Once envelopes were not charged as an extra piece of paper, their manufacture increased and was mechanized. An envelope-folding machine was first patented in the United States in 1849.[26] If the prophylactic symbolism of the envelope is reinforced by the reliability of fine paper that "never is known to tear a hair's point," then such fine paper is also vital for the protection of an important business interest whose expansion and profitability are enhanced by the coordination of paper and postal technologies.

David Henkin has estimated that after money and photographs, "the next most popular enclosures in mid-century letters may have been agricultural samples—typically in the form of seeds." This was not just because of businessmen like the narrator but because individuals exchanged seeds once postage rates fell. Increasingly the post became a place where the words of individuals and of businesses came into contact and circulated alongside one another. This has important consequences for thinking about the relationship between writing and the market, since it reverses our understanding that a preexisting culture of writing was altered by the market's increasing influence; in the case of letters, it is individuals who are intruding on an existing system. Correspondents were, as Henkin suggests, "entering a terrain stamped by the culture of the market."[27] And Melville was certainly already conscious of the connections between paper and the post. Ishmael claims that the classification of whales in terms of paper sizes in *Moby-Dick* is "a ponderous task" to which "no ordinary letter-sorter in the Post-Office is equal" (*MD* 136).

This relationship between paper and the post in the United States is historically even more entwined, since the postal routes that developed in the first half of the nineteenth century often duplicated the rag routes by which paper manufacturers transported old rags to their mills. Alvin Wolcott, one of the early post riders in Berkshire County, who delivered mail as well as newspapers, advertised his services in the *Berkshire Chronicle* in 1788 and 1789 and made clear that he would "take in linen rags in pay for the newspapers at the store of his brother" and that "linen rags will be taken in lieu of cash."[28] A depot was eventually established in what doubled as the post office of West Stockbridge early in the nineteenth century; it became the center for rag-collecting activity after "bins went up in stores and taverns around every small village and hamlet" and "every fortnight a designated teamster traveled the county stopping in turn at each collecting site."[29] So developed did this Berkshire County network become that the routes were divided into franchises.

Owners of paper mills also followed the tradition set by Benjamin Franklin by combining their paper interests with postal administration. While Franklin's training as a printer and his newspaper editing are well known, he also established the first rag warehouse in Philadelphia, helped establish or supply many more paper mills, and co-owned with Anthony Newhouse the Trout Creek paper mill, on whose paper he printed the 1748 edition of *Poor Richard's Almanack,* complete with his personalized watermark. In 1793 he published a pamphlet on the skills of Chinese papermakers, and in Melville's classification of whales by paper size in *Moby-Dick* there is the echo of a poem attributed to Franklin that classifies men and women by paper quality. While the fop, according to Franklin, is gilt paper, poets are "the mere waste-paper of mankind." And if "Mechanics, servants, farmers, and so forth / Are copy paper of inferior worth," then the maiden is "innocently sweet / She's fair white-paper, an unsullied sheet."[30] Franklin also took full advantage of his position as postmaster for Philadelphia to help the circulation of his own newspaper. As Wayne Fuller points out, "editor-postmasters could, by special arrangements, send their newspapers with their mail carriers and at the same time prevent their competitors from doing so."[31] While papermaking, newspaper editing, and the postal service had become specialized and more discrete enterprises in the nineteenth century, there were still several instances of mill owners becoming local postmasters in Berkshire County. Thomas Hurlbut, of the Owen & Hurlbut firm in South Lee, was appointed postmaster for that town in October 1826; Samuel Sturges, who owned the Greenwater Mill, was made postmaster in East Lee in September 1848; and Thomas Carson, son of David Carson, became postmaster in Dalton in 1857.[32]

As the mill-building boom exhausted the local supply of rags, the sourcing of rags also became a major problem for papermakers. This was as true in Europe as it was the United States. Melville is alert to it in "The Paradise of Bachelors and the Tartarus of Maids" when Cupid tells the narrator that, of the rags in the mill, some come "from the country round about; some from far over sea—Leghorn and London" (*PT* 330). Making the connection to the bachelors he knew in London, the seedsman speculates that the rags may be the shirts of those same bachelors. While this moment serves as a handy pivot to link the two parts of the story and draws the maids into the orbit of the bachelors such that the gendered discussion of sexuality and sterility is given further impetus, it is another example of how following the allegorical reading of "Paradise" sidesteps the economy of papermaking. Leghorn provides not just an alliterative connection to London, but a very practical connection to the papermaking taking place in the mill.

Leghorn (the anglicized name for Livorno) is a Tuscan port city that in the nineteenth century became a major exporter of linen rags. Fine-paper manufacturers like those in Dalton preferred linen. It was more expensive than cotton but its fibers were thicker and stronger. The paper produced from linen had a "hardness, or 'rattle,'" which "gave it that most enduring quality" according to Valente.[33] Italy was a good source for these manufacturers because linen was still the preferred fabric in the making of traditional clothing. As the 1850s saw an increasingly competitive international market for rags, many countries began to impose export restrictions. In 1855, in response to complaints from British paper manufacturers that the United States was buying up foreign rags, the British Parliament increased the tax on rag exports to reduce the number of British rags going overseas. The same had happened in the Netherlands the year before, and in 1857 France banned all rag exports. Spain and the German states also took steps to protect their domestic supplies. The papal states banned exports in 1857. In contrast, Leghorn opened a new port to replace the old Medici port in 1854 as a way of coping with increased trade to the United States.

The accretion of these details is an important part of Melville's engagement with the material economy of paper. In the contemplation of his subject, Melville's emphasis on fine paper shows an imagination that does not "reduce paper to the function or topos of an inert surface laid out beneath some markings, a substratum meant for sustaining them, for ensuring their survival or existence," as Derrida claims is often the problem with reductive treatments of paper. To think of paper in this way would be to see it only as the material support for printed products whose workings and exchanges take precedence over what lies beneath the surface. Rather, according to Derrida, paper is "a labyrinth whose walls return the echoes of the voice or song it carries itself" and thus "is utilized in an experience involving the body, beginning with hands, eyes, voice, ears." The result is that paper "has always proclaimed its inadequacy and its finitude."[34] With this appreciation of paper and Melville's paper knowledge in mind, what is there to say of "Bartleby" and "The Paradise of Bachelors and the Tartarus of Maids"?

The "Huge Folio" of "Bartleby, the Scrivener"

Of "Bartleby," the first thing is this: Melville gives us not a writer refusing to write, but a writer writing. Reading the story as a parable of walls in 1953, Leo Marx's central premise was that "Bartleby" "was written in a time of deep hopelessness" after the disastrous reviews of *Pierre.* At the same time, Marx first imagined the correspondence that indelibly linked "Bartleby" to the economy of print: Bartleby is Melville, and Bartleby's refusal to check and write copy is the refusal of a writer who wants to grapple with difficult philosophical questions rather than reproduce conventional genres.[35] Despite the "Bartleby" industry that has been booming since the 1950s, the general thrust of Marx's reading remains intact. But if the biographical correspondence is tenuous then so is the impetus for thinking "Bartleby" corresponds to Melville's alienation from the economy of print.

"Bartleby" is one of three examples in Melville's magazine work of a narrator who is not telling but writing the story he is narrating.[36] The writer we should attend to in this story is not the copyist or refusenik Bartleby, but the lawyer who uses paper for his "briefs"—one of the uses the later narrator in "The Paradise of Bachelors and the Tartarus of Maids" imagines for the paper he watches being made—but paper on which he also creates original text as he remembers the young law-copyist he once employed; the lawyer is a writer whose interaction with paper is hidden in plain sight. Critics have not neglected the lawyer. The discourses he uses to tell the story of his acquaintance with Bartleby are well understood to show his own ideological disposition: a professional man of business whose bad faith makes him incapable of understanding Bartleby's predicament. As a writer and handler of paper he is little understood. That Melville intends his lawyer-narrator to also be a writer is clear from the first paragraph of the story, where the act of writing predominates. Biographies of other scriveners the lawyer waives in favor of "a few passages in the life of Bartleby"; the fuller life "is an irreparable loss to literature," and so the reader must settle for what the lawyer's "own astonished eyes saw of Bartleby." In general, law-copyists or scriveners are the "interesting and somewhat singular set of men, of whom as yet nothing that I know of has ever been written" (*PT* 13). Until now, that is.

As a writer, the lawyer is alert to—one might even say obsessed with—the uses and abuses of paper in his office, the implements used for marking it, and how writing is or is not carried out upon it. Bartleby is not the only character whose relationship to this paper world is idiosyncratic. As his temper frays in the afternoon, so Turkey blots the lawyer's documents when "incautious in dipping his pen into his inkstand." The pens themselves are "impatiently split . . . to pieces," and Turkey's papers are boxed "in a most indecorous manner." He gesticulates and makes violent thrusts with his ruler (*PT* 15). When Turkey uses a moistened ginger cake to seal a mortgage document, the lawyer comes "within an ace of dismissing him" (*PT* 19). Nippers tries in vain to find the correct height for his writing table, using chips and blocks of wood and pasteboard before going "so far as to attempt an exquisite adjustment by final pieces of folded blotting-paper" (*PT* 17). When the lawyer finally packs up his belongings to escape his office, the last item he removes is the screen behind which he places Bartleby when he first arrives. The screen is "folded up like a huge folio" and, thinking himself free of Bartleby at last, the lawyer writes, "I tore myself from him whom I had so longed to be rid of" (*PT* 39). To represent separation as tearing aptly summarizes an office where all the confrontations—between the lawyer and his scriveners and among the scriveners themselves—are confrontations over what should be done with paper.

Chief among these confrontations, of course, is Bartleby's refusal to read or to write. Although central to the author's profession, reading and writing need not necessarily be the occasion to make a connection between Melville and the economy of print; Bartleby's refusal is also a reminder that the legal profession is one of many that rely on reading and writing. In "Bartleby," Melville was already imagining how the paper that drops off the machine in "The Paradise of Bachelors and the Tartarus of Maids" would have nonliterary uses. Before becoming a writer Melville had long observed and experienced the handling and accumulation of paper. Sent to work at the New York State Bank as a twelve-year-old boy, he filed and copied surrounded by the paper money, bonds, and mortgages on which the bank's business relied. Following that, he moved to work at his brother Gansevoort's cap and fur store, where, among other things we know he wrote out receipts; later, he likely wrote *Typee* in the law offices of Gansevoort and his younger brother Allan, where the raw materials he needed for his authorship—paper, pens, and desk space—were all available because they were same raw materials lawyers required to carry out their business.

In a world of work that more generally relies on paper interactions, Bartleby's refusal can be seen as an aversion not to the reading and writing that is the stuff of authorship but an aversion to interacting with paper itself. The lawyer admits he has "never seen him reading—no, not even a newspaper" (*PT* 28). Twice the lawyer asks Bartleby to go to the post office for him: the first time to collect mail, the second to deliver mail (*PT* 25, 32).

On both occasions Bartleby prefers not to. Bartleby uses words only sparingly when he communicates with his trademark perfunctoriness; he will have nothing to do with words at all if that means engaging with paper. Ultimately, once he has given up each of his clerking duties, Bartleby will not check copy to ensure correspondence between different versions; he will not write copy to ensure correspondence between a source and a written, shared version; and he will not deliver or collect the letters by which written correspondence takes place. The repeated refusals of Bartleby to change his mind on this matter become a problem for the lawyer because his writing of the story has to grapple with consequences for which he can discern no legible causes.

As I reiterate later in this chapter when discussing "The Paradise of Bachelors and the Tartarus of Maids," paper's role as a medium of communication, as the place where abstract thought takes physical form, makes legibility a problem for Melville. "Bartleby" proleptically imagines what in "Paradise" is represented by the seedsman's apoplexy in the face of paper whose uses are without end. For the narrators of both stories the problem of legibility is made manifest in similar circumstances: when workers merge eerily with their material surroundings and the narrators are oddly affected.

In "The Paradise of Bachelors and the Tartarus of Maids" this occurs most vividly when the narrator contemplates the abstract force driving the papermaking machine, stands "spell-bound and wandering in my soul," and sees the pallid faces of the maids in the "pallid incipience of the pulp" (*PT* 334). In "Bartleby," when the lawyer enters the office while the scrivener is out, he contemplates the loneliness of Bartleby's life and is gripped by an "overpowering stinging melancholy," following which, he says, "sad fancyings—chimeras, doubtless, of a sick and silly brain—led on to other and more special thoughts, concerning the eccentricities of Bartleby. Presentiments of strange discoveries hovered round me." As the maids appear to the narrator in the later story, so the lawyer sees Bartleby: "The scrivener's pale form appeared to me laid out, among uncaring strangers, in its shivering winding sheet" (*PT* 28). *Sheet* here means a cloth or shroud; elsewhere in the story *sheet* only means paper, as when the lawyer tells Bartleby "I want you to help me compare this sheet here" (*PT* 20). The narrator in "Paradise," when he asks what makes the girls so "sheet-white," is told by Cupid that their "handling of such white bits of sheets all the time makes them so sheety" (*PT* 330–31). Where the seedsman hurries his exit from the paper mill and retreats to an "inscrutable nature," in the lawyer's imagining of Bartleby's pale form against the sheet "did that same melancholy merge into fear, that pity into repulsion" (*PT* 29). At this point he determines to separate himself from Bartleby. Like the seedsman who escapes the paper that has uses without end, so the lawyer, as he writes, "tore" himself from the object that confounds his trust in legibility.

In "Bartleby," the lawyer who relies on paper to seal agreements becomes the writer of a story where agreement—between employer and scrivener, between Bartleby's actions and their cause—is hard to discern. The narrator attempts to make up the deficit between what he sees and what he can explain by grasping, in the sequel, for the rumor that Bartleby once worked at the Dead Letter Office in Washington. He does so at the same moment he reiterates his status as a writer rather than a lawyer: just "ere parting with the reader" of this "little narrative" does he repeat the "vague report" that is of "a certain strange suggestive interest" to him. The suggestion is wrapped up in that perennially confusing question: "Dead letters! Does it not sound like dead men?" The obvious answer is "no," and by confounding the possibility of any redemptive correspondence between even the sound of letters and men it provides a fitting conclusion to a story in which the relationship between the lawyer and Bartleby develops through the reading and writing (or nonreading and nonwriting) of marks on paper.[37] But the lawyer also asks himself a further question: "Conceive a man by nature and misfortune prone to a pallid hopelessness, can any business seem more fitted to heighten it than that of continually handling these dead letters, and assorting them for the flames?" (*PT* 45). As much interpretation as question, the lawyer's words give shape to the story he is writing by suggesting that one's personality is confirmed when one is brought into contact with an environment that shares similar qualities: hopelessness by hopelessness equals hopelessness squared. Bartleby's fate is the fate of the dead letters only according to the lawyer's written narrative.

And yet the correspondence for which the lawyer searches is not confirmed by the rumor he finds so suggestive. All the lawyer can give the narrative is questions that either make little sense (dead letters do not sound like dead men) or rely on some assent outside the text never given: yes, working in a dead letter office might heighten the feeling of hopelessness if one is predisposed to this outlook. The lawyer's narration defers correspondence, and the reader knows well enough not to believe a narrator who has already demonstrated his partiality and provided reason enough to judge harshly his ethical prevarication. Between Bartleby's fate and what is known of him there is only the paper on which the narrator writes his story.

By taking paper as his material, in both senses of that word, Melville avoided the precipice that Fitz-James O'Brien warned would await him unless he wrote more like Addison to make his notch. O'Brien was wrong. Melville did not need to write more like Addison; he needed to satisfy himself as a writer. Leo Marx saw that in the lawyer-narrator, rather than in Bartleby, the reader finds what affirmation the story contains. This is not because he is a writer—for Marx, Melville is Bartleby and Bartleby is the writer—but because, unlike the stubborn writer Bartleby, the lawyer does not turn his back on society. "The eerie story of Bartleby," Marx writes, "is a compassionate rebuke to the self-absorption of the artist, and so a plea that he devote himself to keeping strong his bonds with the rest of mankind." Marx was wrong too. Not because he saw some affirmation in the lawyer but because he argued that affirmation results from the lawyer's belief in "human brotherhood."[38] "Bartleby" affirms writing and the writer. The lawyer may reach for correspondences like the narrator of "The Paradise of Bachelors and the Tartarus of Maids," but even if writers may always fail to achieve such a goal that is no reason to stop writing.

The "Intolerable Allegory" of "The Paradise of Bachelors and the Tartarus of Maids"

Melville continued his fascination with paper in the second part of "Paradise" by using a genre well known to readers of *Harper's* in the early 1850s. The factory or works tour was a popular way of introducing the marvels of the industrial age. I discuss the importance of the sketch genre to magazine writing in chapter 2, but these tours were contemporary versions of the sketch tradition that emerged out of the eighteenth-century magazine, through Washington Irving, Mary Russell Mitford, Charles Dickens when he was still Boz, and William Thackeray. Some of the examples *Harper's* published were reprints from British magazines, but the magazine clearly thought there was enough appetite for this kind of sketch irrespective of national setting. In the August 1850 issue, the *Harper's* reader was given a vicarious tour of the railroad works in Crewe, one of the major railway manufacturing towns in nineteenth-century Britain. The lead article in the May 1851 issue was a description by Jacob Abbott of the Novelty Iron Works in New York City, which manufactured "marine steam-engines of the largest class." In an article titled "Galvanoplasty" the narrator invited readers to "enter the workshop of M. Coblentz, in the Rue Charlot de Paris." Those readers also found themselves in the Weovil (a misspelling of Yeovil) Biscuit Manufactory in southern England and the Hounslow Mills to see the making of gunpowder.[39] An industrial paper mill was an eminently suitable subject for a *Harper's* article.

But this story has wrong-footed critics who prefer to read forward from the occasion of its magazine publication rather than backward to consider how it dramatizes a writer's imaginative labor with the materials of his trade. Paper surfaces as a topic in this story, McLaughlin argues, where "the literary text as a self-contained work is itself shaken by the distracting force of a mass mediacy to which it is inextricably linked."[40] But how inextricable is the link? Melville writes about paper on paper, and the magazine in which the story appeared was also manufactured and circulated in paper form. But that does not mean Melville prioritizes the end function of exchange and circulation—the engines of mass mediacy—the moment he composes a story with paper as its subject. Reading backward rather than forward refuses the inextricability of the link between literary text and mass mediacy.

The paper manufactured in the New England mill of Melville's story has yet to reach an exchange system. And it is a raw material that will never be made into books and magazines. Other professions use the paper on which Melville writes; the words on that paper might at some future point, in the abstracted form of books and magazines, pass into a culture of exchange.[41] But they may not even make that journey, as Melville's lost novel *The Isle of the Cross* did not. For Melville, then, as for Derrida, "paper is in the world that is not a book."[42] In "The Paradise of Bachelors and the Tartarus of Maids," Melville gestures toward a generalized circuit of literary exchange in the first part of the diptych, but he is most preoccupied with the manufacturing process and laboring environment that sees paper, rather than books and magazines, entering the world.

Because of this, the story anticipates and short-circuits the two key correspondences of which critics make so much in order to establish Melville's place at the heart of a literary market: the internal correspondence between the two parts of the diptych; and the external correspondence between the story's symbolic or allegorical form and 1850s America. The story's narrator is central to the short-circuiting process. Also vital is a series of distinctions the narrator witnesses between the abstract force driving the papermaking machine and the purposes to which users will put its paper. While some may find its way back into the hands of those "dreamy men" who write upon it for *Putnam's,* the paper will also end up in the hands of people like the seedsman narrator, who use it for purposes beyond the literary marketplace. Moments considered to serve a symbolic function in this story, then, are actually deeply embedded in Melville's understanding of the manufacture and nonliterary uses of paper. These facts collectively shape the interplay between the story's imaginative and material domains to the extent that paper rather than print becomes the story's subject.

The tendency of critics to move forward from "The Paradise of Bachelors and the Tartarus of Maids" to broader cultural conditions is driven partly by the perceived allegorical nature of the story itself. The distinctly gendered nature of the different worlds of leisure and work in the story is now well served by readings noting a subtext that denies in biological and artistic terms "the idea of female originating power" or envisions a nightmare "division of labor so pervasive that it would divide the sexes and sterilize mankind."[43] The narrator completes the circle of sex and gender in the story, and the paper he uses to distribute his seed duly takes on its prophylactic role in the context of the machine room, which the narrator describes as "stifling with a strange, blood-like, abdominal heat, as if here, true enough, were being finally developed the germinous particles lately seen" (*PT* 331). Sexual difference has an impact on industrial labor and the authorial labor from which, Michael Newbury argues, it "is not separate," but on which it "has already intruded . . . as a trope."[44] But if this work helps extend the significance of "The Paradise of Bachelors and the Tartarus of Maids" to an antebellum context in which writing, reading, and authorship were becoming subject to gendered market conditions, the critical labor expended to locate the story in this context remains paradoxical. On the one hand, it is convincing and sophisticated; on the other, it is too easily led by a story that does so much of the critical work itself and by the nature of the symbols at the critics' disposal.

Given the static representations of men and women offered by the story, it is hard to disagree with Sylvia Jenkins Cook that this is Melville's "'outside' story that embodies his most extreme sense of the otherness that existed for him in both women and poor people."[45] The effort to read these static figures also leads to interpretations that overreach the material at hand. David Dowling's claim, for instance, that "the women factory workers are significantly both book producers and victims of capitalism" is driven more by his need to make an argument about the entrepreneurship of authors faced with market conditions than it is by the story itself.[46] In abstracting paper production to book production Dowling misrepresents the fact that the paper made in the mill is for several purposes—"sermons, lawyers' briefs, physicians' prescriptions, love-letters, marriage certificates, bills of divorce, registers of births, death-warrants" (*PT* 333)—but not for books.

The impulse to read Melville's symbols as coherently connected is taken one stage further by Cindy Weinstein. She reads the story as an allegory and part of a more pervasive and self-conscious attempt by American writers to contest the ideology that labor and the work ethic could lead to personal progress and fulfillment, especially when jobs were becoming increasingly mechanized and monotonous. By revealing its own artifice, Weinstein argues, not only is Melville's literary labor entwined with the labor of the factory girls, but the self-evident artifice of allegory and the flatness of the story's characters "is itself allegorical . . . of cultural anxieties about changing relations between labor and agency."[47] "The Paradise of Bachelors and the Tartarus of Maids" has inspired a criticism that makes use of Melville's symbols of sex and gender, labor and leisure, for the purpose of allegorizing in the broadest possible fashion the story's representations of hierarchies of gender difference and of market conditions for writers.

Casting the internal contents of a story as an allegory and then making claims about the external allegorical function of these contents, however, is a particularly gratuitous separation of a text from its conditions of production. It is a method that relies too heavily on an unbroken chain of correspondences both internal, between the symbols and imagery of the two parts of the story, and external, between the story's imagery and symbols and the historical conditions of labor, gender, industrialization, and commercialized authorship. So how is the story different if the plain facts of paper are brought to the fore?

In watching the paper being made on the machine, the seedsman narrator of Melville's story is brought into contact with the economy of paper in which the paradoxes of its labyrinthine qualities, its "inadequacy" and yet its "finitude," are made evident to him. The production of this material is given a life before it enters the economy of print and the process of exchange; the narrator's contemplation of this time of production dominates the second part of the diptych. If one important strand of the treatment of this part of the story is to see it as an allegory of the dangers of mechanization, such treatments rely unquestioningly on linking the mechanization of papermaking and the marketization of writing and authorship. It is this chain of correspondences I want to uncouple and which "Paradise" itself, through the figure of the narrator, snaps apart. One starting point is to make a distinction between the machine-produced paper and the more abstract concept of continual movement that emerges in Melville's treatment of papermaking, since the latter is "so specially terrible" to the narrator as he observes the machine. While "machinery of this ponderous, elaborate sort," he says, "strikes, in some moods, strange dread into the human heart," the machine itself is subject to some more dramatic "metallic necessity," or an "unbudging fatality which governed it" (*PT* 333).

The narrator reveals himself here to be quite familiar with operating machinery. The fact that it is only in "some moods" that machinery can have this effect suggests an experience of machinery in other moods. The first half of the story too easily creates an image of the narrator as a dreamy character, rather than the experienced and successful businessman he becomes in the second part. Someone who distributes hundreds of thousands of letters is no stranger to the objects of mass production or the demands of a mass market. The narrator is certainly not represented as an innocent coming into contact with machinery for the first time. To distinguish between the mechanical apparatus of papermaking and the mysterious force that seems to control it is not just to raise questions about mechanization itself; it also questions the reliability of a correspondence between abstract process (the invisible force) and literal instantiation (the machine). Or, one might say, between "hideous and intolerable allegory" and "plain facts" (*MD* 205) Readings of the story too often rely on assuming the viability of correspondences of this kind, between the representation of mechanized papermaking in the story and the reality of marketized authorship in mid-nineteenth-century America.

The role of fine paper in this process is also significant. In contrast to the "autocrat cunning of the machine" that sends the narrator giddy and makes him see the pallid faces of the maids in the "pallid incipience of the pulp" (*PT* 333, 334), the cut paper that drops off the end of the machine sets the narrator thinking in different ways. In Melville's words, it sets him "wondering" rather than "wandering." As the narrator watches the paper "dropping, dropping, dropping" off the machine he says that his "mind ran on in wonderings of those strange uses to which those thousand sheets would eventually be put"; while considering the abstract force driving the machine he stands "spell-bound and wandering in my soul" as he watches the forming paper go past him (*PT* 333–34). So only at the end of the papermaking process, when the paper is subdivided into the raw material of cultural usage in all its myriad dimensions—the "sermons, lawyers' briefs, physicians' prescriptions, love-letters, marriage certificates, bills of divorce, registers of births, death-warrants" (*PT* 333)—does the paper stop being a part of that "unbudging fatality" one might argue is at the root of the correspondences I discussed earlier. Correspondence between mechanically produced product and abstract process is broken at this end point because, as the narrator says, "all sorts of writings would be writ on those now vacant things" and, as if to substantiate this, at the end of his list of examples he concludes, "and so on, without end" (*PT* 333).

There is no correspondence, then, between the mass-produced paper sheets and the uses to which they will be put. While the narrator thinks of John Locke when he sees the blank sheets of paper, when he contemplates the "autocratic cunning of the machine" he sees in the pulp the faces of the factory girls. In the first instance there is an associative thinking that delegates the metaphor of blank mind and blank paper to Locke; in the second there is a kind of mesmerized thinking that sees the maids literally embodied on the paper. The loose connection of the first is juxtaposed against the strict correspondence of the second. The very lack of connection as the paper drops off the machine between paper, process, and end use undermines a reading of the story that tries to make a virtue of allegorical equivalence between story and cultural condition. The narrator's "wonderings" at this point are suggestive and imply multiplicity and unknowability in the "strange" uses that might be made of the paper; his "wandering" is, paradoxically, not at all mobile and all too fixed like the "unbudging fatality" driving the machine. He is, as he says, "spell-*bound.*"

The chronological sequencing of the story, which draws to a conclusion through the narrator's linking of the maids and the pulp, might appear to give this moment diegetic privilege. But this is only because it appears to ratify the story's internal correspondences between the bachelors, the maids, and the papermaking process, the seeds of which the narrator has been planting all the way through the second part of the story. Thus when he first sees the maids he notes that "at rows of blank-looking counters sat rows of blank-looking girls with blank, white folders in their blank hands, all blankly folding blank paper." Of the two maids responsible for ruling the paper, the one handling the blank paper has a brow that is "young and fair," while the one handling the ruled paper at the other end of the process has a brow that is "ruled and wrinkled." Seeing the maids embossed on the pulp ratifies the narrator's earlier belief that the girls "did not so much seem accessory wheels to the general machinery as mere cogs to the wheel" (*PT* 328).

The issue here is whether to grant precedence to the ending of the narrative or the ending of the papermaking process and whether the strategic organization of correspondences in the narrator's account outweigh the one moment when correspondence is most clearly broken. The fact that Melville visited the paper mill in Dalton and the pointedness with which he drew attention in his letter to Duyckinck to the papermaker's stamp, the papermaking industry of Berkshire County, and his identification as a writer among other writers in the area, are decisive factors here. They help identify Melville's own understanding of his place within an economy and a culture of paper. The annotation might simply add some biographical interest to the letter were it not for the fact that the purpose of the rest of the letter, as I mentioned in the introduction, is to refuse Duyckinck's request that Melville submit a contribution and a daguerreotype of himself to *Holden's Dollar Magazine.* In the context of this refusal to participate in magazine culture, the purpose to which paper is put becomes all the more significant. Against the paper as it exists in the mill, ready for "all sorts of writings . . . without end," stand the pages of *Holden's Dollar Magazine,* which Melville refuses to fill not only with his image but also with the kind of popular sea piece for which he was known in the early part of his career but from which he was trying to distance himself at that very moment in his writing of *Moby-Dick* on fine paper bought in Dalton. By differentiating so pointedly between the paper that marks a "great neighborhood for authors" and the paper of printed magazine culture that he thinks will bring about his oblivion, Melville draws the sharpest of distinctions between the economy of paper and the economy of print.

The figure of the narrator in "The Paradise of Bachelors and the Tartarus of Maids" also becomes all the more intriguing if, as I am suggesting, the end of the papermaking process rather than the end of the narrative should take interpretative precedence. What exactly are we to make of the emphasis on those correspondences that have given the story its symbolic and allegorical leverage and produced such creative critical accounts of gender and biology and labor and authorship? The narrators in Melville's other short fiction—particularly in "Bartleby" and "Benito Cereno"—offer a version of events that is as interrogative of the narrators themselves and their subject positions as it is of the events narrated. A narrator who continually reaches for symbolic correspondence when faced with the plain facts of papermaking is not necessarily to be trusted; the symbols belong to the narrator more than they do to Melville, and the clumsy groping for connection the narrator undertakes is what the narrative questions rather than ratifies.

One can almost hear the seedsman's mind spinning when he picks up the reference to London in Cupid's response to his question about the sourcing of the rags in order to make the link with the bachelors. And Cupid's misunderstanding of the narrator's question about bachelor's buttons—taking him to mean the flowers of that name rather than the buttons from the shirts of bachelors—only emphasizes the idiosyncrasy of the narrator's perspective and the effort required on his part to produce correspondences that are not obvious to Cupid. Establishing, with another question, that the factory manager is a bachelor, it is the narrator who appears to be inventing rather than merely reporting the connections. He, after all, describes the "white, wet, wooly-looking stuff" as "not unlike the albuminous part of an egg" and then immediately describes the machine room's "abdominal heat" in which "were being finally developed the germinous particles" (*PT* 331); and he, more generally, constructs his experience in the second half of the diptych in the light of the first.

The opening part of the story has attracted much less critical attention than the second primarily because its role in the text is ancillary; it is the pretext upon which the second part of the story is stamped in relief. The seedsman is not just a businessman whose profession locates him as a cipher of coition, fertilized or obstructed; he is also a seedsman in his role as narrator, planting the literary images and scenes which he tends and harvests in the second part of his story.

In "Bartleby" and "Benito Cereno," we find narrators whose blind spots and misreadings are the object of analysis as much as they are the literary architecture by which that analysis proceeds. In "The Paradise of Bachelors and the Tartarus of Maids" Melville offers up a narrator with a different reading practice, one who proliferates connection and correspondence to such a degree across the two parts of the diptych that he too becomes a narrator whose partiality and idiosyncrasies the reader is asked to contemplate. If Melville delegates to the narrator the connections between bachelors and maids, leisure and work, in order to unmoor them from secure surroundings, then the very rigidity of the narrator's compulsion for correspondence in the diptych form resembles the "unbudging fatality" he contemplates as he watches the machine and as Cupid tells him that the machine "must go . . . just that very way, and at that very pace you there plainly *see* it go" (*PT* 333).

Standing in stark juxtaposition is the alternative the narrator touches on but refuses: the "strange uses . . . without end" to which the paper dropping off the end of the machine might be put. In "Bartleby," the retrospective contemplation of his scrivener serves the purpose of enabling the lawyer's observation of his own identity at a distance safe enough to prevent damage. A similar process occurs for the seedsman. When pacing before the machine in contemplation the narrator is "struck . . . by the inevitability as the evolvement-power in all its motions." This passage follows immediately after he contemplates Locke's understanding of the human mind at birth as a sheet of blank paper and as "something destined to be scribbled on, but what sort of characters no soul might tell" (*PT* 333). The shift here between inevitability and indefiniteness is one that clearly unnerves the seedsman and causes him to stand spellbound and wandering in his soul.

What I am suggesting the narrator sees when he watches the paper dropping off the end of the machine, and what Melville is asking the reader to see in the narrator, is something that confounds trust in correspondence and inevitability. The machine illustrates for the narrator in physical form the rigidity of his own mental need for control, harmonization, and correspondence. Yet despite being driven by the inevitable force of continual motion, the machine still produces blank paper, which, at this stage before reaching the maids in the folding room, is literally and philosophically unruly. What confounds the narrator is not the force driving the machine but the failure of this force to replicate itself in the object produced: fine, high-quality paper of substance that has uses "without end." In this reading, the story becomes almost a paean to the possibilities of paper before it enters an economy of print. Paper as a material form is what fascinates Melville; the manufacture and social embeddedness of this material is what the story so subtly and meticulously details. Rather than merely a topos to support the markings of print culture, paper in "The Paradise of Bachelors and the Tartarus of Maids" becomes the location of the narrator's discomfort and his recognition that writing, or scribbling, will only, as Christina Lupton writes, "disavow an absolute referent and gesture to a world of correspondences over which the writer has no control."[48]

Correspondence, of course, can signify both a sense of relation or agreement as well as communication by letter. This double meaning helps when thinking about Melville's imagination of paper and the post in "The Paradise of Bachelors and the Tartarus of Maids." The narrator's discomfort follows almost immediately upon his writing Cupid's name on a scrap piece of paper and dropping it into the pulp to test the speed of the machine. As the piece of paper containing yet another form of correspondence—of name to person—drops off the machine, "with my 'Cupid' half faded out of it, and still moist and warm," the narrator concludes, "my travels were at an end, for here was the end of the machine" (*PT* 332). Lupton suggests that "the more closely we look at ink on paper, the more the meaning of the characters recedes from us; the more we think about paper and print, the more cause we have to suspect that they fall beyond the reach of intellection."[49] In "Paradise" the narrator is pitched into a crisis of certainty after just such an observation of the marks he has cast on paper. Against all attempts at regulation—intricate machinery, the schedule of the workers, the nine-minute cycle that turns pulp into paper, the foolscap size of the uniformly blank paper, the narrative voice that seeks balance through symbol and correspondence—stand all those kinds of writing that will unpredictably and inadequately get scribbled upon the paper dropping predictably off the end of the machine.

The narrator's solution is to hurry his exit and retreat to an "inscrutable nature" that can be trusted not to pass judgment on his final efforts at harmonization when he exclaims, in an ending that echoes the final words of the lawyer in "Bartleby" and ties the two parts of the diptych together, "Oh Paradise of Bachelors! and oh! Tartarus of Maids!" (*PT* 335).

Melville's visit to the Old Berkshire Mill in Dalton in the winter of 1851 and his imagining of what he saw there in "The Paradise of Bachelors and the Tartarus of Maids" actually say very little about the economy of printing and publishing, which by 1860 had become the leading industry in New York. Instead, these events situate Melville in rural western Massachusetts, in a county dominated by the production of paper, and as a purchaser with a specialized knowledge about the material on which his writing career flowered and wilted. His letter to Duyckinck shows that paper was as important to Melville's understanding of himself as a writer as was the antebellum book market or the commercial understanding of authorship David Dowling suggests generated so many anxieties about "the craft" of writing.[50] Traveling to a paper mill by sleigh and buying his own store of fine paper is just as likely to have confirmed Melville's sense of himself as a craftsman; there is little anxiety in his letter to Duyckinck at any rate. Michael Newbury claims that in "Paradise" Melville "suggests that meaningfully legible texts and acts of writing simply do not or cannot emerge though mechanical production on an industrial scale."[51] The fact he completed *Moby-Dick* on machine-produced paper surely proves otherwise. Legibility is a problem for Melville not because of mechanization but because of the status of paper as a medium of communication.

The purpose of Melville's writing, so far as one can understand it in these two magazine stories, is not to make his notch or to satisfy some abstract obligation to society. Melville, thankfully, becomes more self-absorbed, not less; he turns to the material on which his writing life relied to reaffirm his own sense of himself as a writer even as he was writing for the magazine market. Ultimately, the success of the two stories is that they do more than mundanely echo the shrill economy of the commercialized print culture in which they appeared and in which Melville was failing. They are not noisy empty vessels. Melville's stories quietly reiterate that writers are not confined by the paper containers in which their work circulates. Magazine stories might tell something of the economy that gives them a public life, but that is not all, and certainly not the most interesting thing, they can tell. Pressing one's ear to Melville's paper stories one hears the stiff linen fibers bend under the pressure of his hand and the decelerating capillary motion as the paper's sizing stops Melville's ink from spreading too far. These noises constitute the soundtrack of a paper life. Melville understood that paper offered no guarantees to writers; his faith in it was not unconditional. But only someone who understood paper so intimately could explore how it mediated the writing life. To recuperate from the strains of writing novels, Melville continued writing, continued to write deeply, and embedded himself in the economy of paper.

2

"What Nots" and the Genres of Magazine Writing

The final number of the first volume of *Putnam's Monthly Magazine* appeared in June 1853. The magazine took stock and congratulated itself for encouraging Americans to pick up their pens: "from voluntary contributors" during the previous six months, the magazine reported, it had received "four hundred and eighty-nine articles, the greater part from writers wholly unknown before. They came from every state and territory in the Union."[1] More readers with literary ambitions subsequently responded to this announcement. But exactly what kinds of literature they sent to the magazine is not clear even from their own descriptions. "After considerable hesitation," Philip Brown wrote in January 1855, "I venture to offer the accompanying sketch for publication in your magazine. I know it is quite inferior to the articles that usually appear in 'Putnam', but . . . it is what it purports to be, a true story told at the fireside,—and therefore does not need so much the graces of composition, as a more pretentious essay." In October 1854, Eve Wilder asked whether the editors of *Putnam's* were prepared to say, "'Miss Eve, send on your stories, sketches, or what not, and we will try hard to find some merit in your productions.'"[2] Simultaneously stories, sketches, tales, essays, articles, or productions, these magazine "what nots" appear only loosely and interchangeably attached to specific narrative effects.

Melville's own vocabulary shows him embedded in the generic instability of this magazine world. The word "article" appears repeatedly in letters he sent to *Putnam's* and *Harper's* (*C* 248, 275, 281–82). In May 1856, Melville wrote to his father-in-law, Lemuel Shaw, explaining, "My immediate resources are what I can get for articles sent to magazines" (*C* 295). While he was comfortable enough when discussing *Israel Potter* to use "M.S.," "story," and "serial," and to refer to the parts he submitted as "chapters" (*C* 268, 270, 264, 273), when he sent two stories to *Harper's* in September 1854 Melville gave in to definitional uncertainty and stopped using literary terms at all: "I send you by express a brace of fowl—wild fowl. Hope you will like the flavor" (*C* 269). Like the other hopeful writers sending their material to *Putnam's,* Melville was making his way through the dense foliage of short prose forms variably and imprecisely described as sketches, tales, essays, and articles, whose conventions developed fitfully in annuals and gift books during the 1820s and 1830s, and then in magazines during the 1830s, 1840s, and 1850s. When he collected his *Putnam's* "articles" for publication, Melville originally suggested *Benito Cereno & Other Sketches* as the title for what would become *The Piazza Tales* (*C* 285). By changing the title, he registered how the leaves of the branches of sketch, tale, and essay traditions overlapped as he grasped at them in his writing.

The one term never used in Melville's letters or anywhere else in the 1850s is "short story." In this chapter, I show that Melville succeeded where many other writers in the 1850s failed: building on the achievements of writers working in the 1830s and 1840s, he developed and combined sketch and tale traditions to help invent the short story. Melville was not alone in this project. There are parallel and comparative lines of development: in Russia, Ivan Turgenev and Leo Tolstoy; in Britain, George Eliot; all were magazine writers in the 1850s. What distinguishes Melville in this company is that the short form did not mark the beginning of his writing career. Melville came to magazine writing after he was a published novelist.

Melville had briefly been a newspaper writer before he was a novelist, when in May 1839 he published two "Fragments from a Writing Desk" in the *Democratic Press, and Lansingburgh Advertiser,* an upstate New York weekly. But these pieces of stylized juvenilia bear little scrutiny. Melville first showed his adeptness as a magazinist in the summer of 1847, a year after Putnam published *Typee,* when he contributed nine brief satirical sketches to *Yankee Doodle,* a weekly humor publication edited by his friend Cornelius Mathews. "Authentic Anecdotes of 'Old Zack'" parodied Zachary Taylor, best known at that point for his military career during the war with Mexico but soon to become president in 1848. As he would do through his later magazine career, Melville remained anonymous as the sketches were published through July, August, and September. Embedded in the squabbles between New York City's literary Whigs and Democrats, the whimsical sketches linger over Taylor's personal habits and score points from the quotidian punch and counterpunch of a local political milieu that now seems distant and alien. The sketches remain landlocked in their moment of publication.[3] But Melville proved he could pull humorous satire from his writing bag in response to the commission from Mathews. Such a facility for style and genre would shape Melville's later novels; it also foreshadowed the adaptability that would make him a magazine staple for *Putnam's* and *Harper's* in the mid-1850s.

The first pieces he wrote for *Harper's* and *Putnam's* in the spring and summer of 1853—"Bartleby," "The Happy Failure," "The Fiddler," and "Cock-a-Doodle-Doo!"—were all very different in style, tone, and subject matter. What links them is a dexterousness with genre. The writer who adapted the sea narrative in *Typee* and *Omoo,* combined the sea narrative with allegory in *Mardi* and with natural history and the adventure story in *Moby-Dick,* and set about the domestic, the sentimental, and the gothic city-mystery in *Pierre,* brought to his magazine writing a similar restlessness with genre. The magazine writing is a bridge from *Pierre* to *The Confidence-Man,* where Melville would set about the unlikely fusion of metaphysics and southwestern humor.

Magazines accommodated Melville's idiosyncratic talents because of a capaciousness in which distinctions between failure and success for individual pieces carried little meaning. Magazine production could legitimately be called an industry by the 1850s, but it remained understandably disorderly and speculative. Reputations were difficult to create and even more difficult to sustain. Magazines like *Harper's* and *Putnam's* were also distinctively miscellaneous. They included essays, fictions, reviews, travel writing, filler pieces, and visual as well as written material. To describe the situation as chaotic does a disservice to magazines like *Harper's* and *Godey's Lady's Book,* whose operation was innovative and bureaucratically efficient enough to manage tens of thousands of subscribers.[4] But as in other febrile areas of development—the settling of land, gold prospecting, manufacturing, and urban expansion—magazine production during this period worked in the haze of uncertain future developments.

Imitation and Innovation in Magazine Writing

What existed instead of the short story in the 1830s and 1840s was the legacy of Washington Irving's success in combining the essay and sketch genres in his early magazine work for *Salmagundi* (1807–8) and then more famously in *The Sketch Book of Geoffrey Crayon, Gent.* (1819). The origins of these genres lay in the wit, philosophy, and morality of the British writers Richard Steele and Joseph Addison, the satire of Jonathan Swift, and the peripatetic narrators of Daniel Defoe and Oliver Goldsmith. Irving also drew on the Germanic folktale revitalized by Romanticism—and Romanticism's transition into realism—in the tales of Ludwig Tieck and E. T. A. Hoffmann. Transferring these tales across the Atlantic, Irving opened up the American continent to tales of the fantastic, while ingeniously preserving the integrity of his narrator Geoffrey Crayon by having the fictional Diedrich Knickerbocker narrate "Rip Van Winkle" and "The Legend of Sleepy Hollow" at another diegetic level. Irving's genial and amiable style certainly influenced American magazine editors and contributors. Published collections of magazine pieces borrowed the idea of the pictorial sketch in their titles. Eliza Leslie gathered together her stories as *Pencil Sketches; or, Outlines of Character and Manners* (1833) and Fanny Fern collected her magazine pieces as *Fern Leaves from Fanny's Portfolio* (1853). Nathaniel Parker Willis's debt to Irving is evident in his *Dashes at Life with a Free Pencil* (1845). When Willis offers the reader "a portfolio of sketches for a picture never painted," Irving's influence becomes visible as imitation.[5]

The Irving blueprint lived on in the figure of the educated, gentlemanly narrator, or the bachelor given to quiet disquisitions on seemingly random or obscure topics, especially in magazines like the *Knickerbocker* and later in *Putnam's* too. In retrospect, often forgotten authors and editors who wrote or published material of this kind—Donald Mitchell, George William Curtis, Willis Gaylord Clark, William Cullen Bryant—look like part of a residual culture in a literary world changing rapidly around them. They were ill equipped for the literary future because, unlike Irving, they looked backward without carrying their influences forward in adaptions of the genres to which they were so attached; in their hands, the sketch and the essay ossified.[6] But literary cultures rarely know their futures, and these men remained powerful actors in the magazine world in which

Melville published. Amid this magazine world, Hawthorne and Poe are the best-known innovators before Melville. Hawthorne transformed the historical tale into a psychological exploration of contemporary New England's relationship with its past; Poe created new genres (the detective story) and mastered others (sensation and comedy) while producing vivid and memorable characters and tales at the same time as diagnosing the literary qualities of the tale, or what would become the short story. But other lines of development emerged at the same time, and women writers proved some of the most popular and innovative inheritors of Irving.

Eliza Leslie's *Pencil Sketches,* for example, is full of whip-smart social satire that dissects the foibles and weaknesses of urbanizing middle-class men and women. Leslie was already a successful food writer before she started publishing fiction and also wrote children's stories and etiquette guides. After winning a fiction contest in *Godey's Lady's Book* in 1832 she became a regular contributor to the magazine as well as to *Graham's Magazine* in the 1840s. She edited the *Violet* and *Gift* annuals, took up a position as Sarah Josepha Hale's assistant editor at *Godey's,* and briefly in 1843 was the editor of *Miss Leslie's Magazine.* A pioneer of female authorship, Leslie was clearly adept at moving between the demands of fiction and nonfiction genres. But while her social observations skewered the vain, the priggish, and the conformist, they offered little social distance; the world is not a dangerous or mysterious place, just one with minor irritations that do not threaten to disturb the natural order of things. Even in "The Travelling Tin-man," in which an itinerant salesman is discovered to have abducted a black girl to take her to Maryland and sell her into slavery, order is restored when the benevolent white family foils the plan and adopts the girl themselves to replace their inadequate black servant.

In her sketches Leslie does, however, show a self-awareness about the readership of periodical literature shared by Catharine Maria Sedgwick, another important bearer of the short-form magazine tradition in this period. Leslie's "The Escorted Lady" is the story of a wealthy older businessman who escorts the beautiful but vain, provincial, and self-absorbed Miss Fairfax from Boston to Philadelphia. Miss Fairfax constantly delays their progress, but the businessman forgives her and flatters her because of her beauty. Her intellectual deficiencies are highlighted by her boredom with books, especially novels. When the businessman gives her a book he adds an explanation: "In recommending this to your perusal, I can assure you that it is not a novel, but a series of instructive and entertaining tales. I think it will afford you much amusement." Miss Fairfax takes the book "coldly" and is unimpressed: "When they are travelling with ladies under their care," she tells a hotel guest, "instead of keeping always with them, and trying to make themselves agreeable, they go and talk all the time to their own acquaintances, and leave the ladies sitting alone by themselves, thinking it sufficient to put them off with a foolish story-book."[7] Leslie's satire flatters the putative female reader of *Pencil Sketches* by showing that admirable rather than vain womanhood does not despise the "foolish story-book" but relishes it and reads it.

Female authorship is the subject of Sedgwick's "Cacoethes Scribendi," meaning "the itch for writing," first published in *The Atlantic Souvenir* gift book in 1830. In a village deserted by men and where "every woman . . . was a widow or maiden," Ralph Hepburn returns from Boston after "the season of the periodical inundation of annuals." He delivers "two of the prettiest" to Alice, the daughter of Mrs. Courland. But it is Mrs. Courland who is taken with the annuals. She feels the call of authorship and persuades her three sisters to follow her. So obsessed is Mrs. Courland that she "divided the world into two classes, or rather parts—authors and subjects for authors; the one active, the other passive." She is keen that the reluctant Alice become a writer too and sends a composition Alice once wrote at school to a periodical. The piece is accepted and when the magazine is delivered, Mrs. Courland "cut the string, broke the seals, and took out a periodical fresh from the publisher" to pass proudly to Alice. Who promptly throws it in the fire.[8] Mrs. Courland forgets her author ambitions, remembers she is a mother, and consents to her daughter's marriage to Ralph. Sedgwick was an experienced novelist by 1830; she wrote about history, about Indian encounter, and about domestic life with a seriousness and intensity that Leslie did not. In "Cacoethes Scribendi" she subtly demonstrates that female authorship requires artistry and is more than simply a response to the writing "itch."[9]

Neither Leslie nor Sedgwick were straightforwardly sentimental writers. Sentimental or domestic fiction was certainly the most popular genre of magazine writing into the 1850s, and many of the best-selling women writers of the period—Fanny Fern, E. D. E. N. Southworth, and Harriet Beecher Stowe—all published in magazines. But they were as different from each other as they were similar, and only a retrospective and masculinized critical temper impatient for the arrival of realism could characterize the period as one beset by scribbling women.[10] Sentimental fiction's roots were deep and well established in the transatlantic circulation of eighteenth-century writers such as Henry Mackenzie and Oliver Goldsmith. The sentimental tradition also leeched into the realism of Dickens that proved so popular in America. We now understand the cultural work achieved by sentimental fiction and its sensational sideshoot. Promoted and developed in the United States, the genre served—in the hands of a writer like Lydia Maria Child, for instance—the various causes of domestic morality and political reform, at the same time as providing popular entertainment.

More overtly sentimental in style than Leslie or Sedgwick, Child nevertheless still managed to address a range of difficult and controversial themes in her novels and her magazine writing.[11] One of the most powerful examples is "Elizabeth Wilson," Child's stories of a fallen women, published in the *Columbian Lady's and Gentleman's Magazine* in February 1845. As a young woman, Wilson is discarded by her lover for an older, richer woman. Her pregnancy ends with a stillbirth. She moves to Philadelphia for work and again gets pregnant, although there is no sense who might be the father. She gives birth to twins who are subsequently found strangled. Wilson denies killing them, but she is tried and executed after a pardon arrives too late to save her. When the story was published in book form, Child replaced a poem about Elizabeth's ascent to heaven with a damning judgment: "The poor young creature, guilty of too much heart, and too little brain to guide it, had been murdered by law, and men called it justice."[12] The story foreshadows some of the more famous literary infanticides in nineteenth-century literature: Cassy and Lucy in *Uncle Tom's Cabin,* Cora in Stowe's *Dred* (1854), and Hetty Sorel in George Eliot's *Adam Bede* (1859). Even if her style was unremarkable, Child helped diversify the subject matter of magazine fiction for later writers.

These are just a few examples of how innovative writers adapted Irving's sketch and tale legacy. If the stories lack the kind of character development that will mark the short story as it started to incorporate more realistic modes of psychological representation, this is partly because the stories and their authors have an eye on more immediate concerns affecting women and women readers. They may not have taken Irving's legacy forward in original formal directions, but they expanded the horizons of short magazine fiction in ways that were just as vital to its continued success. I choose these particular stories also because, however tangentially, they suggest motifs that reoccur in Melville's stories. The itinerant salesman in "The Lightning-Rod Man" is reminiscent of Leslie's "The Travelling Tin-man"; the strange village of H. in "Cacoethes Scribendi," made up entirely of widows and maidens, is a precursor of Melville's Devil's Dungeon in "The Paradise of Bachelors and the Tartarus of Maids." The tragic tale of Elizabeth Wilson, whose sexual encounters the narrator reveals with little sense of Elizabeth's consent, foreshadows the harrowing rape suffered by Hunilla in "The Encantadas." I do not claim influence here, but writers drew on an archive of imagery that evidences their connections rather than their distinctions, even if ultimately it is how writers represent this imagery that distinguishes them.

As writers continued to absorb Irving's legacy, by the 1850s his status as the premier American author was set in stone. Putnam and Irving both profited from the republication of his entire work in a new series in the late 1840s; Putnam's share of the profits helped his publishing business achieve the status required to launch a venture like *Putnam's Monthly*. But the 1840s also saw the beginnings of a backlash against Irving's influence. His reliance on European models sat uneasily with young New Yorkers—bookish Democrats like Evert Duyckinck and Cornelius Mathews—excited by the gathering changes of the Jacksonian city and averse to the literary traditions of New England. They looked to make their names by identifying and promoting American voices, founded *Arcturus* as a rival to the *Knickerbocker* in 1840 (although the magazine ran for only two years), and then worked with John Louis O'Sullivan on the *Democratic Review*; Duyckinck became an editor for Wiley & Putnam (George Palmer Putnam's earlier joint publishing venture) and finally fulfilled his ambition to produce a literary magazine worthy of national repute by having Wiley & Putnam finance *The Literary World* in 1847.[13] Outlets now existed both for old traditions and new voices.

The differences between the generations were real enough, as were disagreements about the purpose and value of literature, whose backdrop was the political antagonism between Democrats and Whigs. Writers fit less easily into the two camps. Was Hawthorne, for instance, an inheritor of the New England tradition or a nationalist? He was a Democrat but published his work in the *Knickerbocker* as well as in *Arcturus*. Melville had cause to thank Irving at the start of his writing career. After dinner with him in 1847, Evert Duyckinck claimed that Melville "models his writing evidently a great deal on Washington Irving," but Melville's faith in Irving waned by the early 1850s. In "Hawthorne and His Mosses" he accuses Irving of imitating Oliver Goldsmith's geniality. In the same letter to Duyckinck where he points out what "a great neighborhood" for authors is Pittsfield, Melville writes that "Irving is a grasshopper" compared to Hawthorne (*C* 181). He would reverse this assessment in a late unpublished prose poem, "Rip Van Winkle's Lilac," which sympathetically rewrites Irving's tale. But Melville was himself caught in the intellectual clash of old and new America; his writing prospered and suffered in its midst, notably at the hands of the promoter-turned-critic Duyckinck. In his magazine writing, Melville continued to work within the gravitational forces of taste cultures pulling against one another in the galaxy of American magazines, many of whom were caught between conformity and experimentation: on the one hand they must offer what was familiar to avoid alienating readers; on the other they must distinguish their content in order to create a commercial readership. Magazines found different ways to address this dilemma and generate audiences.

The *New York Ledger* bought up talent. Fanny Fern began her association with the magazine in 1855, and Robert Bonner, the *Ledger*'s owner and editor, advertised openly that Fern would be the country's highest-paid magazine writer—at $100 per column—in the hope that readers would identify remuneration as a marker of quality. They did: four hundred thousand of them by 1860, by which time the *Ledger* also owned exclusive rights to E. D. E. N. Southworth's fiction and claimed the imprimatur of other popular writers, such as Henry Ward Beecher, Henry Wadsworth Longfellow, Louisa May Alcott, and Harriet Beecher Stowe. The only fiction Charles Dickens published in America before publishing it in Britain—the three-part tale "Hunted Down"—appeared in the *Ledger*. The magazine paid Dickens the astronomical sum of £1,000.[14]

Harper's New Monthly took a different approach by distinguishing the product readers held in their hands. The firm invested in the expensive process of engraving to offer more illustrations and produced a magazine slightly smaller than competitors like the *Knickerbocker* but with more pages—144 as opposed to the more usual 80, 96, or 112. With the advertising and distribution support of a large and successful publishing house,

Harper's quickly gathered a readership unconcerned by the reliance on British authors that other editors and owners despised. George R. Graham, the publisher of *Graham's Magazine,* dismissed *Harper's* as "a good foreign magazine" of which even "the veriest worshipper of the dust of Europe will tire," while the *American Whig Review* thought the Harpers "anti-American in feeling as concerns literary development" and too keen on "pampering British writers" in their magazine.[15] So successful was *Harper's,* and so ready was the publishing house to support their new venture, that such "pampering" meant the magazine was able to buy, and not just reprint without payment, the work of British writers such as Dickens, Thackeray, Charles Lever, and Edward Bulwer Lytton. Despite brickbats, the combination of quantity, quality, and publishing know-how proved a winning combination in *Harper's.*

The articles of faith for *Putnam's* were indigeneity and quality. For George Palmer Putnam, the best way to recognize and showcase the quality of American writing was in a magazine whose excellence was visible in both content and design. The magazine soon established the reputation Putnam desired for it. The editor and publisher David M. Stone forwarded a manuscript to Putnam from Mary Hubbel, who, he told Putnam, "is ambitious of appearing between your 'green immortal' leaves." One *Putnam's* reader, Theodore Johnson, claimed that the magazine, "among all periodicals of this kind is the best and most valuable," not only because "it surpasses all of them by its popular character" but also because of "its typographical appearance and its excellent articles." Quality alone, however, did not ensure the survival of *Putnam's* beyond 1857.[16]

As they battled for market share and visibility, the capacity of magazines and editors to distinguish between imitative and innovative versions of the sketch and tale genres cannot be taken for granted. If magazine sketches were popular, writers—like Leslie and Willis—might follow Irving's example and resell their portfolio in book form. Encouraging the voices of prospective writers—the Philip Browns and Eve Wilders of the mid-nineteenth century—also meant broadening the range of experiences represented in magazines. Consequently, as Kristie Hamilton notes, authors "who could achieve an appropriately modulated private voice made this genre a field of conflict and accommodation for competing formulations of American authorship and cultural legitimacy."[17] This understanding of the sketch suggests that the literary culture of magazines was not monolithic but diverse; its taste cultures less exclusive and more open in the face of the realities of magazine expansion and competition. As long ago as 1977 Marvin Fisher wrote about Melville "going under" in his short prose writing, but even in much more recent criticism of Melville's magazine writing the belief persists that Melville stole the subversions of his writing into orthodox magazine forms.[18] The truth is that magazines were much more tolerant of formal and ideological idiosyncrasy.

Melville's short magazine pieces slice two ways into predominantly sketches and tales. In the first group are "Cock-a-Doodle-Doo!" "The 'Gees," "I and My Chimney," "The Happy Failure," "The Lightning-Rod Man," the multi-part sketches of "The Encantadas," and the three diptychs—"Poor Man's Pudding and Rich Man's Crumbs," "The Two Temples," and "The Paradise of Bachelors and the Tartarus of Maids." The second group comprises "The Fiddler," "Bartleby, the Scrivener," "Jimmy Rose," "Benito Cereno," "The Bell-Tower," and "The Apple-Tree Table." But Melville's imaginative mixing and juxtaposition of genres in the cosmic inflation of magazine culture defies such easy categorization. Some of these pieces are patchwork quilts stitched together out of garish material; others blend genre distinctions seamlessly into the warp and weft of a single fabric.

Disunited Genres in "Cock-a-Doodle-Doo!"

The December 1853 issue of *Harper's* contained several pieces of fiction in addition to "Cock-a-Doodle-Doo!" The first appeared a third of the way into the magazine, after two pictorial travelogues—Jacob Abbott's memoir of a trip to Bethlehem and Calvin Philleo's account of his visit to Plymouth, Massachusetts—and the pseudonymous "The Virginian Canaan," a report of an excursion into rural Virginia that I come back to later. "Sweet Bells Jangled" is the tragic tale of Edward Angelo, a sensitive young man whose misplaced infatuation with the much less sensitive Boadicea Fleurry results in his death. The reputation of *Harper's* fiction at this time was for sentimental conventionality. One or two stories per issue told tales about the stoical suffering that comes with love, poverty, illness, or family commitments; if suffering is alleviated, this usually occurs through sympathy, benevolence, or philanthropy—or more suffering; readers learn moral lessons, and inequalities of class and status are smoothed over in a bleak and redemptive, but static, moral universe.[19] "Sweet Bells Jangled" added to the quota for December along with the next story, G. P. R. James's "Four Sights of a Young Man," which tells of the sad decline and suicide of William Hardy through the narrator's four meetings with him.

"Cock-a-Doodle-Doo!" was sandwiched between these two tales and the unattributed "Brackley House," whose author we now know to be William Cowper Prime, and an installment of Thackeray's *The Newcomes.* Prime's story is a tragic tale of a family torn apart by feuding, and premature death strikes the central characters. Merrymusk's death in Melville's story, then, is only one of many in this issue of *Harper's.* Swinging back and forth between sentimental and tragic stories and earnestly and lightheartedly informative sketches and travelogues, *Harper's* sets a rhythm with which "Cock-a-Doodle-Doo!" is only partly in time; the story is notable in Melville's earliest batch of short pieces because sentimental, tale, and sketch genres stand so abruptly against one another. The generic structure of "Cock-a-Doodle-Doo!" plays fast and loose with their conventions.

The piece begins in sketch mode with a first-person narrator who drills down from worldwide revolts against "rascally despotisms" quickly crushed in recent times, to the casualties of industrial-age locomotives and steamers, to his "own private affairs" and the landscape he sees from his position sitting on a log at the top of his hillside pasture (*PT* 268). The narrator's eye ranges "over the capacious rolling country, and over the mountains, and over the village, and over a farm-house here and there, and over woods, groves, streams, rocks, fells." This is no pastoral idyll, however; the narrator soon turns to the miseries of modern life—the accidents and stupidity that lead people to be "disembarked into the grim hulk of Charon" (*PT* 269)—and to which he feels himself connected by a creditor who pesters him for payment. He has also suffered a reversal of fortune: his charity—giving up a berth on a boat to a sick woman—forced him to spend a night on deck in the rain, which gave him a case of "the rheumatics." The observational sketch mixes local knowledge of the countryside and the philosophizing of an educated man comfortable with classical allusion (Xerxes and Socrates follow Charon) but downtrodden by the intrusions of the fast-moving modern world, or the "gigantic gad-fly of a Moloch—snort! puff! scream!" that is the train (*PT* 270).

By the end of "Cock-a-Doodle-Doo!" the scene is quite different: the narrator visits the shack that is home to the poor woodsman Merrymusk and his wife and family and finds "the whole house was a hospital now" (*PT* 286–87). Merrymusk dies; his wife soon follows; the children quickly thereafter. "The pallor of the children was changed to radiance," the narrator observes, and their "faces shone celestially through grime and dirt. . . . Far, deep, intense longings for release transfigured them into spirits before my eyes. I saw angels where they lay. They were dead" (*PT* 287–88). The sketcher is now firmly transplanted into the sentimental mode. Bachelor reverie turns into misty-eyed mourning for a dead family; from railing cantankerously against modernity the narrator is pitched into a death scene from which he creates a new outlook on life; no longer, he claims, is he prone to "the doleful dumps" (*PT* 288). Linking these two states is the incongruous comic tale of Signor Beneventano—christened by the narrator after the opera singer Ferdinando Beneventano—the cockerel whose "smooth and flute-like" crowing enraptures the narrator (*PT* 274).

So inspiring is this crowing that the narrator faces down his creditor. Heard but not seen, the cock also forces the narrator to abandon his hillside repose and go wandering at ground level to find the source of the bird's "triumphant thanksgiving of a cock-crow" (*PT* 271). The bird's owner, he learns, is Merrymusk, the poor woodcutter whose life of poverty is ameliorated by having the bird for comfort. The narrator describes how the bird "irradiated the shanty" where Merrymusk lives: "He glorified its meanness. He glorified the battered chest, and tattered gray coat, and the bunged hat. He glorified the very voices which came in ailing tones from behind the screen" where the sickly children lie (*PT* 284). Merrymusk does not think himself a poor man while he owns the bird; he considers himself "a great philanthropist" for giving "all this glorification away gratis" (*PT* 286).

There are several ways to read "Cock-a-Doodle-Doo!" symptomatically: as a satire on transcendentalism's faith in nature to overcome material shortcomings, or as a piece of sexual innuendo charting the recovery of virility—the narrator, after all, is crowing at the end of the story after the cock dies along with the Merrymusk family; or as a piece of sentimental tourism that represents the nobility of poverty seen often in *Harper's* while keeping readers at a safe distance through the gentlemanly and detached narrator.[20] The story certainly made sense to one of Melville's relatives in terms of spiritual uplift. Clearly reading it without irony, Melville's brother-in-law John Hoadley wrote to Melville's sister

Augusta in December 1853, soon after *Harper's* published the story: "Tell Herman I thank him with all my heart, for that noble spiritual lesson of hope,—enduring, triumphant,—never-desponding,—in the 'Crowing of the noble Cock Beneventano.'"[21] All of these readings emphasize the story's unity of effect. Paradoxically, only the disunity of genre in "Cock-a-Doodle-Doo!" makes such readings possible.

The dramatic effects of the story are achieved in the morphing between genres, not through Melville writing steadfastly in one generic mode. The narrator offers no explanation for why the cock's crowing lifts his mood; the reader knows some change takes place when the sketch suddenly meets the new genre of bathetic comedy, which intrudes—like the cockerel—unexpectedly into the narrative. A similar impetus to infer meaning occurs with the coincidence of the narrator's visit to Merrymusk's home and the death of the entire family. Suddenly dropped into the sentimental occasion at the piece's denouement, meaning seems expected. In this formal juxtaposition, "Cock-a-Doodle-Doo!" wears its genres on its sleeve to generate meaning. If short stories like "Bartleby, the Scrivener" and "Benito Cereno" build dense webs of irony, where meaning emerges through a careful elaboration of consciousness, "Cock-a-Doodle-Doo!" patterns in bright blocks.

So why, in stories written at much the same time, does Melville write in such different ways? Why does he not write all his stories like "Bartleby, the Scrivener"? Sheila Post-Lauria suggests that Melville is instructing a particular audience in *Harper's* and that "Cock-a-Doodle-Doo!" conforms to the sentimental structure preferred by the magazine and its readers: sharing the joy of the cockerel that ennobles the suffering of Merrymusk and his family morally redeems the narrator. But if the purpose is to instruct, why does Melville not use genre in a way more consistent with the sentimental instruction available in *Harper's*? There may be angels in "Cock-a-Doodle-Doo!" but there are no tears; distinctions are more obvious than similarities. *Harper's* stories began, continued, and ended in the sentimental mode. So "Blind Man's Wreath," for instance, starts: "'My boy, my poor blind boy!' This sorrowful exclamation broke form the lips of Mrs. Owen."[22] A story Post-Lauria uses to show similarities with "Cock-a-Doodle-Doo!" opens with the following scene: "Just then a little child came running along—a *poor,* ill-clad child; her clothes were scant and threadbare; she had no cloak, and no shawl; and her little bare feet looked red and suffering."[23] Against the wide-ranging eye of the narrator in "Cock-a-Doodle-Doo!" these stories begin in close-up and stay there to generate moral instruction.

Melville's narrator comes out of a different tradition. The rural settlements of "Cock-a-Doodle-Doo!" that exist beside "a lagging, fever-and-agueish river," and over one of which hangs "a great flat canopy of haze, like a pall" (*PT* 269), are not exactly Sleepy Hollow but bear a family resemblance. The slapstick cockerel would fit well in Laurence Sterne's "cock and bull" story *Tristram Shandy,* a book the narrator is reading and whose "cock and bull" reference he would no doubt spot in his other reading matter: *The Anatomy of Melancholy,* in which Robert Burton coined the phrase. Rather than with the sentimental narrators of *Harper's,* Melville's narrator shares much more with the sketch narrator and the mischievous satirist as those figures emerge out of the eighteenth century, partly through Irving, and then twist themselves around each other's tendrils during the nineteenth century.

Overstating the structural unity of "Cock-a-Doodle-Doo!" ignores how the genres of sketch, comic satire, and the sentimental bump against one another so loudly. There is no steadfast sentimental mode as one might find in the writing of Lydia Maria Child, for instance. The sentimental comes to the fore only at the story's very end; the wrapping up enacted there is conventional but hardly offers closure in the light of what goes before. Merrymusk might claim spiritual wealth despite his penurious state, but the narrator, after hearing Merrymusk tell him this, then tells the same reader who will watch the sentimental climax only a page or so later, how he "returned home in a deep mood" and was "not wholly at rest concerning the soundness of Merrymusk's view of things, though full of admiration for him" (*PT* 286). The detached narrator with whom the story begins, high on his hillside, is not brought down to earth nor incorporated so easily into the sentimental mode. As such, the story lacks the formal and generic security that assures its place in the conservative magazine world of *Harper's.*

The sketch tradition was, in fact, alive and well in the pages of *Harper's* and sat happily beside sentimental writing. "The Virginian Canaan," which I mentioned above, attributed to "A Virginian," was the work of David Hunter Strother, who wrote under the blatantly Irvingesque pseudonym Porte Crayon (literally, from the French, "pencil holder") who appears as a character in this and the connected pieces Strother contributed to *Harper's* through the 1870s. In the spirit of the eighteenth-century travelling sketchers, Strother both wrote and illustrated; the two forms were integral to his magazine persona. The pieces themselves are mainly adventure travelogues and transplant Irving's wandering sketcher from Britain to Virginia and the South, where he finds friendship and excitement in backwoods escapades, regionalizing Irving's style along the way. The component parts of Crayon's identity are available in "The Virginian Canaan": "Every day added to the treasures of Porte Crayon's sketch-book. The author reveled in a poetic existence, basking on moss-covered rocks, among foaming rapids and sparkling water-falls; and if his haggard and unshaven countenance and dilapidated wardrobe presented a strong contrast to his mental beatitude, it only exemplified the more strikingly the predominance of mind over matter, and the entire disconnection that sometimes exists between the ideal and the material world."[24] Cerebral but at the same time a man in a physical environment, Crayon—just like the narrator of "Cock-a-Doodle-Doo!"—shows that short-form writing in American magazines drew on, and could accommodate, different traditions.

Magazines were unified neither generically nor philosophically in the 1850s. Magazines were collaborations, contained multitudes, and Melville fit not because he flew his ideas under editorial or reading detection systems by coating them with radar-absorbent irony—although the writing is often, of course, ironic—but because the delimiting of the air space in which he glided was enforced less effectively than it was espoused. *Harper's* spoke of the "unbounded treasures of the Periodical Literature of the present day." Although recognizing the impossibility of making all this material accessible to the magazine's readers, *Harper's* set itself the equally improbable task of placing "every thing of the Periodical Literature of the day, which has permanent value and commanding interest, in the hands of all who have the slightest desire to become acquainted with it."[25] Such confidence is almost as ridiculous as expecting the crowing of a cockerel to change one's moral character. But that was the magazine world of the 1850s: boundless ambition trying to cope with "unbounded treasures." It may seem that the bagginess of the novel is much more accommodating to experiment than the short story; that novels showcase writing, short stories formal precision. Yet without any agreed guidelines about what constituted a short story, the terrain for writing in shorter forms easily accommodated Melville's switching from sketch to satire to sentimentality in "Cock-a-Doodle-Doo!"

Roughening Genre's Smooth Edges in "The Encantadas"

After completing his first batch of "articles" with "Bartleby" in mid-September 1853, Melville spent the following months, through April 1854, writing a series of multi-part pieces whose generic origin is the sketch and whose dramatic and intellectual effects result from contrasting different points of view. These pieces are Melville's three diptychs—"Poor Man's Pudding and Rich Man's Crumbs," "The Paradise of Bachelors and the Tartarus of Maids," and "The Two Temples"—and "The Encantadas," ten connected sketches serialized in three parts by *Putnam's* from March to May 1854.[26]

The diptychs fused pictorial and literary sketch traditions but offered few ways to move that tradition forward. They do not achieve what Irving achieves over the course of his multiple sketches or what Dickens and Thackeray achieve in their regular sketch contributions to newspapers and magazines: the depiction through a roving narratorial point of view of a social world distinguished by contrasts. The results in Melville's diptychs are relatively static panels. In the jargon of narratology, the sketch "is a form in which catalyzers exist without cardinal functions."[27] The steady accumulation and consistency of narrative voice can offset this absence, but the diptych's brazen shifts and binary contrasts are a generic dead end. Melville's only novel twist is to set one panel in America and one in Britain in each of the pieces.

"The Encantadas," the first written of Melville's multi-part experiments with the sketch, is an altogether different proposition. "The Encantadas" offers a sustained experimentation with narrative perspective that makes the diptychs look like afterthoughts in the way they take up the same theme. "The Two Temples," rejected by *Putnam's* and unpublished in Melville's lifetime, deals primarily with a narrator who observes scenes in a New York City church and a London theater and draws attention to the process of looking. From aloft in the church, he says, "I seemed inside some magic-lantern" (*PT* 304) and "through some necromancer's glass, I looked down upon some sly enchanter's show" (*PT* 306). The real "enchanter's show" takes place in Melville's representation of the Galapagos Islands, christened by Spanish travelers "the Encantadas, or Enchanted Isles." In the shadowy half-light of the history and nature of these islands, where one encounters all manner of "ocular deceptions and mirages" (*PT* 142), Melville builds his own magic lantern whose narrative activity surpasses the static panels of the diptychs. As sketches he publishes in a magazine, "The Encantadas" also have their own mysteries; they provide "A Pisgah View from the Rock"—the title of the fourth sketch—from which to look at the place of the sketches in the magazine world and *Putnam's* in particular.

Melville sent the first batch of sketches to *Putnam's* on February 6, 1854, along with a terse and odd note: "Herewith I send you 75. pages adapted for a magazine. Should they suit your's, please write me how much in present cash you will give for them" (*C* 256). Melville's use of the word "adapted" here is ambiguous: it may simply refer to writing Melville thinks suited to a magazine, although he shows little confidence that *Putnam's* is the magazine it best fits; but "adapted" also suggests writing changed from one form to another. In an earlier letter sent to Harper & Brother in November 1853, Melville claimed to have written three hundred pages of a new book: "partly of nautical adventure, and partly—or, rather, chiefly, of Tortoise Hunting Adventure. It will be ready for press some time in the coming January." Melville then asks for an advance of $300. He duly received the advance within two weeks, despite the poor sales of his previous books and the word "Declined" penciled across the top of the letter (*C* 249–50). There was later correspondence about this project, but the book never appeared. The Galapagos Islands is home famously to giant tortoises. Melville clearly took an advance from the Harper firm and "adapted" either what was already written of the "Tortoise Hunting Adventure," or what he intended to write, and sold the material again for publication in *Putnam's*.

Melville's motives in this episode are not clear. If he was intentionally duplicitous then he beat Harper to the punch: the firm would charge him for reprinting his own books after a warehouse fire in December 1853 at its Cliff Street premises. And like the narrator of "Cock-a-Doodle-Doo!" Melville had creditors to pay: John Brewster, from whom he bought Arrowhead with the help of a $1,500 mortgage charged at $90 interest each year; and Tertullus Stewart, from whom Melville took out a second mortgage. Melville paid Brewster after his windfall but not Stewart. Changes were also taking place in the Melville household. In September 1853 Melville's sister Catherine married, and another sister, Helen, married in January 1854. This put a further strain on Melville's finances and interrupted his work; he was now down to one copyist, Augusta, who was also occupied with household chores. It is possible Melville deceived neither the Harpers nor *Putnam's* if the "Tortoise Hunting Adventure" and what *Putnam's* published as "The Encantadas" were two different works. As Hershel Parker points out, when the first installment of "The Encantadas" appeared in March 1854—almost immediately after Melville submitted his "75 pages," so suitable was the piece for *Putnam's*—the tortoises were in full view and the Harpers must have noticed them. But there is no evidence of recrimination; Melville continued to publish work in *Harper's* over the next two years, although *Pierre* proved his last novel with the firm. The biographical and chronological record goes cold at this point. Unlike the Galapagos tortoises, the truth of this magazine conundrum has no "citadel wherein to resist the assaults of Time" (*PT* 131). It is an epistemological dilemma that well serves "The Encantadas," whose own epistemological concerns Melville uses the genre of the sketch to elaborate.

"The Encantadas" nods to the sketch tradition most visibly in the titles of each of the ten sections: "Sketch First," "Sketch Second," and so on. Certainly in the work of Irving, Dickens, and Thackeray, the sketch also nominally protects authorial identity through the use of a pseudonymous narrator: for Irving there is Geoffrey Crayon; for Dickens, Boz; and for Thackeray, Michael Angelo Titmarsh and George Savage Fitz-Boodle. "The Encantadas" is the only piece of Melville's magazine writing to appear with authorial attribution. The three installments do not carry Melville's name, however, but appear under the pseudonym "Salvator R. Tarnmoor." As Geoffrey Crayon is to Irving, so, it seems, Salvator R. Tarnmoor is to Melville as he places himself in the lineage of the sketch tradition. And yet the value *Putnam's* placed on anonymity makes the situation less straightforward.

The three issues in which "The Encantadas" appeared carry no other attributed pieces; more than this, "The Encantadas" is the only attributed piece by a living writer to appear in any issue of *Putnam's* between the first issue of January 1853 and the final issue of September 1857. *Putnam's* published "Old Ironsides" in May 1853 in honor of James Fenimore Cooper, who had died in September 1851, a piece the magazine's publisher understood to be "the only posthumous publication of his writings which will be given to the world."[28] *Putnam's* did not deal in attribution, real or pseudonymous. Francis Underwood, a prospective contributor, anticipated the reason for this in a letter sent to the magazine just as "The Encantadas" reached its readers: "As your contributors are anonymous, it follows, I suppose, that you pay for articles instead of reputations, and therefore, that a nameless man has an equal chance with Hawthorne or Longfellow."[29] *Putnam's* was the residual incarnation of an earlier republican periodical culture where, as Jared Gardner puts it, there existed a "mutual contract inherent in anonymous periodical publication that bound the author to defend himself by words alone and the reader to judge the writer by the same criterion."[30] Melville reprinted "The Encantadas" in *The Piazza Tales* with the pseudonym removed, though whether this resulted from Melville's request or the printer's error is also unknown. Melville never addressed the issue in his letters to *Putnam's* and the ghostly magazine avatar lasts but three months, from March through May 1854.[31]

What, then, to make of this pseudonym in a sea of anonymity?[32] Without primary evidence on which to make an argument, conclusions are by necessity speculative, but one approach is to think about the peculiar qualities of the sketch pseudonym. Unlike other pseudonymous authors, the pseudonymous sketch author is also the narrator and a character in the narrative. Mark Twain does not appear in novels written by Samuel Clemens, nor George Eliot in novels by Mary Anne Evans. But Geoffrey Crayon is the "I" of the *Sketch Book* and Boz the "we" of *Sketches by Boz.* Salvator R. Tarnmoor is certainly the "I" of "The Encantadas," a character in the sketches and more an alter ego than a pseudonym, one who creates an extra diegetic layer between content and anonymous author.

Melville registers the importance of a sketch tradition by using a pseudonym for "The Encantadas," and Marvin Fisher is right to say that Melville "uses the resemblance to emphasize several important literary and pictorial contrasts between his portfolio of sketches and that of such a genteel predecessor as Irving."[33] The contrasts are not just with predecessors but with contemporaries. Salvator R. Tarnmoor stands out in the pages of *Putnam's* like Rock Redondo in "Sketch Third" of "The Encantadas" as it climbs "two hundred and fifty feet high, rising straight from the sea ten miles from land" (*PT* 133). Conspicuously authorized, "The

Encantadas" is unlike any other pieces in *Putnam's*. Tarnmoor localizes the content of the sketches by attributing them to a specific character and to a specifically learned sailor, although he may be a "tar no more."[34] Just as Tarnmoor looks from Redondo Rock at the surrounding terrain from a great height, so the attribution makes us look hard at the rest of *Putnam's* and prompts the question, What is the difference between a world seen from the anonymous authority of *Putnam's* and the position of the sketcher Salvator R. Tarnmoor?

In some respects, the world looks the same because the magazine reader might have traveled this way before; the colorful, exotic, and often dangerous Galapagos existed already in the American imagination. In 1846, *The Living Age*, a popular weekly that republished articles from British and American periodicals, printed a review of John Coulter's *Adventures in the Pacific* (1845). The reviewer reported:

> Willing Crusoes are scattered throughout this vast ocean; and though many soon get tired of their island solitude and escape from it when opportunity offers, men are yet found who prefer it to such civilization as they can have access to. . . . One of such settlements Dr. Coulter fell in with, at the Galapagos, a group near the Equator, and not very far from the coast of Peru. On one of these islands a Spaniard of the name of Vilamil had taken up his quarters; having some claim upon the government, he was paid by a grant of black criminals, and permission to establish a colony in the Galapagos; which he did upon monopoly principles, with unfortunate results.[35]

The conflict over island resources was the object of a *Harper's* report in September 1852, when the magazine informed its readers that "painful intelligence has been received of the massacre of the crew of the American sloop Phantom, and the destruction of the vessel, by the convicts of one of the Gallipagos islands, in November last."[36] The *Friends' Review* in August and September 1854 reprinted from the *National Era* William Seward's speech to the Senate urging the adoption of steam power to help the United States compete commercially with Britain, whose flag one meets, he says, "fixed, planted, rooted into the very earth" when one travels northward, southward, or even when "you ascend along the southwestern coast of America, [where] it is seen at Galapagos, overlooking the Isthmus of Panama."[37] In an age of scientific and natural history discovery, the Galapagos feature both as a destination—as in *The Pioneer; or California Monthly Magazine* article "A Trip to the Galapagos Islands"—or as a site of special geological or zoological interest. In December, 1850, for instance, *The Eclectic Magazine of Foreign Literature* reprinted an article from *Fraser's Magazine* called "Facts and Wonders of the Tortoise Family," in which Charles Darwin and the Galapagos tortoise feature prominently.[38] The publication and reprinting of this material ensured that Melville's writing was not freestanding; as with "Bartleby," there existed a magazine base-camp from which he could set off.

The route Melville scales, however, leads in another direction. Even the title renders from another angle what might be a familiar world to the magazine reader. Not until the bottom of the second page of the first sketch as it appeared in *Putnam's* is it clear that this island world is better known by a different name, and then only in an aside: "For concerning the peculiar reptile inhabitant of these wilds—whose presence gives the group its second Spanish name, Gallipagos—concerning the tortoises found here, most mariners have long cherished a superstition, not more frightful than grotesque" (*PT* 128). Squeezed between the repetition of "concerning," the Galapagos only interrupt Tarnmoor's narration of a world known more readily to him as the Encantadas.

Melville's reimagining of the islands is thoroughgoing and decidedly partial, especially in the way Tarnmoor's narration privileges sources written before Darwin's visit and publication of *The Voyage of the "Beagle,"* the one source most likely to have informed American readers about the islands. The only "eye-witness authorities worth mentioning," Tarnmoor claims, are "Cowley, the buccaneer (1684); Colnet, the whaling-ground explorer (1798); Porter, the post captain (1813). Other than these you have but barren, bootless allusions from some few passing voyagers or compilers" (*PT* 143). The bogus population table for Albermarle Island in "Sketch Fourth" pokes in the eye scientific claims to know the islands. By disregarding and satirizing scientists like Darwin, Denise Tanyol argues, "Melville's work wrests the Galapagos from the grasp of the naturalist, revealing that the marvels of the world are not to be easily mapped, counted, and classified."[39] Nor so easily managed and colonized. One of the pleasures of his journey, Darwin wrote, was that "the world ceases to be blank; it becomes a picture full of the most varied and animated figures." The world Melville creates—the "heaps of cinders" that look "much as the world at large might, after a penal conflagration" (*PT* 126)—is uninhabitable and far removed from the vibrant ecosystem Darwin imagined in his *Voyage,* whose conclusion expresses a colonizing spirit: "To hoist the British flag, seems to draw with it as a certain consequence, wealth, prosperity, and civilization."[40] Tarnmoor's uninhabitable and mysterious Enchanted Isles are not such willing beneficiaries.

Tarnmoor's narrative also charts an island territory that sits ambivalently in the midst of *Putnam's*. In literary terms, the magazine followed Seward's approach by raising the American flag in competition with the British and strived to claim the legitimacy of American writing. The magazine was also part of George Palmer Putnam's larger publishing business, which, as Hester Blum shows, consisted of books and series whose purpose was to register, tabulate, and systematize knowledge of the world from an American perspective in works such as *American Facts: Notes and Statistics Relative to the Government of the United States* (1845), *The World's Progress—A Dictionary of Dates* (1850, republished in 1852 as *Hand-Book of Chronology*), the six-volume *Home Cyclopedia* (1852–53), and in Wiley and Putnam's Library of American Books, the series in which Putnam published Melville's *Typee*. But while "The Encantadas" challenges Darwinian taxonomy, and by extension also mocks the ideological aim of *Putnam's* and its parent company to see the world anew from an American perspective, this mocking is not so loud that "The Encantadas" departs from that aim; on the contrary, the eagerness with which *Putnam's* accepted the sketches suggests Tarnmoor's narrative fulfills the magazine's purpose.

Putnam's was a magazine of both the sciences and the arts; it valued material knowledge as well as the imaginative engagement of this material. So much so, Blum argues, that it operated in a way that could "accommodate both rootedness and fluidity." Salvator R. Tarnmoor's imaginative rendering of the geologically and zoologically captivating Galapagos Islands not only "underscores the importance of active labor over received knowledge"—knowledge like that found in *American Facts*—but is also part of a process to which *Putnam's Monthly* was committed: transforming "existing materials into other usable qualities" in a process that "is never static or complete but always generating matter, printed and physical."[41] In this belief, *Putnam's* was more forgiving of individuals like Melville who experimented with reimagining the world. The multi-part sketch is vital to this process and to the mobilization of Tarnmoor's imaginative eye. Unlike the static panels created in the diptychs, "The Encantadas" generates fluidity and movement in ways that regenerate the sketch genre and also elaborate a way of seeing that is exceptional—like their attribution—in the pages of *Putnam's*.

"The Encantadas" also goes beyond some other famous stories that test the boundaries of literary perspective. In "The Minister's Black Veil," for instance, Hawthorne condenses epistemological uncertainty into the symbol of the veil, whose appearance and continued visibility in the community trigger the search for explanation and meaning. In Poe's "The Purloined Letter," the eponymous letter is hidden in plain sight, and only Dupin's ratiocinative brilliance can find it. "The Encantadas" does not rely on symbolism; like "The Purloined Letter" it projects the issue of perspective onto narrative form. Unlike Poe's story, however, which relies on the twin temporal sequences that will define the detective genre—the time of the crime and the time of the investigation—time in "The Encantadas" does not work so fluently; like the perspectives it presents, time is fractured in Melville's twisting of the sketch form.

Melville's sketches presented no problems to *Putnam's*. As I noted earlier, the tastes of the editors operated respectfully of conservative transatlantic literary influences. This ambivalence even echoes in the magazine's founding editorial: "The genius of the old world is affluent; we owe much to it, and we hope to owe more. But we have no less faith in the opulence of our own resources." "No less faith" only just suggests "more faith." And literary nationalism is more easily stated than enacted when the ideological consistency of the *Putnam's* project had to withstand the periodicity of the publishing cycle and the judgment calls made in the acceptance of each article. The sketch form was a magazine staple and offered none of the potential problems in Melville's structuring of "Benito Cereno," about which George William Curtis complained to Joshua Dix: "It is a great pity he did not work it up as a connected tale instead of putting in the dreary documents at the end.—They should have made part of the substance of the story."[42] The multi-sketch form allows Melville to roam free but from within the confines of a recognizable genre; the ten sketches provide a structure—the simple movement from island to island—that prevents the narrative from spinning out of control; as sketches they require no resolution or forced unity. The multi-part sketch, then, is a structure simultaneously closed and open, or rooted and fluid. When "The Encantadas" arrived at *Putnam's* there was nothing to which the editors might object. Melville's uncertainty that the material would suit *Putnam's* proved ungrounded.

One of the ways Melville generates epistemological fluidity in "The Encantadas"—of narrative voice, of perspective—is by opening the sketches from such a firm and clear point of view that immediately addresses and guides the reader. Sketch dues are paid in the first Spenserian epigraph—Irving's *Sketch Book* is full of such epigraphs—but the first voice is authoritative, suggests a third-person (or first-person plural) rather than a first-person narration, and is heard as the response to a question phrased something like "So, can you describe the islands for me?" The answer is both pragmatic and ornate: "Take five-and-twenty heaps of cinders dumped here and there in an outside city lot; imagine some of them magnified into mountains, and the vacant lot the sea; and you will have a fit idea of the general aspect of the Encantadas, or Enchanted Isles" (*PT* 126). In one way like an instruction for an experiment or a recipe, in another it is also metaphorical; sensitive to its readers' location—an urban scene more familiar to them—it is also otherworldly as the tenor and vehicle of the metaphor pull apart. This phatic opening establishes the perspective of the overview in the first sketch, "The Isles at Large," and the balance of description and allusion continues as the first epistemological dilemma emerges: the unrelenting fixity of the islands—"to them change never comes; neither the change of seasons nor of sorrows" (*PT* 126)—and yet the "apparent fleetingness and unreality of the locality of the isles" that gives rise to the notion of them as the "Enchanted Group" (*PT* 128).

The first sketch establishes that what one sees of the islands depends on one's position: "However wavering their place may seem by reason of the currents, they themselves, at least to one upon the shore, appear invariably the same: fixed, cast, glued into the very body of cadaverous death" (*PT* 128). The narrator stands both on shore and at sea. Where in the diptychs conflicting visions are separated formally in the two panels, here they are combined in a copious, delicate, and reflective narrative eye that takes the stuff of the travel narrative or the natural history and brings it into the impressionistic sketch. Vivid images are fused with history and superstition. The islands are at one moment like "split Syrian gourds left withering in the sun" (*PT* 126), and then the location for fleets of whaling ships and buccaneers; the "self-condemned" tortoises in whom "lasting sorrow and penal hopelessness are . . . so suppliantly expressed" (*PT* 129) are also, so legend has it, the transformed bodies of commodores and captains. The first sketch then offers the delayed gratification of the first-person narrator, Salvator R. Tarnmoor, whose "I" appears only in the penultimate paragraph and is located in yet another position: back in America, from whose cities he escapes into the Adirondack Mountains to recall "as in a dream, my other and far-distant rovings in the baked heart of the charmed isles." Not just from shore and from sea does Tarnmoor imagine the Encantadas; he sees them, too, in the mansions where he socializes and where candles cast shadows on walls: out of the undergrowth of these shadows Tarnmoor sees "the ghost of a gigantic tortoise, with 'Memento ****' burning in live letters upon his back" (*PT* 129).

The late arrival of the first-person narrator in "Sketch First" is a subtle adjustment of the sketch form. The shift of narrative position unmoors the seemingly authoritative and fixed point of view with which the sketch starts. Moving from the omniscient to the personal, Tarnmoor is now not just author of, but actor in, this account; one is moved from an outward-facing view of the world to an inward view of a narrator in whom an impression of that external world is burned like the letters on the tortoise's back. If traditional sketches rely on what Amanpal Garcha calls "individualized figures of quirky, eccentric narratorial personas," this figure is gone in "The Encantadas" because the movement from omniscience to Tarnmoor's "I"—and the delay of this movement—undercuts the idea of the consistent point of view required to establish such a figure.[43] Tarnmoor may trade in empirical reality combined with a sketcher's subjectivity, but in later sketches other voices and stories intrude on his subjectivity—as I show later in this chapter—and his own subjectivity is continually exposed. In these conditions, any consistent position is circumscribed. The sketches in "The Encantadas" are less like quick and individual impressions than contemplations narrated retrospectively; less initial drawings than finished paintings worked up in the studio, or in the hills of the Adirondacks, where Tarnmoor can "recall" and "remember" and where he feels "the vividness of my memory, or the magic of my fancy" and reckons himself the "victim of optical delusion concerning the Gallipagos" (*PT* 129). Subjectivity here seems to be the object of analysis for Tarnmoor rather than the medium for telling the reader about the islands. Where Irving's Geoffrey Crayon keeps the "enchanted region" of Sleepy Hollow at safe distance in the papers of Diedrich Knickerbocker, Melville's

Tarnmoor has himself "slept upon evilly enchanted ground" (*PT* 129).[44] Out of sketches emerge a short story.

The dual components of Tarnmoor's narrative subjectivity—as guide and rememberer—emerge more clearly in "Sketch Second—Two Sides to a Tortoise" and "Sketch Third—Rock Redondo." The first of these begins with a general disquisition on the dark back of tortoises and their brighter underside, before halting formally—"But let us to particulars" (*PT* 130)—at which point the first-person narration again begins. "Rock Redondo" starts similarly: "Now, with reference to the Enchanted Isles, we are fortunately supplied with . . . a noble point of observation in a remarkable rock" (*PT* 133), which is the steep-sided, towerlike islet known in Spanish as Roca Redonda, in the northern Galapagos. Tarnmoor then recounts for the reader "my first visit to the spot" (*PT* 134) and a different "we"—his shipmates—who lower boats from their ship and make for the rock; as he climbs it, the first-person singular gives way to first-person plural: "Let us glance low down to the lowermost shelf," Tarnmoor says. As he observes different birds, he makes the reader follow: "But look, what are yon woebegone regiments drawn up on the next shelf above? . . . Higher up now we mark the gony, or gray albatross . . . As we still ascend from shelf to shelf, we find the tenants of the tower serially disposed in order of their magnitude" (*PT* 135). In "Sketch Fourth—A Pisgah View from the Rock" the multiplication of points of view increases still further as the second person joins in:

> Suffice it, that here at the summit you and I stand. Does any balloonist, does the outlooking man in the moon, take a broader view of space? Much thus, one fancies, looks the universe from Milton's celestial battlements. A boundless watery Kentucky. Here Daniel Boone would have dwelt content.
>
> Never heed for the present yonder Burnt District of the Enchanted Isles. Look edgeways, as it were, past them, to the south. You see nothing; but permit me to point out the direction, if not the place, of certain interesting objects in the vast sea, which kissing this tower's base, we behold unscrolling itself towards the Antarctic Pole. (*PT* 137)

All these shifts in perspective take place in views of, and from, a rock that is itself the viewing platform for the rest of the islands as well as the watery world "unscrolling" as far as the Antarctic. The impressionistic sketch becomes more like a Cubist painting juxtaposing impossible angles of vision.

Finally (if not in the final sketch), there is the story of Hunilla's rescue in "Sketch Eighth." The story is prompted by the unusual angle of vision of one of Tarnmoor's shipmates. Having consumed "a dram of Peruvian pisco" and standing atop rather beside his handspike as he helps turn a large windlass, the "elevation of his eye" spots a fluttering handkerchief on Norfolk Isle. The "long cabin spy-glass . . . thrust through the mizzen rigging from the high platform of the poop" confirms Hunilla's presence on the isle, from which she is rescued by the ship's crew. Between the rescue and Hunilla telling her story to the ship's captain, Tarnmoor inserts a paragraph of reflection that lays bare the sketch tradition in and against which Melville is working: "It is not artistic heartlessness," Tarnmoor says, "but I wish I could but draw in crayons; for this woman was a most touching sight; and crayons, tracing softly melancholy lines, would best depict the mournful image of the dark-damasked Chola widow" (*PT* 152). To conceive of writing as drawing, or crayoning, was nothing new: the literary sketch had long used tropes of visual sketching. But in implying his inability to "draw in crayons," Tarnmoor puts himself at one remove from sketchers like Irving's incarnation of the Crayon-er.

If not crayons, then what? Instead of the smooth geniality one might find in Irving, Melville's Tarnmoor retells Hunilla's story in the stark, rough lines of tragedy as Hunilla watches the death of Felipe and Truxill, her husband and brother. To achieve this, the sketch uses the format of a story within a story common to the sketch, but in a way that manages to look two ways at once: from the narrator's perspective as Tarnmoor relays the scene but also from Hunilla's perspective as the tragedy unfolds. Setting out by raft on a fishing trip, Felipe and Truxill "perished before Hunilla's eyes." As if reinforcing the importance of showing this tragedy from Hunilla's perspective, Tarnmoor's narrative continues by repeating these final words before elaborating the visual manner in which Hunilla observes the tragedy. The accumulation of visual effects is worth quoting at length:

> Before Hunilla's eyes they sank. The real woe of this event passed before her sight as some sham tragedy on the stage. She was seated on a rude bower among the withered thickets, crowning a lofty cliff, a little back from the beach. . . . [U]pon the day we speak of here, the better to watch the adventure of those two hearts she loved, Hunilla had withdrawn the branches to one side, and held them so. They formed an oval frame, through which the bluey boundless sea rolled like a painted one. And

> there, the invisible painter painted to her view the wave-tossed and disjointed raft . . . ; and then all subsided into smooth-flowing creamy waters, slowly drifting the splintered wreck; while first and last, no sound of any sort was heard. Death in a silent picture; a dream of the eye; such vanishing shapes as the mirage shows. (*PT* 154)

The reader watches Tarnmoor reimagine Hunilla spectating on the drama playing out before her and the painting being painted before her eyes. The censure of Irving, John Bryant argues, may show that Melville did "not reject Irving so much as grow beyond him."[45] In "The Encantadas," then, there exist not sketches but paintings; not smooth geniality but the heart-stopping realization of what the painting shows even as the narrator cannot: death. No wonder the narrator is reluctant to intrude further on Hunilla's woe, or on her rape at the hands of passing whalemen evident from her blank responses to the captain's questioning: "'Señor, ask me not. . . . Nay Señor. . . . Ask me not, Señor.'" Tarnmoor "will not file this thing complete" because "it may be libellous to speak some truths," but in truth he has already spoken it, and Tarnmoor's painting of the encounter of a Chilean woman and western whaleboats speaks a truth more accurate than Darwin's faith in the consequences of national flag-planting (*PT* 157–58).[46]

There is nothing smooth about "The Encantadas." Not the recursive diegetic structure, the jagged angles of vision, the multiplying of perspectives during the course of meditations on perspective, or the stitched and sewn-together experiences Tarnmoor tailors from his several visits to the islands. When Tarnmoor describes the sea "unscrolling" toward the Antarctic, he is reminiscent of the narrator in "The Paradise of Bachelors and the Tartarus of Maids," who gazes at the machine that stands before him "rolled out like some long Eastern manuscript" and the paper it produces for uses "without end." For Melville the sea had long been a scroll for his writing. That he turns here in "The Encantadas" to a paper metaphor reinforces a point I made in chapter 1: when writing for the magazine market, the material on which his writing life relied is close at hand when he wishes to reaffirm his sense of himself as a writer. In "The Encantadas" he shows no less ambition with genre than previously in his novels; here the sketch that Irving bequeathed to America crumbles. "The Encantadas" contains sketches but shows that sketches cannot contain the Enchanted Isles.

The form of "The Encantadas" is rarely now the primary focus of critical attention. Yet all that the story achieves is done with genre in mind and was first achieved in *Putnam's Monthly*. The attribution to Salvator R. Tarnmoor may make the story stand proud in that magazine's pages, but Melville was much more closely embedded in the sketches and other "what nots" among which he published. He was also much more closely entwined with Darwin. In Britain, John Murray published *Typee* and *Omoo* in the Home and Colonial Library series; the second edition of Darwin's *Voyage of the "Beagle"* appeared in the same series. The two travelers who both passed through the Galapagos Islands also passed through Murray's publishing house. It is perhaps no more than a serendipitous twist, but Albermarle Street in London was home to Murray's premises. The same Duke of Albermarle who gave his name to this street also gave his name to Albermarle Island in the Galapagos, which two writers—embedded in each other's own sources—brilliantly imagined in wholly different ways.

The Forged Blade of "Bartleby, the Scrivener"

Around the same time Melville wrote "Bartleby" he completed two other stories, "The Happy Failure" and "The Fiddler." Both remained unpublished until July and September 1854, respectively. Neglected for several months, perhaps filed away in someone's drawer, perhaps lost temporarily in *Harper's* offices, the fate of the two stories was to only just achieve the status of fleeting magazine stories. *Harper's* even misattributed "The Fiddler" to Fitz-James O'Brien in four indexes to the magazine published from 1870 through 1885.[47] Both pieces are studies in failure: of a drainage pump that is the result of a decade of labor in "The Happy Failure" and of an acting child prodigy who ends up performing in a circus in "The Fiddler." One can read the stories as Melville's ironic accommodation of his own failure as a novelist reduced to scratching around in the magazine world. Negative impressions of his real thoughts, his magazine sketches are "what nots" whose irony *Harper's* is too shortsighted to notice.[48] And yet in "Bartleby" he simultaneously wrote a story that inherited the same searching questions his novels explored; caught up in the magazine's cultural form, Melville was able to take a generic dramatic situation and then deploy his artful design. In doing so, the familiar and expected become sufficiently less well known that they become intriguing but do not entirely confound. To read "Bartleby" as magazine fiction is to see how the magazine format disciplines and releases Melville's creative energy.

One way to think about the story's magazine qualities is to consider how it first declared itself to the world in quite an ordinary way. The nature of this ordinariness, suggested by the anonymity of its publication and the location of the first installment toward the end of the magazine, is better understood if one pushes the story back against some of the sources often claimed as influences. The most obvious is James Maitland's *The Lawyer's Story,* the first chapter of which appeared in the *New York Tribune* and *New York Times* of February 18, 1853. "In the summer of 1843," Maitland's tale begins, "having an extraordinary quantity of deeds to copy, I engaged, temporarily, an extra copying clerk, who interested me considerably, in consequence of his modest, quiet, gentlemanly demeanor, and his intense application to his duties."[49] In "Bartleby," the lawyer likewise is in need of extra help and advertises for another copying clerk; he also is taken with the sedate, gentlemanly, and industrious qualities of his new employee. Both tales are narrated in the first person by a lawyer, and Bartleby shares his melancholy disposition with the scrivener in Maitland's story. The similarities seem too particular to be the result of coincidence, although, unlike Bartleby, Maitland's copying clerk is easily put out of the lawyer's office once work dries up and the source of his melancholy is identified and resolved through the lawyer's intervention. *The Lawyer's Story* turns into a saga of family separation and lost inheritance very different from "Bartleby." Even if Melville did read Maitland's story, or at least the first chapter published in the *Tribune* and the *Times,* the larger question is, why did Melville think the relationship between a lawyer and a copying clerk would make a suitable subject for a piece of magazine fiction?[50]

The answer is that the particular nature of Maitland's story matters less than its generic qualities. Having a lawyer at the center of a mystery is what the stories share. And with lawyers come clerks. In an essay on Melville in the February 1853 issue of *Putnam's,* Fitz-James O'Brien looks back fondly to *Typee,* in whose island paradise Tommo and Toby "spend as agreeable a life as ever [a] town-imprisoned merchant's clerk sighed for."[51] The second installment of "New-York Daguerreotyped" in the April 1853 issue, an essay about the commercial districts of Manhattan, drew attention to the architecture of the New York Custom House and how "utilitarian panes of plate glass . . . let in light upon the 'attic cells,' where custom-house clerks sit at their mahogany desks."[52] Clerks and the urban world in which they worked were common currency in magazine writing. This was partly because clerking was fast becoming the most common form of employment in 1850s New York City and partly because clerks—just as they did in Dickens—served as markers of status distinction for the readers of these magazines. Young clerks were also literate, committed to self-improvement, and eager consumers of the cultural capital one found in magazines.[53] From "stalls nigh the Custom House," Ginger Nut buys the Spitzenbergs that Turkey and Nippers use to moisten their mouths in "Bartleby" as they work at their own desks while performing the "husky" business of copying law papers (*PT* 14). In vividly imagining the drudgery of clerks who could only daydream of exotic adventures and who were desk-bound in their ill-lit cells, *Putnam's* depicted the world of "Bartleby" even before Melville came to write the story.

To read "Bartleby" as magazine fiction, then, means recognizing how it sat comfortably alongside other tales, essays, and reports dealing in the same component parts; to read it, that is, as embedded in the magazine world as genre writing whose specific sources matter less than the broader literary and magazine tradition of lawyers and clerks on which it draws. The story also serves the aspirations of the magazine by bringing the details of New York City life to the page at the same time as expanding the reader's knowledge of a particular part of a more familiar world of work. And "Bartleby" gives clerks and their acquaintances a story foregrounding the conditions giving rise to their daydreams rather than the contents of the daydreams themselves.

The importance of this clerking milieu is evident in the structure of the story. Bartleby does not appear in person until almost a third of the way through the first installment as it was published in *Putnam's*. The lawyer-narrator's painstaking introductions to himself and the idiosyncrasies of his other clerks—the aging Turkey, the younger Nippers, and the office boy Ginger Nut—make little sense in narrative terms. They make much more sense as a way of establishing the story's generic credentials and the clerking environment familiar to the magazine's readers. They also allow Melville to establish the tone of the story in a way that fulfills one other vital aspect of *Putnam's* prospectus: "A man buys a Magazine to be amused," the first editorial announced, "to be instructed, if you please, but the lesson must be made amusing."[54] For interpretations that privilege endings, Bartleby's fate—imprisonment and death—negates the comedy of the lawyer's narration. The portraits of his clerks, though, are comic sketches or caricatures and work primarily through exaggeration. So after his morning productivity begins to wane, Turkey grows "altogether too energetic" and has a "strange, inflamed, flurried, flighty recklessness of activity about him" that causes him to spill his sandbox and to split his pens and throw them to the floor in a fit of passion as he tries to mend them. Of Nippers, the lawyer observes bathetically that "I always deemed him the victim of two evil powers—ambition and indigestion" (*PT* 16). The latter of these preoccupies the lawyer as he explains Nippers's protracted struggles to find the right height for his desk.

Turkey also shows himself to be a fluent pacifier of the lawyer in moments that work by wry comic reversal. When he complains about the blots Turkey makes on his copy, Turkey offers old age as his excuse: "Old age—even if it blot the page—is honorable. With submission, sir, we *both* are getting old" (*PT* 16). And when the lawyer thinks about dismissing Turkey for "moistening a ginger-cake between his lips, and clapping it on to a mortgage for a seal," Turkey makes an oriental bow and turns the situation to his advantage: "With submission, sir, it was generous of me to find you in stationery on my own account" (*PT* 19). In his dealings with Bartleby, the lawyer also shows himself to be capable of comic intent. When Bartleby refuses various other career options—a clerkship in a dry goods store, bartending, a traveling job collecting bills for merchants—the lawyer asks, "How then would going as a companion to Europe, to entertain some young gentleman with your conversation,—how would that suit you?" (*PT* 41). The magazine reader is left to recognize the lawyer's irony.

The sketchlike qualities and moments of comic exchange in "Bartleby" fulfill *Putnam's* duty to amuse and connect the story to the pieces Melville wrote for *Harper's* around the same time. The figure of the bachelor narrator, this time in the guise of the elderly lawyer, also emphasizes the sketch mode so important to the story. When in the opening paragraph he draws attention to the "biographies" and "histories" of which literature is made, the lawyer confirms a literary heritage on whose traditions he must draw in order to regale his audience with Bartleby's story. "Bartleby" came to publication, then, with specific generic qualities. This is not to diminish the quality of "Bartleby" but to see Melville writing "the *other* way" and to read the story as readers of *Putnam's Monthly* encountered it in 1853.

To be sensitive to the way that a story comes into publication, however, does not mean discounting qualities that allow it to withstand the pressures of obsolescence. The capacity for a story like "Bartleby" to be transformed from ordinary magazine fiction into canonical text across a hundred years may even be a consequence of the manner of its coming to publication. As well as writing within a tradition, Melville writes a story that goes beyond it. The story fulfills the charge *Putnam's* set itself of offering "a running commentary upon the countless phenomena of the times as they rise,"[55] but the ambition of the story is to open up a new world: as the lawyer-narrator immediately suggests, "Bartleby" is about that "interesting and somewhat singular set of men, of whom as yet nothing that I know of has ever been written:—I mean the law-copyists or scriveners" (*PT* 13). Part of the story's enduring quality results from the techniques Melville deploys to examine this new world.

Here the lawyer-narrator distinguishes Melville's clerking story at the same time as he performs the generic functions that establish the sketch and comic elements of the story. As well as a sketcher, the lawyer is a tale teller. "Bartleby, the Scrivener" is not simply a sketch, however, because the story relates—despite the narrator's opening gambit—the partial story of a particular and specific character rather than the lives of that "somewhat singular set of men" in general. In Dickens's sketches, beadles, curates, workhouse masters, and various other characters may have names, but more important are the generic qualities that define their roles; the sketches narrate once what Dickens infers to be occurring in similar ways in various locations. Dickens's constant use in his sketches of the first-person plural pronouns "our" and "we" dramatize characters and events in such a way that they become shared experiences. Such a phatic style endeared readers to the author and his work.

Melville's lawyer-narrator is entirely different, and his first-person narration quickly veers from sketch to tale mode. The descriptions he offers of the idiosyncrasies of Turkey and Nippers are more elaborate than is necessary for most tales, although the predictability of these eccentricities means both characters remain static through the rest of the story. The inability of the narrator to adequately define Bartleby in the same way, however, undermines his reliability as a narrator. The lawyer is a first-person narrator who lacks the confidence and sureness of a sketch narrator like Irving's Geoffrey Crayon; he too readily draws attention to the storytelling process in his addresses to the reader and so differs from the first-person narrators Hawthorne uses sparingly in his tales. The lawyer-narrator is more reminiscent of the first-person narrators one finds in the "Poe-ish" tales to which "Bartleby" was first compared. Here narrators are not separated from the story but integral to its unfolding and themselves become the central characters.

Without a sequence of sketches in which to find familiarity and comfort in the lawyer-narrator's voice, the reader's relationship with the narrator is insecure. The narrator has to resort to his colleagues and acquaintances to prove his credentials: "All who know me," he assures the reader, "consider me an eminently *safe* man"; while "John Jacob Astor, a personage little given to poetic enthusiasm, had no hesitation in pronouncing my first grand point to be prudence; my next, method" (*PT* 14). "Prudence" and "method": little "poetic enthusiasm" indeed. And a recommendation from Astor—nicknamed "Old Skinflint" and despised by many in New York for his greed—is hardly a recommendation to cement the reader's trust in the narrator. The lawyer is a man whose reputation he protests too much.

Given his already questionable status, the narrator's shifts in register also fray rather than stitch neatly together the qualities of his personality. He becomes the essayist when he posits, "Nothing so aggravates an earnest person as a passive resistance. If the individual so resisted be of a not inhumane temper, and the resisting one perfectly harmless in his passivity; then, in the better moods of the former, he will endeavor charitably to construe to his imagination what proves impossible to be solved by his judgment" (*PT* 23).

There are other sections, too, where the narrative presses beyond the sketch; rather than impressions of a scene, what the narration imagines is the unfolding of a consciousness. The narrator turns lyrical when he remembers "the bright silks and sparkling faces" he has seen that day "in gala trim, swan-like sailing down the Mississippi of Broadway." All "happiness courts the light," he suggests, "so we deem the world is gay; but misery hides aloof, so we deem that misery there is none" (*PT* 28). He even shows himself capable of the kind of self-questioning and shifts from first to second person appropriate to a dramatic soliloquy. When Bartleby affirms his decision not to leave the narrator but to "abide" with him, the lawyer is forced to ask what he can now do. His answer, in iambic pentameter, is: "Rid myself of him, I must; go, he shall." He continues:

"But how? You will not thrust him, the poor, pale, passive mortal,—you will not thrust such a helpless creature out of your door? . . . [S]urely you will not have him collared by a constable, and commit his innocent pallor to the common jail?" (*PT* 38). For two paragraphs the lawyer narrates this interior battle from within; in the language of self-examination he pulls aside the curtain on his gentlemanly, bachelor persona to show an ailing, conflicted conscience whose shape is even more ragged for being retrieved by this retrospective narration; the passage of time only exacerbates the vividness with which the "bright silks" and the "misery" stand in juxtaposition.

One of the dilemmas when thinking about Melville is why a writer now so revered was so routinely ignored or undervalued when he was writing and publishing. What do we see in his work that readers did not in the 1850s? The question, though, can be usefully turned the other way: What did readers of his work in the 1850s see that we do not? Apart from the comparison to Poe in *The Literary World,* there is little evidence of any reaction to "Bartleby" as it appeared in *Putnam's Monthly.* When it was reprinted in *The Piazza Tales* reviewers certainly saw the humor, but one word that reoccurs in the reviews is "quaint." The New York–based journal *The Criterion* described "Bartleby" as "a quaint tale, based upon living characters." The *Boston Evening Traveller* wrote of the "quaint explanation" of Bartleby's silence, while the *New York Tribune* noted a "quaintness of expression" across the collection as whole. These positive connotations of *quaint* stand in contrast to *Godey's Lady's Book,* whose disparaging review suggested Melville's "style has an affectation of quaintness, which renders it, to us, very confused and wearisome."[56]

The modern meaning of *quaint* suggests something pleasantly old-fashioned. In all of these reviews, however, the word is used in an archaic sense to indicate something elaborate, detailed, and artfully designed. This is the sense in which Melville uses the word in his own novels: "the quaint old arms on the panel" of a carriage in *Pierre,* for instance (*P* 19), or the tattoos in *Typee* that Tommo compares to "quaint patterns we sometimes see in costly pieces of lace-work" (*T* 78). Perhaps more apparent when "Bartleby" was set alongside his other stories in *The Piazza Tales* rather than buried in the miscellany of a magazine, readers of the 1850s saw quite clearly the intricacies of Melville's writing that distinguished it—for good or bad—from other writing.

To read "Bartleby" as magazine fiction, then, also means recognizing how Melville embeds these "quaint" designs in the story's generic dimensions. So the lawyer-narrator's effort at the beginning of the story to describe Turkey, Nippers, and Ginger Nut sketches and establishes their characters; it also elaborates the characters with detail—the multiplying of their eccentricities—without making them more than supporting characters or exceeding the purpose of a sketch. The lawyer's delineation of his office space likewise locates the reader in the familiar territory of Wall Street and a white-collar working environment. It is then embellished with details—the white wall of the light shaft, the wall black with age at the other side of the chambers, the demarcation of space, and Bartleby's place behind his screen—that go beyond the information needed to position the reader without threatening the reader's familiarity with the scene. The brief references to John Jacob Astor and the Colt-Adams murder might, in retrospect, add contextual weight to the story, but they work as topical asides for the reader of the 1850s without intruding on the central characters or the story's development. All these details reward interpretation without impeding the story's ordinariness that so fit it for the magazine form.

Finally, and most wondrously of all of course, there is the design of Bartleby himself. Melville's master stroke is to keep the reader constantly at one remove from the scrivener, whose character becomes all the more mysterious and intriguing because one only ever encounters him from within the partial and retrospective imagining of the lawyer. In trying to understand Bartleby, the reader is continually confounded by first having to try to understand the lawyer. Both are revealed iteratively: through Bartleby's refrain of "I prefer not to" and his repeated refusal to work; through the lawyer's repeated descriptions of Bartleby as pallid; through the accumulation of incidents—Bartleby's eating of ginger biscuits, his locking himself in the office, his unchanging demeanor—that the lawyer struggles to understand; and through Bartleby's capacity to withstand the lawyer's attempts to be rid of him. In these recurrences the reader follows the lawyer in looking for meaning, only to have that expectation deferred or denied. Unlike the copying clerk in Maitland's *The Lawyer's Story,* and even though his profession is central to his identity and gives him his place in this generic story of lawyers and clerks, Bartleby's melancholy disposition and mysterious personality are never supplanted or explained by hard facts and family history.

In place of these, Melville brings together a series of details, actions, and observations and holds them in relation to one another in a way that refuses to tell the reader what to think. Coming at the end of the story, Bartleby's tragic death appears to be the result of prior events. And yet the lawyer's narration does not connect the causal chain for the reader to show why Bartleby dies. The rumor of his previous employment in the Dead Letter Office tantalizes. The lawyer himself is moved to say, "When I think over this rumor, hardly can I express the emotions which seize me" (*PT* 45). But just as the prospect of clarification seems at hand, the lawyer deepens the mystery still further in his conjectures about dead men, dead letters, and the effects they may have had on his former scrivener. What is reiterated is the partiality and incompleteness of the lawyer's perspective. The rumor about the Dead Letter Office is the final addition to the story's elaborately constructed design. Bartleby is truly quaint in the nineteenth-century meaning of the word, and Melville's artful design of his character (and of his character's demise) becomes part of the larger design of a story intended to function as magazine fiction.

"Bartleby" was one among many stories of lawyers and clerks who, in various forms, were common enough in American magazine culture. *Harper's* published the sensational "Dark Chapter from the Diary of a Law Clerk" in October 1852, while the same magazine also published several lawyer's tales, such as "The Gentleman Beggar: An Attorney's Story" (October 1850), "Jane Eccles; or, Confessions of an Attorney" (April 1851), and "Reminiscences of an Attorney" (August 1851). None of these magazine stories comes close to achieving the degree of narrative complexity Melville creates in "Bartleby." Working with the sketch and the tale, he adjusts and adapts their forms to open new possibilities for the short prose story. The personal impression of the sketch becomes the self-examination of the short story; the character type of the tale, even the more complex characters one finds in Hawthorne's tales, evaporates in the indefinable Bartleby; the familiar and confident voice of the sketch narrator gives way to the unreliable narration of the multivocal short story; the resolution of the tale's ending becomes the open-ended ambiguity of the short story. At all points history intrudes into the scene—not only Astor, but Colt and

Adams, the Tombs, Sing-Sing, Monroe Edwards, Wall Street, the Halls of Justice. Out of the "what nots" of magazine genres, Melville forges a blade against whose razor-sharp edge the outmoded sketch and tale could not compete.

The rich criticism of Melville's writing for *Harper's* and for *Putnam's* is usually preoccupied with more urgent matters than the genre conventions of the midcentury magazine: politics, history, the ideological tapestry of midcentury America beyond the magazine. But thinking about genre shows that one of the reasons stories like "Bartleby," "Benito Cereno," and "The Encantadas" live longer in the critical memory is because they bury their generic past in the moment Melville engages it; the pieces most open to continuing interpretation and analysis are the ones whose relationship to genre is adaptive rather than derivative. Melville's magazine writing gives up rewards in proportion to the distance of travel between convention and iteration, between the genre with which Melville engages and the execution of his version.

3

"Passing Muster" at *Putnam's*

On June 18, 1855, George William Curtis sent one of his near-daily letters to the magazine's new publisher and co-owner, Joshua Dix. At that point coeditor of *Putnam's Monthly Magazine,* Curtis wrote from his home in Providence, Rhode Island, to which he had retreated at the beginning of June to rest his aching eyes after a busy spring in New York City conducting various writing and editorial tasks. Like a latter-day telecommuter, Curtis maintained his obligations no less vigorously from Providence. The June 18 letter recommended that the magazine reject Melville's "The Bell-Tower." Curtis's summary judgment was that the story had "*not* passed muster." Overnight, however, he changed his mind, much like the reader of Curtis's own *Nile Notes of a Howadji* (1851), who, the author boasted in a letter to his father, "thought it dull & wasn't interested when he began," but then "read it aloud to his family & never changed his mind about a book so much & so suddenly, in his life." Writing again to Dix on June 19, Curtis claimed Melville's story, "is, after all, too good to lose.—It is picturesque & of a profound morality" and has about it "the touch of genius."[1]

The exact reasons for his change of heart will forever remain a mystery, but Curtis's letters to Dix open a window on the business of magazine editing. Central to this business were Curtis and his peers at *Putnam's,* Charles Frederick Briggs, Frederick Beecher Perkins, Parke Godwin, and those at *Harper's,* Fletcher Harper and Henry Raymond. Virtually forgotten, their names take up little ink in the writing about Melville and need no blotting in works of literary history. This chapter emphasizes the role of Briggs and Curtis in the story of Melville's magazine writing for three reasons. First, through them we can better understand the nature of two magazines set up in the wake of cultural dogfights about a national literature in the 1840s. Second, the collective and personal judgments Curtis and his fellow editors exercised articulate the aesthetic distinctions of antebellum literary culture in which Melville's writing was embedded. Finally, we can see how decisions of editorial judgment took place in micro-contexts not always in harmony with the ideological macro-contexts critics use to read Melville's magazine pieces. Closer observation of the rest of the two letters Curtis sent to Dix in June 1855 allows an initial glimpse into this world.

Curtis's main concern in the letter of June 18 was not Melville at all but an article *Putnam's* was considering on James Gordon Bennett, owner and editor of the *New York Herald* since the 1830s. Curtis is "decidedly opposed" to the article, he says, because the newspaperman "is not an important man or a representative man." Curtis then turns his attention to the proposed publication of a collection of stories by his close friend William Douglas O'Connor, cautioning that "collections of tales rarely sell well. Hawthorne's did not—nor Poe's." When he then asks Dix, "What is it you are to publish for Godwin?" he means Parke Godwin, one of Curtis's friends and a colleague at *Putnam's* and *Harper's Monthly,* for which Curtis also wrote continuously from the early 1850s through his death in 1892. Only after all this, in a postscript below his signature, and almost as an afterthought, does Curtis inform Dix that "The Bell-Tower" and a story by Frederick Cozzens have "*not* passed muster."[2]

This letter shows the entanglement and prioritization of various elements in the business of magazine editing. That *Putnam's* is considering an article about Bennett, the infamous proprietor of a daily newspaper against which *Putnam's* wished to distinguish itself, shows the stratification of intellectual ambitions and audiences. The reference to O'Connor's collection of tales indicates that the publisher of *Putnam's,* by this point Dix & Edwards, is also trying to compete in the world of book publishing. It would later publish *The Piazza Tales* and *The Confidence-Man.* Curtis's inquiry about Godwin evidences the social network of writers and editors on which regional and national print cultures relied and in whose matrix Melville was just one node. His subordination to a postscript enacts the priorities of that matrix: once a headline act during his early career,

Melville is now American literature's undercard at the bottom of a hastily written business letter.

When he was reading Melville's story in June 1855, Curtis had more reason than previously to give the business of *Putnam's* greater priority. He had returned to the magazine a couple of months earlier after an absence of nearly a year, during which time George Palmer Putnam took over editing responsibilities to save money; when Putnam could no longer continue, he sold the magazine to his former clerk, Joshua Dix, and Dix's associate Arthur Edwards. Offered sole editorship of the magazine—a position Putnam also offered him in May 1854—Curtis chose instead to maintain the variety of his writing and lecturing commitments; he agreed to become coeditor, with more control over content than he previously enjoyed while working under the editorship of Charles Briggs, who stepped down in mid-1854 and left the magazine completely by the end of that year. Curtis's only proviso was that his identity and that of his coeditor—now known to be Charles A. Dana, who passed behind the pseudonym of Mr. Law—remain secret.[3] His desire for anonymity and refusal to commit his full-time energies to *Putnam's* show Curtis's discomfort with translating the cultural capital he possessed as a man of letters into the economic capital that would define him as a professional magazine man. For *Putnam's,* the consequence of this situation was that decisions over content were not deterministically economic; literary and aesthetic decisions were made that had unpredictable financial consequences for the magazine. A conscientious enough editor to make Melville submit to the strictures of his literary judgment, Curtis operated as a mediator of economic and cultural imperatives.

The interaction of these elements in a text's coming to publication is not always well understood, but the letter of June 19 indicates how Curtis could move between the roles of businesslike editor and literary critic. In deciding whether or not *Putnam's* should pay Melville for "The Bell-Tower" Curtis offers a fuller literary and aesthetic justification than he provided in his terse dismissal of the story the day before. Now he considers "The Bell-Tower" to be "rich in treatment, not unlike the quaint carving of the bell" that appears in the story. "I meant to say no," he goes on, "and so wrote you; but looking again, I am converted, and, making some erasures, we cannot afford to lose it. To many the style will seem painfully artificial and pompously self-conscious. But it seems to me well united to the theme. The story has the touch of genius in it—and so—in spite of the style—it should be accepted. . . . In reading 'The Bell Tower' you must remember that the style is *consistently* picturesque. It isn't Addisonian nor is it Johnsonese—neither is Malmsey wine, Springwater."

There is more to say later about the story's picturesque style, the comparisons to Addison and Johnson, and the liquid metaphors; for now, what bears noting is the other reason Curtis is writing to Dix on June 19. Shifting abruptly from his assessment of Melville's story, Curtis tells Dix: "I send with this some verses I wrote 7 years ago in Naples. Margaret Fuller used to like them very much. They are different from 'Putnam' poetry in general! And if Mr Law likes them—but only if he likes them, for I haven't the slightest pride about them—let them go in."[4] The connection between the Italian setting of "The Bell-Tower" and the composition of Curtis's own poems in that same country does not appear to be a coincidence. A day after his initial rejection of the story, Curtis is not only "converted" but moved enough by a picturesque evocation of Italy to resurrect his own seven-year-old poetry. There is much here that is intangible—the linking of reading to memory, affection, and writing—but Curtis is clearly performing a different role than that shown in his letter of the day before.

The letters of June 18 and 19 display very different aspects of Curtis's character and decision-making roles. To dismiss "The Bell-Tower" for not having "passed muster" is to subject it to the inspection of an organizational eye; to emphasize the picturesque and forgive stylistic idiosyncrasy is to apply an aesthetic judgment of a wholly different order, even as that judgment is bound up with the economic success of a magazine that "cannot afford to lose it." Into this alignment of priorities Melville dispatched his writing. To put Curtis's role into context, I want to stir up the waters of magazine culture and show how *Putnam's* and *Harper's*, ostensibly rivals in the magazine market, organized economic and cultural priorities in ways that challenge later assumptions about their status and identity. I then move on to examine more closely the fate suffered by "The Two Temples" at *Putnam's* in May 1854, the only occasion during his magazine-writing career when Melville met with rejection. Finally, I return to Curtis's relationship with Melville's writing through 1855 and 1856, when Curtis was aesthetic gatekeeper at *Putnam's* and saw into print all Melville's later pieces for the magazine: "Benito Cereno," "The Bell-Tower," "I and My Chimney," and "The Apple-Tree Table."

Cross-Pollination in the Magazine Market

Putnam's and *Harper's* both helped advertise the larger publishing houses out of which they emerged. They set about establishing their priorities, however, by taking different approaches and demarcating themselves as different types of magazines. *Harper's* was populist and popular; it reprinted material from British and Irish magazines, serialized best-selling British novelists, and incorporated many expensive woodcut illustrations. Once up and running, average circulation reached over one hundred thousand. The circulation of *Putnam's* peaked at thirty-five thousand in the summer of 1853 before sinking back to the low teens by 1857.[5] The dedication to American content and quality writing, however, earned the magazine a reputation for originality and intellectual distinction. In March 1857, an article in *Putnam's* described *Harper's* as "a repository of pleasant, various reading, of sprightly chit-chat, and safe, vague, and dull disquisitions upon a few public questions."[6] *Putnam's* addressed public questions more frequently and less insipidly, especially in Parke Godwin's political essays, which appeared with greater frequency toward the end of the magazine's first incarnation in the autumn of 1857.

Competition between the owners meant relationships between the two publishing houses were never more than cordial, although Putnam made efforts to cool hostility after the fire that destroyed the Harper premises in December 1853: "This may be a time," he wrote to the Harpers, "when all these things may be properly and easily buried and forgotten if you feel so disposed—and from this time if such be your disposition it may surely be easy to avoid all grounds for complaint on either side."[7] Nevertheless, *Putnam's* and *Harper's* continued to see themselves as different kinds of literary animal.

They certainly had very different management histories during their coexistence. Throughout the 1850s, *Harper's* remained stable under the guidance of Fletcher Harper. But of all the magazines that made a name for themselves in the 1850s, *Putnam's* was the one that most lacked continuity of identity in ownership, production, and leadership. Not one member of the original editorial or ownership team stayed with the magazine during the entirety of its five-year lifespan. There were clearly tensions in the editorial office. Curtis wrote of Briggs that "he has crotchets, & sometimes things get done, which I don't love at all."[8] Briggs was no longer editor by the middle of 1854. Frederick Beecher Perkins was brought on board, but when Putnam sold the magazine to Dix & Edwards in March 1855, Frederick Law Olmsted invested and became a managing editor. Curtis and Godwin returned, and Dana worked in the managing office. In April 1857 the firm of Dix & Edwards was dissolved and new owners—Curtis, Olmsted, and the magazine's printer, John Miller, who was keen to protect money owed to him—bought the company for one dollar. In August, the company failed and Curtis's father-in-law was left with debts of seventy thousand dollars.

Harper's and *Putnam's* shared formal similarities as magazines, but distinctions between their physical makeup and content are evident when one compares what these magazines looked like just before Melville entered their pages. Take the July 1853 issues of both magazines: *Harper's,* in white wrappers, ran to 144 pages; *Putnam's,* in pea-green wrappers, ran slightly shorter at 120 pages. Both sold for twenty-five cents. *Putnam's* described itself as a "Magazine of American Literature, Science and Art," but there was little to indicate this on its understated cover. Stalks of corn and sugarcane flanked the formal serif font of the magazine's title. The cover of *Harper's* declared its educational and intellectual intent in more traditional ways and was altogether louder and more striking. Atop a stone plinth stood two garlanded classical columns surrounded at their bases by objects of learning: books, scrolls, and pen and ink. Inside, both magazines used a double-column layout typical of many nineteenth-century magazines.

By this point, *Harper's* had established a rhythm out of the cacophonous clatter of its early issues. The first, in June 1850, contained sixty-four separate items of mostly reprinted poetry, popular science, fiction, travelogues, history, literary criticism, and essays. The second issue still contained fifty-two pieces; the only features continued from the previous issue were the "Literary Notices" section and illustrations of the latest fashion for women. By July 1853 there were only twenty-four items, less reliance on reprinting, and a degree of continuity. At the rear of the magazine now appeared the regular editorial features: the "Monthly Record of Current Events," the "Editor's Table," the "Editor's Easy Chair," the "Editor's Drawer," "Literary Notices," "Comicalities, Original and Selected," and "Fashions" of the month. Although some of these features fell by the wayside, the "Monthly Record of Current Events," "Editor's Table," and "Editor's Drawer" remained regular features at the end of the century. These final sections amounted to about one-sixth of the magazine in July 1853.

The first pages of the July 1853 issue of *Putnam's* and *Harper's* were remarkably similar. Beneath the magazine title and issue information appeared a large engraved image illustrating the lead article. In *Putnam's* this was a sober account of New York's educational institutions and their buildings; in *Harper's,* a reverent account of a trip to Jefferson's Monticello. In what follows, there is some crossover between the magazines. Both contain travelogues of different sorts: in *Harper's* an account of a trip to Lake George, New York, and "Sketches on the Upper Mississippi," both of which mix history and natural history; in *Putnam's* "Life in Hawaii" and "A Few Days in Venice" take a similar approach, while "Sketches in a Parisian Café" is a lighter, gossipy travelogue. *Harper's* was partway through the yearlong serialization of John Abbott's history of Napoleon, while *Putnam's* offered a natural history of "Fish Hawks and Falcons" and Arthur Clough's philosophical musings in "Letters of Parapidemus."

Both magazines also contained several pieces of fiction. *Harper's* lead with "Love Snuffed Out" by J. Smytthe Jr., a comic story of the romances of Don Bobtail Fandango, a Spanish ambassador. Next came "Extracts from the Portfolio of an Excitement-Seeker," a serial by G. P. R. James, the prolific English novelist and diplomat who settled in the United States and was British consul in Norfolk and Richmond, Virginia, from 1852 to 1856; "Hester," a sentimental fictional tale of a woman's reunion with her father; and for a final populist flourish, an installment of *Bleak House,* which *Harper's* serialized from April 1852 to October 1853. In *Putnam's,* the reader could enjoy "Dinner Time," an episode about gentlemanly dining from what would become George William Curtis's *Prue and I* (1856); the final installment of "Miss Peck's Friend"; and "A Story without a Moral," an installment of Edmund Quincy's romance, *Wensley* (1854).

There were certainly differences in the style and tone of these common features. *Wensley,* for instance, Quincy's only novel, is a historical romance of New England; in *Bleak House,* Dickens was at the height of his realist powers. But significant differences in the content are also obvious. While *Putnam's* continued to publish poetry, there was no poetry in the July issue of *Harper's.* The fifteen-page reviews section of *Putnam's* was serious and cosmopolitan, with sections on American literature, English literature, and French and German literature as well as a section on the fine arts and music. In *Harper's,* the "Literary Notices" ran for only five pages; the section covered American and European literature, poetry, and history, and the format mixed reviews with snippets of information about writers, other literary discoveries, and auctions of old books. Of the first eight books reviewed, Harper & Brothers were the publishers of six. There was less nepotism in *Putnam's.*[9] The most obvious visual distinction between the two magazines was the attribution of articles and the number of illustrations. *Harper's* gave the names of authors for seven of its longer pieces; *Putnam's* gave no attributions, and would never do so for anything it published during the five years it existed. *Harper's* contained sixty-nine illustrations of varying sizes all through the magazine; *Putnam's* illustrated just the first two articles and the whole issue contained only twenty images.

In conception and approach, then, clear distinctions between the ethos of each magazine are obvious. Consequently, Sheila Post-Lauria argues, Melville adapted the style of his stories for each magazine, sending those with more complex political, social, and aesthetic themes to *Putnam's*—to match that magazine's ideological progressiveness—and his more sentimental and lightweight pieces to match the less serious *Harper's.*[10] But Melville's example is actually a good indicator of the incestuousness of magazine production in the 1850s: the heat haze of the monthly composition cycle and culture of anonymity could blur the discrete identity a magazine acquires for both contemporary and retrospective readers. I mentioned in the previous chapter Melville's duplicitousness over the Tortoise Hunting material that turned up in *Putnam's* as "The Encantadas." Melville was certainly not averse to sending the same material to both magazines. He also sent *Israel Potter* first to *Harper's.* When they did not reply to his request to consider the first sixty pages as the first installment of a serial, he immediately sent the manuscript to *Putnam's.* Melville sent "The Apple-Tree Table" to *Harper's* in the autumn of 1855 but did not receive a quick reply. He followed up with an inquiry about the article's fate on December 10; *Putnam's* published the tale in May 1856.

Writing of the rivalry with *Harper's,* Ezra Greenspan notes that "it was never Putnam's intent or expectation to match them but simply to set up operations on their flank." Rather than opposites, either ideologically or aesthetically, it is more useful to think of *Harper's* and *Putnam's* as subsets of a common core. Meredith McGill argues that if *Putnam's* was the avant-garde of a "sea-change in publishers' and readers' estimations of the value of American writing," the Harper organization was not far behind.[11] Their reprint ethos gave way to faith in American authors, and this influenced the content of *Harper's Monthly,* which also started to publish American writers like Melville. And it was not only writers who were mobile and moved between magazines. Different in ideological design, *Putnam's* and *Harper's* were not always so easily distinguished at the level of contributors, editors, and regular feature writers who set the tone for the magazines. As a case in point, Curtis worked for both magazines—at the same time. For him, the priorities of economics and culture met at a personal and institutional level.

Curtis's relationship with *Harper's* began when his travel books *Nile Notes of a Howadji* (1851) and *The Howadji in Syria* (1852) were both excerpted in the magazine, which also published his story "All Baggage at the Risk of the Owner" in September 1852. Most notably, however, Curtis wrote the popular "Editor's Easy Chair" column for *Harper's.* Fletcher Harper, who took company responsibility for magazine affairs and acted as de facto editor, approached Curtis about this job while he was employed at *Putnam's.* Curtis bargained hard: "Probably I shall ask you to pay me more than you will think reasonable," he said, but Harper was not deterred.[12] Curtis's regard for his supplementary employer is evident in his own letter to Fletcher Harper after the fire of December 1853: "Let me say to you how sincerely I sympathize with you and your firm in this sudden and tremendous blow—from which you will show us all how American enterprise can recover without a visible scar."[13] After sharing duties for six months, starting in October 1853, with Donald G. Mitchell, author of *Reveries of a Bachelor* (1850) and *Dream Life: A Fable of the Seasons* (1851) under the pen name Ik Marvel, Curtis took sole responsibility for the "Editor's Easy Chair" from April 1854 until his death in 1892. The point to emphasize here is that Curtis's column was not just a magazine tidbit but "the best of the early departments," according to the magazine historian Frank Luther Mott, who writes that "for forty years Curtis made this section of *Harper's* the most delightful department in an American periodical."[14] Partly on Curtis's writing did *Harper's* establish its credentials.

As evidence of incestuousness, Mitchell was in turn the subject of an article in the first issue of *Putnam's.* "Our Young Authors" was a series that lasted only two months—Melville was the second and final subject—and the review of Mitchell's career, attributed to Fitz-James O'Brien, damns with faint praise and then snarls. Dipping into *Reveries of a Bachelor* as relief following a day's work, "your heart will be no longer arid," O'Brien writes; spending any length of time in this world—"the champaign lands of sentiment"—will induce "terrible lassitude, and mental depression." Mitchell's repetitive, minor-key ramblings leave the reader "sighing for some dark unfathomable pool into which we might gaze and wonder, hour upon hour."[15] Parts of *Reveries* were serialized in *Harper's,* and when Harper & Brothers published the book the review in the company magazine was gushing: "one of the most remarkable and delightful books of the present season," the reviewer claimed; "Mr. Ik. Marvel has opened a new vein of gold in the literature of his country."[16] As a statement of the different requirements *Putnam's* expected of literature compared to *Harper's,* O'Brien's assessment is suggestive. But that differentiation is not clear-cut. The same *Harper's* serializing, praising, and employing Mitchell was also employing Curtis, one of the editors of *Putnam's* whose ethos O'Brien propounded in writing so witheringly about Mitchell. And none of this stopped O'Brien from also writing for *Harper's* in the 1850s.[17]

Neither did Curtis always support *Putnam's.* He was furious with "The Editor at Large" column in the magazine's September 1854 issue: "It is flippant, pointless, coarse and ambitious. . . . And the anti-H. quotation is impolite, and unnecessary. People say 'Why does P. throw mud at H.—which has never dirtied it?'"[18] "H." and "P." here stand for *Harper's* and *Putnam's.* Curtis's evenhandedness and his work for and influence at the two magazines does not overturn the real differences that separated them. But the ease with which he moves between the magazines should caution against exaggerating those differences, particularly in the area over which Curtis came to exercise greatest influence: literature and the arts.

One further example demonstrates Curtis's bipartisan position in the *Putnam's-Harper's* matrix. William Douglas O'Connor, to whom Curtis refers in his June 18 letter to Dix, is best known now as author of *The Good Gray Poet* (1866), his defense of Walt Whitman after the poet's dismissal from a clerking job at the Indian Affairs Bureau of the Department of Interior in 1865. O'Connor and Curtis became friends in the 1850s. O'Connor was responsible for the first, but not the last, time Curtis and Melville were mentioned in the same breath. Reviewing *Nile Notes of a Howadji* for the *Providence Journal,* O'Connor wrote: "We can point with pride to Longfellow and Bryant, to Poe and Melville, to Emerson,

Curtis and Hawthorne, to them as representatives only of many that are, of more that are to be."[19] It was Curtis who placed O'Connor's pamphlet on Whitman with the publisher Bunce & Harrington. But O'Connor and Curtis also corresponded regularly throughout 1855 about O'Connor's magazine writing.

It is to O'Connor that Curtis, in a letter of March 9, 1855, confesses the "secrets, which will come out by & by" about Putnam's sale of his magazine to Dix and Edwards; he also relates the offer to become sole editor made to him by the new owners. In the same letter Curtis maps out his role at the two magazines and the benefits of each to his friend:

> Now the "improvement" of these facts for you is this, that [Fletcher] Harper wants immensely the story of yours that I have, and will pay very generously, that is, he will pay you $100 probably, if I tell him he can not have it for a less sum. . . . But it is hard to make a literary reputation in their mag. because it is read by a class that do not make such reputation. Putnam, under the new regime will pay better, nearly twice as well as before. It would probably give you $65 or 75 for the article; and such a story would have better literary success in P. than in any other periodical. But that would alienate Harpers which is not so well worth while at present.

Curtis then apologizes for not taking sole editorship at *Putnam's,* a position from which "I should have tried to make such arrangements with you that you would write only for Putnam, as would have satisfied you." O'Connor must decide which way to jump, but Curtis can help either way: "But now, you must determine. And will you let me know as soon as possible to which magazine, considering all the circumstances & prospects[,] I shall give your story."[20] Even if not formally an editor at *Harper's,* Curtis clearly carried sufficient influence with Fletcher Harper to place material.

Curtis also acted as O'Connor's literary agent and editor for pieces that appeared in both magazines. In a letter sent later in the month, he advises O'Connor to "send me the 'What Cheer' to dispose of for you, & probably to Putnam under the new regime, which, I hope, is to be better than the old." Early in April, Curtis takes the blue pencil to "What Cheer?" and makes changes that remain in the published version: "It seems to me to end properly within the departure of the Dark Student, upon page 82. . . . I have therefore cut out from page 82 to page 93." The postscript of this letter refers to another of O'Connor's pieces, on which Curtis advises about the title: "I have gone over the first story for the Harper's. It is hard to name it. I should say 'The Knocker'. . . . It will be published in the July no.—So Mr. Fletcher Harper tell me."[21] By July, Curtis has ready a check for eighty-five dollars in payment for "What Cheer?" after it appears in that month's issue of *Putnam's*; by September, presumably in response to O'Connor's inquiry about the payment for "The Knocker," Curtis writes: "'The Knocker' I know nothing about, except that in June I altered the title with my own hand in Harper's counting room. They always delay as much as possible."[22] "The Knocker" eventually appeared in *Harper's* in December 1855.

The image Curtis presents here is a compelling one: the newly appointed coeditor of *Putnam's* standing in the counting room of Harper & Brothers amending accounting records for their magazine. Alfred Guernsey, managing editor of *Harper's* from February 1856, described the counting room and the adjacent proprietors' area as "the brains of the establishment."[23] At the very least this compromises the idea that *Putnam's* and *Harper's* were diametrically opposed magazines. Curtis, O'Connor, Melville, and O'Brien are examples of how cross-pollination rather than separate development shaped magazine culture during this period. Writers produced work for different magazines; editors, often with long careers, moved regularly from one newspaper and magazine to another, between whose audiences and agendas it is not always possible to draw natural links. Magazines were more portable and flexible than often supposed: portable in the sense that a magazine could move between owners and change editors; flexible in the sense that the monthly cycle of production compromised the quest for coherency. Curtis wrote that "it is terrible to feel the periodically recurring necessity of literary labor, if you cannot easily toss it off."[24] Where these magazines stood in relation to the nation they wanted to represent and entertain, and how Melville fitted into their vision, is the next part of the story.

Charles Frederick Briggs, Cosmopolitan Localism, and "The Two Temples"

Briggs was one of the most mobile figures working in magazines during the 1840s and 1850s. He was a veteran contributor to the *Knickerbocker* (1840–46), founder and editor of the *Broadway Journal* (1845) before Poe forced him out, editor of *Holden's Dollar Magazine* (1848–50), and, after his time at *Putnam's,* a newspaper journalist and editor, serving on the *New York Times,* the *Independent,* and the *Brooklyn Union.* His early *Knickerbocker* pseudonym he took from the protagonist in his first novel, *The Adventures of Harry Franco* (1839). Other novels followed, most notably *The Haunted Merchant* (1843), *Working a Passage* (1844), and *The Trippings of Tom Pepper* (1847).

This background as writer and magazinist is important to bear in mind when thinking about two other things for which Briggs was responsible and on which I concentrate here: rejecting Melville's "The Two Temples" in May 1854 and writing the opening "Introductory" that delivered *Putnam's* to its public in January 1853. "It is because we are confident," Briggs wrote anonymously in the first pages of the new magazine, "that neither Greece nor Guinea can offer the American reader a richer variety of instruction and amusement in every kind, than the country whose pulses throb with his, and whose every interest is his own, that this Magazine presents itself to-day." Neither the author of this elegant statement—ostensibly evidence of the magazine's national intent—nor the rest of the founding editorial in which it sits, align themselves straightforwardly with the nationalist project of *Putnam's,* as the rejection of "The Two Temples" demonstrates.

The source of the problem with Melville's diptych, according to Briggs, was "Temple First," in which a corruptible sexton, described as a "great, fat-paunched, beadle-faced man," refuses the narrator entry to a church service (*PT* 303). After finding a side door to the church tower, the narrator instead observes the service from on high, only then to find himself locked inside the church. His discovery by the beadle-faced man leads to a fine and a reprimand from the city justices. Though the tower the narrator ascends is reminiscent of Trinity Church on Broadway in lower Manhattan, the story is usually understood to represent Grace Church, further up on Broadway and not far from Melville's residence at 103 Fourth Avenue. The sexton of this church, Isaac Brown, lived at 107 Fourth Avenue and is thinly disguised as the "beadle-faced man"; according to Matthew Hale Smith he was "immensely popular with the elite of New York."[25]

Briggs wrote to Melville on May 12, 1854, congratulating him on "some exquisitely fine description, and some pungent satire" but telling him the diptych was unacceptable, because "the moral of the Two Temples would array against us the whole power of the pulpit, to say nothing of Brown, and the congregation of Grace Church" (*C* 636). This was exactly the kind of New York audience Briggs did not want to alienate, especially after ructions caused by an article leading off the September 1853 issue. "New-York Church Architecture," part of the "New-York Daguerreotyped" series, included several disparaging comments about the use of gothic ornamentation in church architecture and about church benefactors: "There are two causes for the incorrect and unimposing architecture of the greater number of churches in New-York; the one is the incapacity of the architects who design them—the other is the ignorance of the people who pay for them."[26] In cheerleading for the city, *Putnam's* also took on the role of critic. Where "Bartleby" fit the magazine's aim of telling the life of the city and offered no slights against an identifiable lawyer, the location and the characters in "The Two Temples" were all too recognizable. Satisfying a local constituency rather than a national audience is sufficient to explain why *Putnam's* rejected "The Two Temples." But Briggs also exemplifies the tension between these aims as they developed during the 1850s.

Briggs considered his time at *Putnam's* the highlight of his working life, but he took the earlier parts of his career with him into the new job. Through the 1840s he navigated a route between influential cultural elites; allied to none of them, he instead made a living from undermining the principles on which their identities rested. Briggs was an independent New Yorker. Though born on the Massachusetts island of Nantucket, he despised the Boston-centric philosophizing of thinkers and writers like Bronson Alcott—burlesqued mercilessly in the figure of Dobbins in *The Haunted Merchant*—to the extent, Perry Miller argues, that through all his early writing "runs a hostility to New England transcendentalism more than in keeping with the New York attitude."[27] When he edited the *Broadway Journal* Briggs aimed this hostility more visibly in the direction of Margaret Fuller, whom he (unlike Curtis) loathed.

In three issues of the *Broadway Journal* during March 1845, Briggs lays out his objections to Fuller's *Woman in the Nineteenth Century* (1845). An unflattering engraving of Fuller also appeared, calculated to offend in image as Briggs's review offended in words. The caption accompanying the engraving, presumably written by Briggs, faults the illustrator because "the nose is a little—a *very* little too Grecian" and because "the 'fine phrenzy' of the eyes has not been preserved so decidedly as it should be."[28] Briggs's views on women make difficult reading for a contemporary reader. Though his barbs often resolve to attacks on Fuller's class privilege, his rebuke that "no unmarried woman has any right to say any thing on the subject" of women's lives and roles is particularly cringe-worthy. But the attack achieved its intended effect: to outrage Boston abolitionists and suffragists with whom he disagreed. The result backfired on Briggs, however. Garrison's *Liberator* withdrew support for the *Broadway Journal*—vital to ensure sales and circulation in Boston—and Briggs's co-owner, John Bisco, sold his shares in the magazine to Poe rather than to Briggs as originally intended. Briggs had to leave his own journal after just three months.

In politics, Briggs was idiosyncratic. His disagreements with abolitionists and transcendentalists did not stop, although they often interfered with, his long and close friendship with James Russell Lowell. Briggs opposed slavery and abolition simultaneously, believing industrialization would make the slave system obsolete but objecting to the extension of slaveholding and the annexation of Texas. In the 1844 election he backed Henry Clay over James Polk and blamed Polk's narrow victory on supporters of the Liberty Party candidate, James Birney, whose success in New York he thought cost Clay the presidency: "To think of it! A junta of slaveholders entrusted with the destinies of this country by the efforts of a band of misjudging men who have the enormous effrontery to style themselves abolitionists. My stomach sours at the name of them."[29] Briggs's conservative Whig tendencies did not stop him from rejecting Zachary Taylor in the 1848 election, though this in turn did not stop him from taking a clerkship in the Debenture room of the New York Custom House when Hiram Fuller recommended him after Taylor's election.

Neither was Briggs a great friend of the Democratic Party and its New York cultural wing, the Young America of Duyckinck and Mathews. Briggs considered Mathews a talentless egotist, and the group's connections with southerner William Gilmore Simms, who disparaged the kind of American humor close to Briggs's heart, did not help their cause. Briggs gave Mathews and Duyckinck the same treatment he meted out to Bronson Alcott, lampooning them as Mr. Ferocious and Tibbings in *The Trippings of Tom Pepper*, a novel that more generally satirizes the hypocrisies of New York literary and business life. Although a regular contributor to the Whig *Knickerbocker*, Curtis also despised the New York elites in whose shadows poverty blighted the lives of New York City's lower classes. When they are not turning a comic eye to life, Briggs's novels turn to this theme—on which he drew from personal experience—in proto-realist style, though his magazine writing was always sharp and witty enough to please an editor like Lewis Gaylord Clark at the *Knickerbocker*.

What Briggs objected to most about Young America, as with the transcendentalists, abolitionists, and single-cause reformers more generally, was their doctrinaire factionalism. "I see so much of the belittling influences of sectarianism," he wrote to Lowell, "that I am almost persuaded it is dangerous to belong to a clique of even such enlightened philanthropists as the Garrisonians. The moment you call Garrison a leader you begin to establish a spiritual despotism."[30] For Briggs, factionalism manifested itself in different ways: in the overembellished romantic attachment to nature; in evangelical political crusades; and in Young America's deafening and repetitive demands for a national literature. When Tom Pepper goes to study law with Mr. Ferocious, Briggs makes fun of this obsession. Ferocious even describes Tom's name as "individual, national, indigenous, capital, and spicy too." He asks, "Do you read, Mr. Pepper, imaginative literature, the home article, or foreign trash, in pink covers?" Tom is understandably bemused when Ferocious gives him a book on which he must pass judgment: "Young, unsophisticated, a real, true American, your opinion must be fresh, home-born, and congenial with the better life of the country."[31] The special pleading of factional causes Briggs found objectionable and counterproductive. As a writer, however, he needed to earn a living from chastising individuals belonging to factional groups. In doing so, he perfected the art of engaged satire while himself remaining aloof.

Briggs's distrust of encomiums to national literature, and his chameleon-like ability to shift between different guises as a humorist and satirist, should make us look again at his "Introductory." I wrote in the previous chapter of the ambivalence in this founding statement, where having "no less faith in the opulence" of American resources hardly suggests the superiority of these resources. The "Introductory" also trades in an odd combination of hyperbole and the same kind of rhetoric that elsewhere Briggs uses to satirize the transcendentalists: "Astronomers assert," the "Introductory" begins, "that the nebulous mist with which the ether is charged is perpetually taking form—that the regions of space are but a celestial dairy, in which the milky way is for ever churned into stars. . . . Taking the reader, therefore, by the hand, or rather by the eye, here at the portal, we invite a moment's conversation before he passes within." In his earlier novel *The Haunted Merchant,* the object of Briggs's satire, Dobbins, says, "Nature is every where, she is every thing . . . ; listen to her; she speaks to you in the cataract; in the noiseless dews; the stars, the sun, the moon, all speak to you."[32] The juxtaposition of this earlier piece of astronomical rhetoric against the *Putnam's* "Introductory" makes it difficult to treat the latter as straightforwardly affirmative or unironic; rather than a defense of the visionary impulse we have the hocus-pocus of transcendentalist optics.

The role of a founding statement is to affirm aims and objectives for an audience to which a magazine aspires. Briggs's experience at the *Broadway Journal* taught him that Boston was an important audience to a magazine with literary and artistic ambition, one to whom star-struck rhetoric might appeal. Briggs had little time for such readers, as his earlier writing showed; Curtis, a former resident at Brook Farm, was much better disposed to this audience, and his acquaintance with leading Boston writers and intellectuals played a key role in Putnam's appointing him. In November 1854, the publisher James T. Fields wrote to Putnam, "I will do all that in me lies to inform our Boston world that Putnam's Magazine is the great literary flame."[33] As editor, and for the larger good of the magazine, it is quite possible Briggs projected a position to which he was not necessarily wedded. His long writing and editing career at various magazines and newspapers, together with his ability to exist in the gaps between group allegiances, shows his capacity for this role.

Equally, that he moved in quick succession between posts also indicates the editorial guise was not always sustainable in the long run. In *A Fable for Critics* (1848) Lowell wrote of his friend in a way that makes it difficult to take at face value anything Briggs writes: "There comes Harry Franco, and, as he draws near,/You find that's a smile which you took for a sneer; . . . He's in joke half the time when he seems to be sternest,/When he seems to be joking, be sure he's in earnest."[34] When the "Introductory" claims *Putnam's* is inevitable—just as "Columbus believed in his Cathay of the West—and discovered it" so "our Magazine is a foregone conclusion"—one hears the echoes of Briggs lampooning the nationalist stridency of Duyckinck and Mathews. The "Introductory" may project a magazine identity, but it is rhetoric of the sort wherein what is said and its inverse can both appear true.

When the "Introductory" projects the importance of "an American eye" it is equally clear this eye is not nationally universal. Only the "man who sees through 'American spectacles'" will look with such an eye, not "every man whose birth chanced to fall in America." Making a division between those who do and do not wear "American spectacles" separates the nation in the process of gesturing toward it. Briggs had little time for important sectional groups in America; his was a nation split along several fault lines and his version of what America or the rest of the world looked like did not necessarily correspond to the version Putnam or Curtis saw. The owner and editors breathed the same air of ambition for the magazine, but it was not put together each month in Briggs's image or the image of the "Introductory." Briggs was not a controlling force after the first eighteen months. But neither was the magazine Putnam's project after early 1855, when Curtis came to the fore. To call *Putnam's* a national magazine is to confuse the intention to produce a high-quality magazine containing original American contributions with a coherent project. The number of owners and editors the magazine went through did not encourage coherency; judgments about quality did not readily resolve to any manifesto of nationalism.

There is also more than one way to be a national magazine, and *Harper's* could claim this status for one very good reason: the geographic reach of its circulation. For the Harper organization the expansion of literacy for the national good trumped the promotion of indigenous resources. That *Harper's* for its first twenty years, until 1870, advertised only books published by the magazine's holding company mitigates against any altruism here; Harper & Brothers wanted to clean up where it could. But, as John Dowgray argues, "the Harpers appeared to realize very early the possibilities of a national magazine, a true miscellany with stories and articles designed to appeal to many areas rather than limiting its appeal to one."[35] They did not wait for the appearance of *Putnam's* to put this strategy in place and to replace eclecticism with organization.

The second volume of *Harper's* was bound for sale in book form in May 1851. In the opening pages an advertisement thanked readers and promised that the owners would spare "no effort to insure the succeeding volumes of the Magazine a still wider and more favorable reception among all classes of readers." Then, eighteen months before *Putnam's* saw the light of day, *Harper's* declared that the owners "intend it to be a strictly national work" and to be "devoted to no local interests, pledged to no religious sect or political party, connected with no favorite movement of the day, except the diffusion of intelligence, virtue, and patriotism." Furthermore, "original matter" would enrich the "utility and attractiveness" of the magazine.[36]

For this reason, *Harper's* began publishing American writers like Melville along with Jacob Abbott, Curtis, Benson J. Lossing's popular history articles, Caroline Chesebrough, Fitz-James O'Brien, and David Strother (Porte Crayon). Neither was the magazine in thrall to sentimentalism. Dickens and Thackeray appeared regularly enough that they moderated any sentimental excess. As Jennifer Phegley argues, "*Harper's* supported a melding of the forms of realism and sentimentalism rather than a strict division between the two literary modes."[37] The promotion and defense of Dickens's brand of realism offered Americans a template for adapting sentimentalism to national purpose; the aim was to help Americans produce what the magazine considered better literature. The development of the magazine's idiosyncratic departments—"The Editor's Drawer" began in July 1851, "The Editor's Table" and "The Editor's Easy Chair" in October 1851—also formally located an Americanized perspective in the magazine's structure rather than just the content.

The imperfect implementation of a didactic mandate, especially in the early years, makes the miscellany of *Harper's* look more like an abstract mosaic than a realist still life, where dissonance rather than harmony resulted from the mixing of non-American and American voices. But one principle underlying the work-in-progress of the magazine was, as Thomas Lilly observes, "a strong sense of civic duty, which defined the value of anything worth reading in terms of its utility and availability, not its origin."[38] By 1859, this sense of civic duty meant *Harper's* published Stephen A. Douglas's "The Dividing Line between Federal and Local Authority; Popular Sovereignty in the Territories" (September 1859) but none of the letters objecting to the views Douglas expressed.[39]

Allied to this civic-mindedness, *Harper's* created a national presence by refusing to rely on a subscription model. According to Alfred Guernsey, a longtime Harper employee who worked his way up from compositor to managing editor of the magazine under Fletcher Harper's guidance in 1856, subscriptions accounted for only a quarter of sales. "The remainder," he wrote in 1865, were "sold to booksellers and dealers, who supply their own customers, and usually receive their supply by express." The benefit of this model was threefold: it defrayed distribution costs, because it was much better and cheaper to send a batch of magazines to one bookseller than to individuals; it streamlined cash flow, as larger receipts came from fewer intermediaries; and it helped establish stronger regional outposts compared to magazines that relied more heavily on advance subscriptions. Staggered distribution—copies are sent first to California, next to New Orleans and St. Louis, then Cincinnati, Detroit, and Chicago, before "working toward home by way of Boston and Philadelphia"—ensured that "the Magazine shall come out as nearly as possible at the same time in every part of the country."[40] *Harper's* was a magazine whose national aspirations first manifested themselves pragmatically. Over the course of the 1850s it showed that magazines might be national in more than one way and that native content was not always king.

Under Briggs's editorial guidance, New York City rather than the nation quickly became the focal point for *Putnam's*. The magazine subjected New York to the kind of scrutiny offered of no other American city, primarily in a series of articles commencing in February 1853 called "New-York Daguerreotyped." Built around a collection of specially commissioned engravings, the series promised to provide "a rapid glance, at the progress of New York and its architecture." It began with the business district; later articles were promised on "Hotels and Restaurants; the Churches; the Colleges and Schools; the Benevolent Institutions; the places of Amusement, and the Public Buildings generally; and also the private houses and the domestic life of the commercial metropolis." Some of these duly followed. But Putnam's also promised "similar papers on Boston, Philadelphia, and other places" that never materialized, while it continued to publish fictionalized and nonfictional accounts of life in America's world city.[41] Curtis's writing for the magazine, later published as *The Potiphar Papers* (1853) and *Prue and I* (1856), tells stories about New York City life, and Curtis himself wrote a column for the magazine beginning in January 1856 called "The World of New York." If the initial ambition of *Putnam's* was to represent America's cities and build a picture of national urban development, in practice the magazine felt most at home in New York City.

The local interests that *Putnam's* magazine weighed against the national also needed to compete with more cosmopolitan events and activities from further afield. Putnam himself contacted Melville the day after Briggs sent his letter rejecting "The Two Temples." Supporting his editor, the owner wrote that "some of our Church readers might be disturbed by the *point* of your sketch" (*C* 636–37). While Melville's point was to satirize Brown, Putnam perhaps also takes aim at the larger meaning of "The Two Temples" and the more benevolent depiction in "Temple Second" of the narrator's experience at a London theater, where he watches Charles Macready perform in Edward Bulwer Lytton's *Richelieu; Or, the Conspiracy.* Dennis Berthold argues that such valorization of Macready did not fit the agenda of literary nationalism that *Putnam's* promoted; "Temple Second" instead "challenged nationalist aesthetics with a vital cosmopolitanism that men like Briggs and Putnam preferred to avoid," and that ideological reasons rather than religious ones account for Briggs rejecting "The Two Temples."[42] There are several problems with this proposition.

First, Briggs was far from the latter-day Young American Berthold suggests him to be. Briggs's antipathy to the factionalism of Young Americanism is evident in his satirical treatments of figures like Mathews and Duyckinck. Perry Miller's assessment that "Briggs is no strident isolationist, he simply enjoys this country" is nearer the mark.[43] Second, what literary nationalism *Putnam's* promoted was certainly able to contain dissenting opinions or appreciations of non-American culture. A eulogy for London's Crystal Palace, described as "the first original piece of architecture of modern times" and a "cosmopolitan castle of industry," appeared in August 1853. If Berthold is right and *Putnam's* suppressed references to the Astor Place riot in order to sanitize cultural history, the more likely reason for doing so is that raising the specter of class conflict was hardly likely to appeal to the magazine's readership. Those who had most to lose from the eruption of class conflict were the New York City elites who read *Putnam's* and liked Isaac Brown. And the magazine's praise of the Swedish opera singer Jenny Lind, whose brilliance put to shame lesser acts appearing at the Astor Place Opera House before its closure, surely makes visible what Berthold suggests Briggs and Putnam do not want to see: the promotion of cosmopolitan aesthetic values over nationalist ones.

Putnam's was actually a much more cosmopolitan magazine than writers credit. Putnam made sure that he published the magazine with Sampson & Low in London as well as in New York to guarantee international circulation. Neither is it true that *Putnam's* published exclusively American writers. Arthur Clough, the English poet, published "Letters of Parapidemus" in the July and August issues of 1853.[44] In the same July 1853 issue, there appeared an article on "Life in Hawaii," a poem titled

"Ode to Southern Italy," and other pieces of non-American focus: "A Few Days in Vienna" and "Sketches in a Parisian Café," along with six pages of reviews of English and European literature. While the writers of these pieces were American, the reader they were leading by the eye was one for whom quality and nation were not synonymous. Far from being out of sync with the nationalism of *Putnam's,* Melville's "The Two Temples" was decidedly in tune with the magazine's own cosmopolitanism.

The evidence suggests Briggs and Putnam together rejected "The Two Temples" not for religious or ideological reasons but because of potential offense to a well-known New Yorker in a position of some respect and prominence. If this explanation seems more prosaic than some of the alternatives, then so sometimes is the business of magazine editing. *Putnam's* could ill afford to antagonize readers, having already offended churchgoers with the article on architecture and with magazine sales dwindling after the high-water mark of the first year. Economics took priority over the cultural capital of satire in this instance. In the same way that *Putnam's* rejected hopeful contributors, so the magazine rejected Melville, who so far had only written "Bartleby" and "The Lightning-Rod Man" (published in August 1854). He was not a magazine mainstay. That economics should take priority is not surprising. Putnam knew he must make changes to maintain the magazine's viability; the changes would see Briggs step back, Curtis and Godwin relinquish editing duties, and Putnam take up a greater control that itself proved unsustainable. To make one cultural sacrifice in the cause of longer-term stability is an understandable, if not entirely virtuous, local piece of decision making.

The sinews that attached Melville to the magazine culture of the 1850s were knotty and tough; the fibrous tissue embedded Melville in decisions of quality as well as appropriateness that he did not or could not always anticipate. The fate of "The Two Temples" gives the lie to any argument that Melville was capable of fitting his pieces to the requirements of *Putnam's.* A writer does not always understand as well as owners, editors, and office managers the turbulences of magazine politics and priorities. What Melville found himself up against was a magazine for whom, in this instance, local reputation outweighed the qualities of "pungent satire" or cosmopolitan aesthetics. At other times, that *Putnam's* was both a local and cosmopolitan magazine suited Melville; because the lawyer in "Bartleby" plies his trade on Wall Street rather than State Street in Boston or Broad Street in Philadelphia is one reason why the story fit so well in the pages of *Putnam's* and why readers and editors, and Curtis in particular, liked it so much.

Melville himself did not protest the rejection of "The Two Temples," nor did he send the piece for publication elsewhere, even though *Harper's* published his two other diptychs. He acknowledged the letters from both Briggs and Putnam. His response to Briggs is lost. Putnam's letter, perhaps to keep the author warm after rejection, asked Melville to supply a daguerreotype: "We wish very much to have your *head* as one of our series of portraits. Curtis will be in the July No." (*C* 637). Once more Curtis and Melville are mentioned in the same breath. But Melville refused Putnam's request matter-of-factly. While he told Duyckinck he respectfully declined "being oblivionated," Melville told Putnam: "I don't know a good artist in this rural neighborhood." One daguerreotypist regularly advertised in the *Pittsfield Sun* beginning in August 1853; his studio was near the post office Melville visited regularly. With only a hint of sarcasm, Melville ends the letter: "Ere long I will send down some other things, to which, I think, no objections will be made on the score of tender consciences of the public" (*C* 261). Melville moved on.

"Mr. Melville's younger brother in letters": George William Curtis and "The Bell-Tower"

After the rejection of "The Two Temples" and the serialization of *Israel Potter* between July 1854 and March 1855, Melville next sent "Benito Cereno" to *Putnam's*. I deal with *Israel Potter* in more detail in chapter 5, but in the time it took for the novel to reach its conclusion in the magazine, Melville found himself dealing with different owners and editors. Joshua A. Dix and Arthur T. Edwards signed an article of partnership on March 1, 1855. Edwards agreed to invest five thousand dollars before May 1, 1856. The division of responsibilities put Dix in charge of manufacturing and contracts with editors and contributors; Edwards looked after financial matters. A further memorandum of agreement, signed on April 2, 1855, brought Olmsted into the company as joint partner. Edwards now agreed to put in five hundred dollars by May 1, 1855, in addition to the money due by March 1 the following year. Olmsted agreed to the same terms.[45] In this form, the ship of *Putnam's* sailed on for over a year. Neither

Dix nor Edwards had much pedigree in the magazine world. Dix worked for Putnam from at least May 1853 and left to publish Dickens's *Household Words,* for which he bought American rights; Edwards was a clerk. But their ascension meant that Melville's long relationship with Putnam, publisher of his first novel in 1846, ended with the March publication of *Israel Potter* in book form.

No longer now was Briggs or Putnam casting the first eye over Melville's writing. Curtis joined Dix, Edwards, and Olmsted as an equal partner only in May 1856, at which point he invested ten thousand dollars in cash and signed over to Dix & Edwards the copyright to his earlier books. In return, the firm agreed that Curtis "shall have charge of and conduct the literary department of said business."[46] This formalized the role Curtis took up on his return to the magazine a year earlier. If the financial investment signaled his faith in the *Putnam's* project, it was a faith badly misplaced, although the full horrors of the magazine's financial mismanagement only became clear several months after Melville published his seventh and final story, "The Apple-Tree Table," in the May 1856 issue that marked Curtis's coming out of hiding and formal appointment to the masthead. In the end, Curtis showed himself a better reader of literature than of balance sheets when evaluating cultural and economic matters; when he needed to stop digging the financial hole in which he found himself in 1857 he only made matters worse, for both himself and his wife's family, by persuading his father-in-law to put his finger in the breached dam. Curtis spent the rest of his life paying off debts accruing from the flood that washed away *Putnam's*. But from April 1855 on, his was the eye Melville's writing needed to engage.

The initial signs were promising. On April 17, 1855, Curtis expressed relish to Dix at the prospect of something new from Melville: "I am anxious to see Melville's story, which is in his best style of subject." Presumably Dix told him that in "Benito Cereno" Melville was once more writing about the sea. Curtis's first reaction on writing to Dix two days later was more positive than his first reading of "The Bell-Tower," though still not without criticism: "Melville's story is very good. It is a great pity he did not work it up as a connected tale instead of putting in the dreary documents at the end.—They should have made part of the substance of the story. It's a little spun out but it is very striking & well done. And I agree with Mr Law that it ought not to be lost." The next day, April 20, Curtis's initial enthusiasm begins to wane: "I return Melville's story today. I wrote you yesterday what I thought of it. He does everything too hurriedly now." By July, in advice about what to place in future issues, Curtis's view spirals to a new low and he seems more concerned with value for money. He tells Dix to "take up *Benito Cereno* of Melville. You have paid for it. . . . why can't Americans write good stories. They tell good lies enough, & plenty of'em."[47]

The change of heart about "The Bell-Tower" comes in June. And then in January 1856 Curtis cautions Dix about the planned collection of Melville stories in *The Piazza Tales* while expressing his pleasure about certain of the stories: "I don't think Melville's book will sell a great deal but he is a good name upon your list. He has lost his prestige,—and I don't believe the Putnam stories will bring it up." In the absence of any evidence about "The Apple-Tree Table," Curtis accepted only one of Melville's pieces for *Putnam's* without question during this period. "I and My Chimney," he wrote Dix in September 1855, is "a capital, genial, humorous sketch . . . thoroughly magazinish."[48] The terms of his acceptance indicate the criteria on which he judged Melville's stories. "I and My Chimney" did not appear in *The Piazza Tales,* which suggests Melville's view of its value did not coincide with Curtis's.

What to make, then, of this new editorial eye passing judgment on Melville's magazine writing? I answer this question by looking at "The Bell-Tower," and secondarily at "Benito Cereno" and "I and My Chimney," but without charging them with the task of mediating the complexities of American politics and history. As I mentioned in the introduction, this method is a consistent feature of critical analyses of Melville's magazine writing, as the original magazine publication of the stories is forgotten in the urgency to deliver symptomatic readings of their narratives. The most compelling reading of "The Bell-Tower" is Russ Castronovo's analysis of the story's "ironic construction of national history." Through sophisticated contextualization—of the cracked bell in which is read the history of Philadelphia's similarly flawed Liberty Bell, and of the suggestions of revolt when Bannadonna is killed by his mechanical slave—Castronovo emphasizes the "allusive import" of a story allegorically engaging the founding moments of U.S. national history and their legacy in the mid-nineteenth century. The ironic historiography of "The Bell-Tower" works by insisting "on the continuity of political history even at the cost of uncovering atrocities within sacred origins" and by reminding readers—as the murder of the artisan, Bannadonna's death, and the slave revolt are quickly brushed aside in the recasting of the bell—that "only forgetting can fashion a narrative stable or coherent enough to support the accumulated layers of history from the origins to the present."[49] Castronovo's reading is exemplary in revealing what he argues Melville reveals allusively in "The Bell-Tower."

That "The Bell-Tower" was magazine fiction is not important in Castronovo's reading. But when Curtis revised his judgment in his second letter to Dix, on June 19, 1855, and decided that the story was too good to lose, there is no sense in which he saw the story's "ironic historiography." Curtis is more interested in how the story measures up to his judgment of literary value, his understanding of the picturesque, the unity of style and theme, and whether or not the story deserves a place in *Putnam's*. In the context of such aesthetic judgments and distinctions shaping the magazine world Curtis and Melville emerge as figures very closely entwined, yet fundamentally different; they radically coexist in the 1850s in a way that is no longer the case and hardly recognized in considerations of Melville's magazine writing.

Curtis was the son of a banker but, after a disastrous year spent working in a German importing house, he chose to go to Brook Farm rather than following his father into the world of business. As a boy in the 1830s Curtis heard lectures by Emerson, Richard Henry Dana, John Neal, and Margaret Fuller in Providence, and with his brother, Burrill, he enrolled at West Roxbury as a boarder rather than a member of the Brook Farm Association. He stayed for a year, leaving partly because he disagreed with the Fourierist shift, and moved to Concord in 1844, immersing himself in a social network that would prove invaluable to a future journalist and editor. He befriended Emerson, Hawthorne, and Margaret Fuller, helped Thoreau build his cabin at Walden Pond, and developed an interest in politics that would later dominate his life. After five years traveling through Europe and the Middle East, Curtis returned to the United States and turned his experiences into *Nile Notes of a Howadji* and *The Howadji in Syria.*

So popular were these books that "Howadji" became Curtis's sobriquet. In his preface to *The Blithedale Romance,* Hawthorne expressed his hope that "the brilliant Howadji might find as rich a theme in his youthful reminiscences of BROOK FARM, and a more novel one—close at hand as it lies—than those which he has since made so distant a pilgrimage to seek, in Syria, and along the current of the Nile."[50] Curtis began working as a journalist from his home in Staten Island. He first took a position with the *New York Tribune,* under the editorship of Horace Greeley, to whom he had written letters during his travels in Europe; Harper & Brothers published the letters as *Lotus-Eating* (1852). Curtis soon got out of the unfulfilling world of newspapers. He complained to William Douglas O'Connor that "a Newspaper life is unmitigated slavery. I would rather be a clerk in a shop, with some leisure than be forever tantalized by the neighborhood of things I loved & could not enjoy,—as a literary man is, in a Newspaper."[51] He turned instead to magazines and lecturing. Family money sponsored Curtis's peripatetic adult life, but by the age of twenty-five he was a veteran intern with contacts in all the right places in a cultural milieu where thinking, writing, and publishing were closely connected activities.

It was in this world, where writers turned intellectual labor into modest economic currency, that Curtis and Melville met. While a long evolutionary history is responsible for Melville's assuming his place at the tip of the tree of American letters and for making Curtis extinct, in the primordial soup of the mid-nineteenth century their careers showed many similarities. Both writers based their early work on foreign travel and immersion in non-Western cultures; both made part of their living through the burgeoning magazine culture of the 1850s; both turned to the lecture circuit after the collapse of *Putnam's* in 1857, Curtis successfully, Melville much less so; in later life both made their living through government service, Melville as a customs officer and Curtis as a civil service reformer; and both were poets.

In the sketches that became *Prue and I,* Curtis even enmeshes himself in Melville's magazine fiction by directly engaging it in his own work. One of the recurring figures in Curtis's sketches is the character of Titbottom, a dowdy accountant to the sketches' narrator. In one sketch the narrator notes of Titbottom: "Before I knew him, I used sometimes to meet him with a man whom I was afterwards told was Bartleby, the scrivener. . . . Recently I have not seen Bartleby; but Titbottom seems no more solitary because he is alone."[52] After the failure of *Putnam's* in the autumn of 1857, Curtis and Melville also occupied the same venues and towns during their respective lecture tours, as Curtis helped Melville secure appointments. In correspondence about the sale of the stereotypes of *The Piazza Tales* and *The Confidence-Man,* Melville told Curtis, "I have received two or three invitations to lecture,—invitations prompted by you—and have promptly accepted. I am ready for as many more as may come on" (*C* 316). A business relationship forced them to occupy the same cultural networks.

At another level, however, they were incompatible figures with very different ideas about literature. In noting the "*consistently* picturesque" qualities of "The Bell-Tower" in his letter of June 19, Curtis betrays his allegiance to what George Santayana would later call the genteel tradition. When he coined this phrase at the beginning of the twentieth century, Santayana's description could easily have had Curtis and Melville in mind. "America," he wrote, "is not simply a young country with an old mentality: it is a country with two mentalities. . . . The one is all aggressive enterprise; the other is all genteel tradition."[53] While Melville was deploying his literary aggressions in *Moby-Dick* and *Pierre* in the early 1850s, Curtis was publishing his *Howadji* books. Unlike Melville's genre-busting travel narratives of the exotic in *Typee, Omoo,* and *Mardi,* Curtis's books swerve toward, without being the worst examples of, Wilfred McClay's description of this genteel mode: "odious formalism, superficial sentimentality, elitism, disingenuous optimism, vapid idealism, and Victorian moral sensibility."[54] What we know about Melville's opinion of Curtis's work is limited to one piece of evidence: F. O. Matthiessen pointed out that Melville annotated the initials "G. W. C." alongside Matthew Arnold's observation that "it is comparatively a small matter to express oneself well, if one will be content with not expressing much, with expressing only trite ideas."[55] This damning judgment marks out Melville's disapproval of the intellectual qualities of the literary generation to which he was connected by the necessity of money.

The diametrically opposed methods and styles of Melville and Curtis were also well explored in the pages of *Putnam's* itself. Under Curtis's editorship, Fitz-James O'Brien published "Our Authors and Authorship: Melville and Curtis" in the April 1857 issue, weaving his discussion around the premise, paraphrased from Goethe, that "to praise is easy, to judge is hard—to suit our praise to our judgment troublesome." Melville is upbraided in the essay "for hiding his light under such an impervious bushel" and for being "a man born to create, who resolves to anatomize;

a man born to see, who insists upon speculating," one who has "turned away . . . to cultivate his speculative faculties in a strange, loose way." In a manner that sounds odd to contemporary ears, Curtis is described as "Mr. Melville's younger brother in letters." He is too superficial for O'Brien's tastes. Whereas Melville "throws himself off his balance by an over-eagerness to be prophetic and impressive, Mr. Curtis loses his through an over-anxiety to be moderate, judicious, and experienced." Having seen Curtis lecture in support of the Republican Party, O'Brien suggests that Curtis "emancipate himself from the mistaken direction which he took in the *Potiphar Papers*" by throwing himself "back resolutely upon himself" to "study the positive qualities of his own mind, and learn afresh how clear and fine a field there is for him to till," not in fictional satire but in essays.[56]

That Curtis allowed such a critical assessment of his writing to appear in *Putnam's* says something positive about his lack of writerly preciousness. Either that or he just thought O'Brien wrong. The one novel he published subsequently—*Trumps* (1861), serialized in *Harper's* between April 1859 and January 1861—certainly showed no signs he took the criticism on board. The same genteel and sentimental horizon noticeable in his earlier work hangs heavily on his last attempt to fictionalize New York City life. But as O'Brien suggests, Curtis was by no means uninterested in issues of substance. Parke Godwin was charged with writing many of the most effective political articles, but Curtis also built a reputation as one of the leading antislavery lecturers of the period.

Opposition to slavery was part of Curtis's upbringing. In one of his final speeches as senator for Rhode Island, Curtis's grandfather James Burrill set out his objections to the Missouri Compromise; in 1856 Curtis married Anna Shaw, the daughter of the abolitionist Francis George Shaw. Curtis also followed Godwin's and Olmsted's lead as *Putnam's* became more partisan in its support of the Republican Party during 1856.[57] And while Curtis lectured on sober literary topics such as Bulwer Lytton, Disraeli, Kingsley, and Dickens, during the election campaign of 1856 he spoke for John Fremont on several occasions. After Fremont's defeat and following the Dred Scott decision, his lectures turned increasingly to the issue of slavery. Delivering a lecture titled "The Present Aspect of the Slavery Question" in Philadelphia, Curtis continued as hecklers in the audience tried to shout him down while thousands of protesters massed outside the hall, throwing bricks through the windows and attempting to set fire to the building.[58]

Curtis emerges from this juxtaposition with Melville as a figure whose efforts to translate between economic and cultural capital are marked by a desire to clearly demarcate literature and the arts from history and politics. While Melville was speculating in "a strange, loose way," Curtis was exercising his propensity "to be moderate, judicious, and experienced" both in his editorial activities, which he fitted around his lecturing and literary commitments to *Harper's,* and in his gentle satires of metropolitan socialites, which themselves maintained this distinction as they fell far short, as O'Brien also pointed out, of the "faithful anatomization of a corrupted social order" one found in the work of Curtis's close friend Thackeray.[59]

This distinction between different domains of intellectual activity and writing are important when thinking about Curtis's acceptance of "The Bell-Tower" and Melville's other stories published in *Putnam's.* The thrust of Castronovo's reading, of course, is precisely the way in which Melville's narrative manages to conjoin the literary with American history and the politics of slavery in "The Bell-Tower." Indeed, critics admire Melville's writing more generally now because it resonates so vibrantly with those issues defining American history in the 1840s and '50s—race, empire, capitalism—and because he fuses a literary with a philosophical and political consciousness. What marks out Curtis as a writer, editor, and lecturer is the almost mechanical separation of these domains.

In all of his literary judgments Curtis shies away from invoking the discourse of politics that so dominated his lecturing and whose engagement, in one of his addresses, he describes as the scholar's main responsibility. Curtis delivered "The Duty of the American Scholar to Politics and the Times" at Wesleyan University in 1856; a published version appeared shortly thereafter with Dix & Edwards. Pivoting on the crisis over Kansas, and the divisive question of whether the newly created state should allow slavery, Curtis summons the imagery of race as he argues that "drifting across a continent, and blighting the harvests that gild it with plenty from the Atlantic to the Mississippi, a black cloud obscures the page that records an old crime." He goes on to suggest that "every scholar degrades his order, and courts the pity of all generous men, who can see a just liberty threatened, without deserting every other cause to defend liberty."

Without this defense, he asks, "of what use are your books? Of what use is your scholarship?" In the main an extended history lesson that continually attacks "the Slave Power" of the southern states, Curtis concludes by claiming that "while we read history, we make history." He cites Milton as an exemplar, someone whose "sublime scholarship . . . began in literature and ended in life" and who pursued truth while others pursued what was expedient. The blending of literature, history, and what Curtis calls "the eternal law of justice" in Milton is what distinguishes him.[60]

Curtis is a conundrum. The views expressed in this address isolate qualities in Milton similar to those found by contemporary critics in Melville. When added to the views about slavery and abolition Curtis propounded in his lectures, why then is he not more positive in his assessment of "Benito Cereno"? Why does he seem to prefer the qualities of "I and My Chimney," a piece of writing Melville had no desire to republish in *The Piazza Tales*? Curtis discusses his conception of scholarship through English dramatic and poetic literary figures—Jonson, Addison, Swift, Pope, and Gray, for instance—but there is no sense in the address that Melville, nor any other writer Curtis could call a contemporary, should be part of this calling. Contemporary literature and contemporary politics are ruptured in Curtis's imagination; American writers play no role in his discussion. The editor reading and assessing "Benito Cereno" for a magazine whose ideological stance was hardening in support of abolition and Republicanism was an editor who favored the literature of gentility and sentimentality removed from issues of substance. This must modify any existing sense of how "Benito Cereno" does cultural work for *Putnam's*.

One straightforward explanation of "Benito Cereno" would see its politics matching the politics of *Putnam's*. It is certainly hard to imagine "Benito Cereno" appearing in *Harper's*. But there are problems with having a magazine context determine the meaning of the story. First of all, *Putnam's* may well have followed an editorial policy—though the editors were rarely in the same room together—when it came to political commentary, but this policy did not overlap with the acceptance or rejection of tales, sketches, and poetry. Second, *Putnam's* was not a single entity. This point is worth reiterating. Ownership and editorial changes fractured unity; monthly publication in the midst of such changes made coherency difficult; different editors performed different roles. Curtis and Godwin shared views, but their views also differed. Godwin's Fourierist roots lingered on after the 1840s, while Curtis never had much time for this strand of liberal thought. And Godwin had nothing to do with Melville's submissions to *Putnam's*. Finally, there is the problem of Curtis: an editor for whom the politics of race, or the politics of anything for that matter, blew hardly at all on the weathervane of his literary judgments.

Curtis's ambivalent reaction to "Benito Cereno" is more telling about *Putnam's* than the politics of *Putnam's* is telling about Melville's ambivalent representation of race. What Curtis first anticipated in "Benito Cereno" was Melville's "best style of subject." This subject was the sea, but also a particular approach to the sea: one that makes the reader hesitate about the balance between fiction and reality. In rewriting part of Amasa Delano's narrative of his voyages Melville gave *Putnam's* a piece of writing grounded in a nonfictional form he then brings to life. Melville's original title for *The Piazza Tales—Benito Cereno & Other Sketches*—suggests what Curtis was anticipating. "Benito Cereno" would be a sea sketch just as "The Encantadas" were sea sketches. Curtis was right to prepare himself for Melville's "best style," and such a sketch would have fit comfortably in the pages of *Putnam's* given its enjoyment of travel sketches.

Where Curtis balks is when he sees the "dreary documents." This is a structural problem. The balance of fictive imagination and nonfiction crashes too heavily on the latter side. While sketches sometimes cede narrative responsibilities to third persons—the story within the story—what kind of sketch cedes responsibility toward the end of its work to such documentary evidence? Geoffrey Crayon recycles the papers of Diedrich Knickerbocker, but Knickerbocker is left to speak for himself through Crayon; in "Benito Cereno" the reader is distracted and disoriented by what is "compiled from certain recovered documents of Aranda's, and also from recollections of the deponent, from which portions only are extracted" (*PT* 104). The wonder is that Curtis did not suggest edits and ask Melville to either drop or rework the documents into the "connected tale" he thought "should have made part of the substance of the story." Curtis was keen enough to help his friend William Douglas O'Connor chop off the end of his story "What Cheer?" But he is impatient with Melville for not taking the time to properly carry out the working up of these documents that we can understand now as another iteration of the sketch's examination of perspective and reliability, and one intimately connected with the representation of race. Curtis's advice to Dix to "attenuate the dreadful statistic of the end" went unheeded.[61]

Curtis's fading enjoyment of "Benito Cereno" hardly suggests that the story nestled snugly in the mutual conviction of magazine and author against racism and slavery. Instead, Curtis comes to question "Benito Cereno" because the narrative breaks the decorum of the sketch frame he thinks would make it "connected" and ready, presumably, to fulfill the anticipation he expressed to Dix. What Curtis demands of literature is what makes him a figure forgotten by literature. Not for him the bold experiments of "Benito Cereno," in which there are "too many allusions, too many references, to surely determine political analogs" and where meaning "is as much sunk in silent depths as drowned in a deluge of discourse."[62] "Benito Cereno" appears in the pages of *Putnam's* despite, not because of, its representation of the politics of slavery. Curtis is forgiving enough and satisfied enough by a mixture of anticipation and partial fulfillment to wave the story through.

Much more to Curtis's liking was "I and My Chimney," a sketch at the opposite end of the spectrum of narrative experiment from "Benito Cereno." Nothing more is known of Curtis's reaction to "I and My Chimney" other than that he found it "thoroughly magazinish," but the emphasis on domestic matters and the gently humorous tone are similar to Curtis's own preoccupations in his genteel satires of family life in the city. As plot gives way to characterization, so "I and My Chimney" leans firmly toward the sketch tradition. The narrator is stubbornly attached to his chimney, the more so as his wife tries to persuade him to demolish it. Even the possibility that within the chimney lies a secret closet put there by the previous occupant, a sea captain, that might contain money is not enough to make the narrator knock the chimney down. Defiantly, he says at the end of the sketch, "I and my chimney will never surrender" (*PT* 377). The chief appeal of the sketch is the humorous defamiliarization of the chimney and the subordination of the narrator to its charms: "in everything" but the phrase "I and My Chimney," the narrator says, is "my chimney taking precedence of me" (*PT* 352). Curtis held "Bartleby, the Scrivener" and "The Encantadas" in high esteem; that he found "I and My Chimney" so suited to *Putnam's* suggests his struggles over "Benito Cereno" and "The Bell-Tower" resulted from their unsuitability for, not their fit with, the magazine's literary aim. What fit best was the lightest, the most insubstantial of Melville's magazine writing; Curtis the *Putnam's* man, it turns out, was always a *Harper's* man.

The Curtis who withstood the bricks and fire-starters in Philadelphia to talk about slavery, who issued a call to arms to the literary societies of Wesleyan University, appears incompatible with the figure who enthuses over "I and My Chimney." This latter Curtis is the man who expressed himself so well and yet on such "trite" subjects as found in the "Editor's Easy Chair" columns he wrote for *Harper's.* Writing in a consistently erudite and conversational style, Curtis assumed the persona in these pieces of the educated and genteel man about town. The politically engaged, principled abolitionist is absent, just as American writers were absent in Curtis's Wesleyan address. In the pages of *Harper's,* in his own magazine writing, and in his editorial judgments, Curtis drew on a mode that followed more obviously from his earliest published work.

Curtis inherited a picturesque tradition that in the United States went back at least as far as Charles Brockden Brown and came to underscore the imagination of other romantic writers, including Hawthorne and Thoreau, with whom Curtis was well acquainted.[63] Curtis's own travel writing in his Howadji books fashioned a quiescently picturesque version of the landscape of North Africa, and *Putnam's* became a ready publisher of similar travelogues. While the imperialist and ideologically containing nature of this picturesque aesthetic is now well understood, much of the work on Melville and the picturesque has emphasized the ways in which he circumvents this tradition and offers a critique of the picturesque mode from within its clichés and figures.[64] That Curtis found enough to admire in the picturesque qualities of "The Bell-Tower" to commit to publication therefore raises questions about the extent to which Melville's critique of the picturesque was visible to Curtis.

The critique is visible to Castronovo, of course, who locates in the narrator's surveying of the ruined landscape of the Italian setting "a founding contaminated by murder, fraud, and slavery" and "a genealogical investigation bearing him back to the origins."[65] Much more visible to Curtis, as the submission of his own poems written in Italy during the period of his reacquaintance with Margaret Fuller suggests, is the picturesque Italian setting of Melville's story rather than its undermining. In comparison with Castronovo's view, watching Curtis reading "The Bell-Tower" is like watching someone content to wander through a terrain with which he is familiar and in which he feels at home; to watch, that is, a reader who reads not for deep meaning through an act of unveiling, but a reader for whom "profound morality" is etched into the surface of a style whose picturesque qualities—pomposity and self-consciousness notwithstanding—simultaneously enact a judgment on a story's central character.

From the justification he offers in his letter of June 19, it appears that Curtis changes his mind about "The Bell-Tower" because he now better understands the connection between style and theme and is willing to forgive the stylistic flaws that presumably he could not on first reading the story. The flaws are similar to those identified by O'Brien. In cultivating "his speculative faculties in a strange, loose way" Melville produces prose that is, in Curtis's words, "painfully artificial and pompously self-conscious." O'Brien was following up an opinion about Melville that he first expressed in *Putnam's* in 1853 in the second of a soon-to-be-dropped series called "Our Young Authors." A mainly hostile account of the "interregnum of nonsense" from *Mardi* onward, O'Brien's review criticizes Melville for language that is "drunken and reeling" and a style that is "antipodical, and marches on its head." Preferring the plainer style of *Typee* and *White-Jacket,* O'Brien concludes by counseling Melville: "Let him diet himself for a year or two on Addison, and avoid Sir Thomas Browne."[66] Wayne R. Kime suggests that "The Bell-Tower" is Melville's defiant response to O'Brien's review.[67] Curtis's judgment is likewise that Melville has made no Addisonian concessions in his style. And yet despite the importance to Curtis's culture of gentility of an Augustan tradition in which the clarity and wit of periodical writing were important constituents, Curtis forgives Melville his stylistic excesses. He does so not because Melville is undermining the picturesque but because he is strengthening it: "In reading 'The Bell Tower' you must remember that the style is *consistently* picturesque. It isn't Addisonian nor is it Johnsonese—neither is Malmsey wine, Springwater." Addison may provide the clarity and purity of springwater, but Melville gives the substance and heady effects of fortified wine.

Curtis's willingness to make compromises in his editorial judgment should modify any polarizing argument about Melville's stylistic defiance in "The Bell-Tower" and the genteel quality of *Putnam's.* For Kime, the story is willfully obscure. The historical setting, the extensive use of classical allusion, and the ostentatious style all contribute to the refusal of the story to fulfill O'Brien's advice. At the same time, *Putnam's* is characterized as a magazine with popular aspirations, readers of limited literary awareness, and an editor in Curtis "who is not remembered for his penetration as a reader of Melville."[68] And yet this defiant story was still published in this genteel and popular magazine. Curtis was a perceptive enough reader to see Melville's stylistic defiance but a sympathetic enough reader to recognize the story's qualities.

Neither would the Italian setting of the story have been odd to a reader of magazines in the 1850s. There were numerous pieces about Europe, including Italy, in *Harper's,* because it reprinted, and in *Putnam's,* because it was cosmopolitan.[69] And Melville's style is not all defiance. Elements of the lush and poetic syntax are similar to Curtis's own prose style. This is the second paragraph of "The Bell-Tower": "As all along where the pine tree falls, its dissolution leaves a mossy mound—last-flung shadow of the perished trunk; never lengthening, never lessening; unsubject to the fleet falsities of the sun; shade immutable and true gauge which cometh by prostration—so westward from what seems the stump, one steadfast spear of lichened ruin veins the plain" (*PT* 174). The use of alliteration, assonance, and consonance bears some resemblance to this paragraph from the opening of Curtis's *Nile Notes of a Howadji*: "In a gold and purple December sunset, the Pacha and I walked down to the boat at Boulak, the port of Cairo. The Pacha was my friend, and it does not concern you, gracious reader, to know if he were Sicilian, or Syrian; whether he wore coat or kaftan, had a hareem, or was a baleful bachelor. The air was warm, like a May evening in Italy. Behind us, the slim minarets of Cairo spired shiningly in the brilliance, like the towers of a fairy city, under the sunset sea."[70] Melville and Curtis were obviously very different writers, but their differences did not separate them completely. There were points of intersection; Curtis's change of heart about "The Bell-Tower" and his coming to the conclusion that the story does pass muster is one example.

The uneasy presence of the experimental and rebellious Melville in the pages of magazines like *Putnam's* and *Harper's* is usually explained by crediting Melville with the capacity to fit his expansive literary preoccupations to magazine forms. He was certainly expert at adapting the genre of the story of working life in the city, the sea narrative, and the travelogue in, respectively, "Bartleby," "Benito Cereno," and "The Encantadas." Even if "The Bell-Tower" did not pass initial scrutiny there was enough in it for

Curtis to eventually publish. It is tempting, then, to characterize Melville as a writer capable of anticipating a reader like Curtis who would simply misread the "The Bell-Tower." At the moment of judging, his reading eye would see only the textual surface and miss the substantial meanings Castronovo and later critics identify. Melville knew well enough that it was Curtis whose professional eye he needed to satisfy; the fact that he published regularly suggests he was successful. So the Italian setting would be key to this distraction rather than an obscurity, something that would draw Curtis's attention and prompt his sympathy. The issue in which "The Bell-Tower" appeared was the first to have a reviews section, albeit brief, devoted specifically to Italian writing.

For further evidence of this technique of distraction one might also turn to "Hawthorne and His Mosses," published anonymously in *The Literary World* in August 1850, in which Melville addresses the relationship between surface and depth in outlining a theory of Hawthorne's method. In Hawthorne's stories, the essay argues, "bright gildings but fringe, and play upon the edges of thunder-clouds" (*PT* 243), while the sublimity of Hawthorne's writing is "lost in his sweetness" (*PT* 252); genius appears in the stories "by cunning glimpses" like the "sacred white doe in the woodlands" (*PT* 244). If one sees this essay as a blueprint for his own method in his short fiction, then Melville smuggles complex ideas past superficial readers like Curtis.

This argument does not stand up to scrutiny. First of all, Curtis was ambivalent enough about "Benito Cereno" to suggest that Melville could not easily steal things past him. His doubts about the style of "The Bell-Tower" are evidence of this too, and his editorial decisions were necessarily compromises given the problems of filling space and meeting copy deadlines. The acceptance and valuing of Melville's stories was not straightforward, and we can draw no easy conclusions about distracting surface and deeper meaning. The example of "The Two Temples" shows both that Melville's stories did not align so easily with the requirements of *Putnam's* and that editors, in that instance Briggs, were not easy to hoodwink.

A second reason to be cautious about relying on a narrative that sees Melville smuggling deeper meanings past magazine editors is that "Hawthorne and His Mosses" does not provide unmediated access to Melville's thoughts. Also well known for its disquisition on literary nationalism, the essay voices opinions that seem to align with the project of a magazine like *Putnam's* where a nationalist agenda sat alongside exercises in literary distinction. The narrator of "Mosses" who writes that "we want no American Goldsmiths; nay, we want no American Miltons" appears to anticipate Curtis's judgment of "The Bell-Tower" as Malmsey wine in comparison to the springwater of Addison and Johnson (*PT* 248). Yet Ida Rothschild argues that "Mosses" is notable not for affirming the ideas about literary nationalism often claimed of it but for undermining such ideas as it displaces them onto the persona of the essay's narrator, the "Virginian Spending July in Vermont."[71] The Virginian also extends his discussion to literary evaluation. He suggests that "you cannot know greatness by inspecting it" and "there is no glimpse to be caught of it, except by intuition; you need not ring it, you but touch it, and you find it is gold" (*PT* 244). If the opinions on literary nationalism in "Mosses" cannot be trusted, then the narrator's judgment of Hawthorne's method of writing short stories and methods of literary evaluation also begin to look less secure. Indeed, the Virginian may be an early example of those partial narrators who figure so prominently in "Bartleby," "Benito Cereno," and "The Bell-Tower." To read "Mosses" ironically means treating with skepticism not only the opinions about literary nationalism but also the Virginian's claims about the separation of light and dark, gilding and thunderclouds, and inspection and intuition.

In this context, Curtis's letters of June 18 and 19 look much less like misreading. The paradox of the letter of June 19 is that even given more time to read and think about "The Bell-Tower" Curtis's aim is neither to read contextually nor more deeply but to read more superficially; that is, he shows no evidence of reading for dark thunderclouds. Instead he comes to more concrete and satisfying conclusions about the story's "unity" and sees the gilding in "The Bell-Tower"—an ornateness that he likens to the "quaint carving of the bell" in the story—but does not reach for the metaphorical "gold" of substance that lurks in the thunderclouds Castronovo identifies beyond the gilded fringes.

In trying to carry out what O'Brien calls "the troublesome office of suiting praise to judgment," Curtis shows no appetite for the kind of political engagement he advocated in his lectures.[72] I am clearly not suggesting that Curtis's aesthetic judgments were made outside of ideology, but I do want to distinguish between modes of critical speculation that—in Castronovo's case, and in symptomatic reading more generally—work to prioritize the inevitability of connections between the political and the aesthetic, and cases like Curtis's where the two domains were demarcated because of different aesthetic and political priorities. Curtis is a dissociative reader. He is an interesting figure not because he lacked political affiliation or purpose but precisely because he believed in political change and the abolition of slavery. When Curtis read "The Bell-Tower" he did not consider it vital to make the connection between literature and formal politics or history. Melville's stories had to pass through a different orientation of criticism to political commitment when they reached Curtis, one where dissociative rather than symptomatic reading held sway. If one follows Castronovo's reading of "The Bell-Tower," Melville is offering *Putnam's* a radicalized version of U.S. history. What made "The Bell-Tower" magazine writing, however, was its picturesque style rather than its radical allegory or the unity of this style with a theme Curtis identified but did not, or could not, articulate.

Even so, it would be a mistake to equate Curtis's dissociative reading style and his criteria for publishing literature with either superficiality or social disengagement. That Curtis finds himself "converted" by "The Bell-Tower" suggests the heightened effect the story creates in him overnight and his understanding of literature as a cultural form with the capacity to change minds. His differentiation between the "many" who will find the style problematic and his own more forgiving judgment is clearly full of social as well as cultural distinction. At the same time, it is a judgment that what best changes minds is a literature whose point is made not just by transparency or force of argument but by a subtlety of persuasion that is contained in some correspondence between theme and style.

We better know now the thunderclouds rather than the gildings of "The Bell-Tower" because of the prevalence of symptomatic criticism that opens up Melville's magazine writing to new analysis. But at what cost? In creating "The Bell-Tower" as so stable a narrative that it does the work he claims for it, Castronovo has to perpetrate his own forgetting. Of what kinds of experience, for instance, are those "accumulated layers of history" constituted? And, if it is impossible to incorporate them all, on what basis does selection occur? There is also rigidity in the critical language by which these readings proceed. If it does not quite construct a monumental narrative out of an "ironic historiography" that Castronovo argues cripples such narratives, then there is certainly little room for any deviation: Melville's narrative "insists"; "a generation cannot inherit a coherent legacy"; "only forgetting can fashion" a stable narrative. But if the terms in which Curtis first read the story no longer resonate or make sense, then what does that say about the capacity of symptomatic criticism to contextualize? Curtis's reading of the story now looks odd, or misaligned with the story as it has become known, and this is because symptomatic criticism tends better to contextualize the time of a narrative's interpretation than the time of a narrative's composition and publication. But "The Bell-Tower" was a magazine story and a material object embedded in the contingencies of publication.

Watching Curtis pass judgment on Melville is, from one perspective, like looking at a world turned upside down. When Fitz-James O'Brien identifies Melville's insistence on being "prophetic" he anticipates later critics who make much of Melville's prescience as a writer and the proleptic capacity of his fiction. Under these circumstances, a world in which so ephemeral and forgotten a writer as Curtis is in a position to exercise literary judgment is difficult to conceive. Even more unlikely is that his judgment is worth taking seriously. One of the problems of symptomatic reading is that such an inversion is dealt with in only one way: restore order by asserting the power of Melville's narratives while forgetting Curtis and how "The Bell-Tower" stumbled into print. That Curtis wavered over "The Bell-Tower," however, and that his judgment turned the story into magazine writing, are important considerations if one wants to understand the history that shapes literary judgment and the texture of literary history itself.

The Curtis who emerges at the intersection of his various occupations, judgments, and interests is someone who could appeal, as he did during his lectures, to the most serious of causes and the most exacting standards of ethical and political commitment while also being able to deal in the trivia of urban social satire and conversational gossip. His ability to regularly fulfill his writing, editing, and lecturing duties at the same time showed he was capable of spontaneous acts of writing and of speaking in front of different audiences during his lecture tours. A man of letters and a man of business, he played off these roles as he mediated the demands of, and his investment in, the economic and cultural capital of writing and intellectual life. Perspiration rather than inspiration generated his multifaceted and often mundane work, and there is nothing in him of the romantic artist; nevertheless, we should not undervalue his role in the literary culture of the mid-nineteenth century.

To factor out Curtis is to underestimate the capacity of literary cultures and cultures of criticism to be different than our own. In the 1850s the literary differences between Melville and Curtis were well enough understood but were part and parcel of the machinations of a literary network that hindsight is not always careful enough to observe. If the balance of cultural taste in the 1850s favored Curtis, neither he nor Melville had careers in the writing of fiction beyond the end of that decade. With the benefit of hindsight, the superiority of Melville's vision might seem obvious. But the reason Melville's magazine writing appeared at all is because it did not do in the 1850s what it does now for readers and critics. According to Castronovo, "the political message" of "The Bell-Tower" is "that once authority effaces its past it can only be subject to the debilitating mistrust of all citizens."[73] Juxtaposing Curtis's reading of "The Bell-Tower" and "Benito Cereno" against such a claim helps to show that the stories were, and still might, be read otherwise, even by someone like Curtis who was expert at holding and expressing political opinions. The urge to make such large claims for stories that originally passed almost unnoticed, or in the case of "The Bell-Tower" almost unpublished, risks lifting Melville out of his context into our own. What then gets lost is the contingent chain of events that shaped Curtis's dissociative reading of Melville's story on those two days in June 1855.

4

The "Unbounded Treasures" of Magazine Paratexts

Reading Melville's magazine writing as pioneer readers once read it in the 1850s is no longer possible. Contemporary critics cannot recreate, for want of resources, how those readers chanced upon anonymous stories in *Putnam's* and *Harper's* and skimmed, dismissed, or perhaps even reread them in the drawing room, the railway carriage, or the library. The opinions of professional reviewers of *The Piazza Tales* are poor substitutes; like us, they could never not know they were reading Melville. The book cover and the contents page of whatever edition we present-day Melville readers hold in our hands remind us that we are trapped in what psychologists call ironic processing: try not to think about Melville's authorship when reading "Bartleby, the Scrivener" or "Benito Cereno" and all one sees is Rodney H. Dewey's 1861 photograph, from which Melville stares back defiantly, arms folded, hands withdrawn.

This chapter offers alternative speculations on how to cope with this dilemma rather than a solution to it. Primarily I concentrate on the one thing a contemporary reader can do: read Melville's work as magazine writing by also reading the other material among which it was embedded when first published. The different magazine pieces that appeared in *Putnam's* or *Harper's* may not have been written in dialogue with one another, but for the reader they were all part of her or his experience of the magazine; they were the paratextual apparatus readers often take for granted—titles, subtitles, prefaces, epigraphs, illustrations, book covers, blurbs, dust jackets, and so on—that in Gérard Genette's words "surround" and "extend" a text "to ensure the text's presence in the world."[1] While magazines exhibit many of the same paratextual components one finds in books and book publishing, they also have their own paratextual systems.

A magazine is most like an edited book that contains pieces by different authors, but unlike an edited book, because it has a title—*Putnam's Monthly Magazine of American Literature, Science and Art,* for instance—that reappears periodically with new sections written by sometimes the same but also different authors. One reason why *Putnam's* was not a book in the 1850s was because it paginated continuously—six issues to a volume—and printed two columns to the page rather than one. Each article published within an issue one might consider a text, but each issue of *Putnam's* is also a text formally sealed by front and rear covers. And the collection of six issues into a volume creates another text when that volume is bound and published in book format. Genette describes paratextuality as "first and foremost a treasure trove of questions without answers."[2] The first questions one might ask of magazine paratexts are: What exactly constitutes a magazine text? Where exactly does a magazine text begin and end? And how viable is it to think of Melville's magazine pieces as self-sufficient texts one can extract from the pages of *Putnam's* and *Harper's* without fundamentally altering their constitution?

The textual boundaries of magazine writing are not immediately obvious. Consider the example of Melville's "The Encantadas." Where and what is this story? In Melville's lifetime, something titled "The Encantadas, or Enchanted Isles" appeared five times. Three of these occasions were the monthly installments *Putnam's* published in March, April, and May 1854, which appeared under the pseudonym Salvator R. Tarnmoor. To ensure readers did not lose track of the whole of which each installment was a part, *Putnam's* added a suffix at the end of the first two months: "(To be continued)." In parts 2 and 3, after the title and pseudonym but before the sketches restarted, the magazine reminded readers these sketches had antecedents: "(Continued from page 319)"; "(Concluded from page 355)." The division of the sketches between issues probably owed more to the physical space each took up than to natural breaks in the story. *Putnam's* operated on the basis that articles were no longer than ten to twelve pages. The division of "The Encantadas" into sketches certainly made breaks less intrusive than in either "Bartleby, the Scrivener" or "Benito Cereno," whose narrative impetus this limit suspended. With its multi-sketch format, "The Encantadas" is actually a rare form of magazine writing: a serialization within a serialization.

Alert readers no doubt also spotted that *Putnam's* made a mistake by jumping from Sketch Sixth to Sketch Eighth in the April issue, a mistake repeated when "The Encantadas" appeared for the fourth time: the compilation of the six issues from January to June 1854 that was volume 3 of *Putnam's.* This mistake remained because the volume bound together coverless issues of the magazine (or reprinted them from the same stereotype plates). The fifth appearance of "The Encantadas" was in *The Piazza Tales,* published by Dix & Edwards in May 1856. Minus the pseudonym and with the numbering of the sketches corrected, the book of collected magazine pieces introduced Melville on its title page as "AUTHOR OF 'TYPEE,' 'OMOO,' ETC., ETC., ETC." The etceteras give some sense of the quantity of Melville's output, but by hiding *Mardi, Moby-Dick,* and *Pierre* they also skip conveniently across works whose qualities many readers and critics struggled to discern, to the extent that they were clearly not worth advertising. The full title of "The Encantadas" gained a semicolon and moved a comma to become "The Encantadas; or, Enchanted Isles." And *The Piazza Tales* did correct one omission from the magazine version: a symbol in Sketch Fourth meant to indicate the shape of Albermarle and Narborough Island. The magazine version prepared readers for this symbol—"A familiar diagram will illustrate this strange neighhourhood"—but what followed was two blank lines.[3] The missing "letter" restored to *The Piazza Tales* version was an upper-case E rotated ninety degrees clockwise, although this still incorrectly visualized the shape of Albermarle Isle. The E needed to rotate 180 degrees (*PT* 609).

Each encounter with these iterations of "The Encantadas" marks a different reading event. At each point the nature of the text is different. The treasure trove of questions about these events might include: What responses did serialization produce? Did readers rejoice when they reached the end of the first installment and saw there was more to come of "The Encantadas"? Or did they sigh with disappointment because they knew next month's issue would contain one fewer readable article? What was the consequence of the missing "letter" and the absence of Sketch Seventh? Did readers sit bemused and give up on a story and a magazine proofed so incompetently? Or did they move on forgivingly because the sketches were so enjoyable? How did readers respond if their subscription to *Putnam's* started with the April or May issue? Did they track down earlier issues or remain satisfied with reading only part of some larger work? What nods of recognition did the buyers of *The Piazza Tales,* or readers of reviews of that book, exhibit—and how did it make them reassess their first reading of Salvator R. Tarnmoor's story of the same name—when they saw Melville's name? Or had they never heard of him before now? And had they forgotten reading the serialized version of the story? Did they not know, or care, that the sketches appeared first in *Putnam's*? Or did they, after reading *The Piazza Tales,* rush out and buy the "entirely New and Uniform Edition"—all five volumes—of the works of George William Curtis advertised along with other books and journals at the end of the volume?

Genette is right to suggest that questions of this sort have no answers. But asking them is important nonetheless. They help remind us that our reading habits and expectations of writing are often stubborn, predictable, and partial; that a text is a material object with which we interact and not merely language and narrative we interpret. When Melville reviewed a new edition of James Fenimore Cooper's *The Red Rover* for *The Literary World* in March 1850, he took the opportunity to concentrate his entire review on the book's "sober hued muslin" binding (*PT* 237). He was particularly enthused by the care taken by the book's publisher in stamping in relief on the covers a "horse-shoe," an object which "in all honest and God-fearing piratical vessels is invariably found nailed to the mast" (*PT* 237–38). How one defines a text—as content, as cover, as inside or outside—alters the interpretations and thoughts one deploys to make sense of that text.

The textual boundaries of Melville's magazine writing are much less fixed than the subsequent reprinting of stand-alone stories suggests. In later collections they appear only to stand in relation to one another, but when first published they bled into their surroundings. And like a territory subject to state and federal laws, at some crossover point each of Melville's magazine pieces is also part of another text whose estate is the broader contents of an issue, a volume, or a whole run of *Putnam's* or *Harper's*; the cosmos of magazine publishing, in which Charles Briggs saw *Putnam's* as one speck of star-dust, is an even larger master text. Melville's magazine writing and the content adjacent to it were for readers of *Putnam's* and

Harper's all part of the magazine text. The individual pieces published in a magazine—each poem, tale, sketch, and essay—were therefore paratexts for each other in the same way that titles, subtitles, footnotes, and illustrations within each piece were paratexts to those pieces.

This is a more liberal interpretation than perhaps Genette intended when defining paratexts. But few of Melville's pieces for *Putnam's* and *Harper's* were reprinted during his lifetime. There is little work to do, therefore, in assessing the paratexts of reprinting as Ryan Cordell has done for Nathaniel Hawthorne's "The Celestial Railroad."[4] But magazines bring paratextuality much more closely into the ambit of intertextuality; magazine texts reside together more intimately than do book texts, and the magazine is a different kind of textual system that requires its own parameters.[5] Magazines embedded Melville's writing among a host of other material, and these are the paratexts this chapter engages. This sometimes means looking at pieces directly preceding or following Melville's writing in pages of the magazine, sometimes pieces in different issues or across different magazines; and sometimes Melville's writing is its own paratext.

One role of magazines was to strike up conversations with readers. This took the form of founding statements, publication of readers' letters and work by unknown writers, and editorial reviews of past volumes and projections of future contents. The subscription method of paying for a magazine established a reader's investment and a publisher's commitment to continue the conversation over the next year. The pieces in each month's issue also spoke to one another for the reader just as one part of a novel's narrative speaks to another. In this chapter I listen to Melville's writing as it was part of these conversations. The thoughts and feelings of pioneer readers of Melville's magazine writing may be lost, but one line of productive speculation is to ask, What meanings does Melville's writing accrue when juxtaposed against fellow-traveling magazine writing? This kind of paratextual criticism can supplement a contextual criticism that treats Melville's writing as most adjacent to the tides of historical and social events. His writing was certainly adjacent to these tides, but it was borne across their currents in the holds of *Putnam's* and *Harper's*. These magazines were not rudderless and drifting ghost ships; they were sturdy vessels that plotted courses through storms. *Harper's* claimed to offer the American people "the unbounded treasures of the Periodical Literature of the present day."[6] Embedded among the cargo of these treasures, Melville's writing sparkles anew when caught in their reflected glister.

Conversing with Science in "The Lightning-Rod Man" and "Israel Potter"

The August 1854 issue of *Putnam's* was the only occasion during Melville's magazine career when he published more than one piece of writing in the same number. The second installment of "Israel Potter; or, Fifty Years of Exile" appeared as the third item in the magazine.[7] Picking up the eponymous war veteran's story after his escape from English captors, chapters IV through VII follow him on his journey toward and through London and his subsequent dispatch to Paris, where he meets Benjamin Franklin. The preceding item in the magazine was Melville's "The Lightning-Rod Man," a four-page sketch about the standoff during a New England thunderstorm between a pushy salesman of lightning conductors and a skeptical narrator. In this instance, and unbeknown to the magazine's reader, the proximity of a lightning-rod man and America's very own lightning-rod pioneer meant that Melville's anonymously published writings acted as their own paratexts.

Melville wrote "The Lightning-Rod Man" in the spring of 1854, and Hershel Parker suggests he delivered it to *Putnam's* sometime close to April 1.[8] Melville sent sixty pages of his suggested new serial to George Palmer Putnam on June 7, 1854, nearly two weeks after he first sent it to *Harper's*. Melville wrote the pieces, then, at roughly the same time. There can be no question of authorial intentionality in the proximity of "The Lightning-Rod Man" and Franklin's first appearance in chapter VII of "Israel Potter"; Melville had no control over when *Putnam's* published his work. No proof exists, either, that the juxtaposition of Melville's two musings on Franklin was the result of someone in the editorial office connecting up the dots. But it is not impossible to rule out editorial intentionality, especially when the first item in the August 1854 issue of *Putnam's*—directly preceding "The Lightning-Rod Man" and "Israel Potter"—was an essay titled "The Smithsonian Institution: Its Legitimate Mission." The essay's author we now know was the doctor turned journalist and ornithologist Thomas Mayo Brewer. In the air and on the pages of this issue of *Putnam's* were science, the history of science, the advancement of knowledge, and the

American men on whose ideas future development would proceed. And electricity was central to this discussion.

When his *Putnam's* essay appeared Brewer was editor of the *Boston Atlas*. He first corresponded with George Palmer Putnam in December 1852, when he offered to advertise the new magazine and other of Putnam's publications in his newspaper. Appealing to Putnam's faith in quality, Brewer ventured that the *Atlas* "is the largest of any of the large commercial papers, of permanent subscribers among the best classes of our citizens, a much more valuable list than that of the penny, or the two-penny journals, even though the latter may boast a numerical advantage."[9] In his next contact with Putnam Brewer discussed the possibility of an essay on the Smithsonian, and Putnam clearly agreed to publish it.

Brewer's essay is sober but evangelizing. Bolstered with the kind of discursive footnotes one finds in *Putnam's* at this time but never in *Harper's*, it argues that the purpose of the Smithsonian Institution is to advance and disseminate knowledge. Congress was impeding this mission by decreeing the institution spend half its income on a gallery of fine arts, various lecture series, and the building itself. In supporting Joseph Henry, the institution's first secretary, the essay intervened in a long-running dispute over resources between Henry and the Smithsonian's librarian, Charles Coffin Jewett: Henry wanted more money for research and original publication; Jewett wanted more for the library and museum. Jewett lost, and Henry dismissed him in July 1854, just as *Putnam's* published Brewer's essay. The tone of Brewer's assessment of Henry was very different from an earlier depiction of him in the September 1853 issue of *Putnam's Monthly*. Edward Bissell Hunt described Henry as "a hale and rather portly man, with a face alternating between abstraction and a very kindly consciousness." Although recognizing his skills as a scientist, Hunt indulged in underhand criticism of Henry by arguing that he was much better qualified as a researcher than an administrator; the implicit judgment in Hunt's belief that "he is busy with what others, doubtless, could do as well" is that there were men with more suitable qualities who would better do the job of running the Smithsonian.[10]

These turf wars between researchers and administrators, advancers and institutionalizers of knowledge, are pertinent to Melville's depictions of science and Franklin, given Joseph Henry's area of research expertise. In the International System of Units, the "henry"—or the symbol

H—measures inductance. Henry was a pioneer of electromagnetic science. He and the British scientist Michael Faraday both discovered electromagnetic self-induction during independent experiments in 1831. Faraday is better known than Henry now by virtue of publishing first, but Henry was the early nineteenth-century inheritor of Franklin's experiments with electricity. Faraday himself once assured one of Henry's former Princeton students, Theodore Cuyler, that "by far the greatest man of science your country has produced since Benjamin Franklin is Professor Henry." Samuel Morse's telegraph put to practical use Henry's work on the electromagnetic relay. We also know that Henry taught Melville at the Albany Academy in 1831.[11]

Franklin is the subject of a good deal of comment in critical treatments of both "The Lightning-Rod Man" and *Israel Potter*, but only Joshua Matthews brings the two pieces together. Even then the juxtaposition is fleeting; they are simply examples of "other uses of Franklin in fictional pieces composed and published at the same time."[12] Brewer's essay attracts no attention. But the contiguity of the three pieces can add to our understanding of Melville's magazine writing. Perhaps rather than two texts, "The Lightning-Rod Man" and the four chapters of "Israel Potter" make sense as a new hybrid text. Elements of a larger text purchased and read as the August issue of *Putnam's*, this hybrid text has consequences for the reading of its own elements. Rather than trying to interpret the two pieces separately in their own contexts and traditions, their publication as pieces of magazine writing in the same number alongside Brewer's essay affects the interpretation of them against and within each other. The paratext of "The Lightning-Rod Man" puts into new light the depiction of Franklin and Franklinesque lore in chapter VII of "Israel Potter" and vice versa. Brewer's essay on the Smithsonian provides a new frame for understanding Melville's pieces. Putting the paratexts to work opens a new dialogue.

Melville does not sugar-coat Franklin's legacy in either story. "The Lightning-Rod Man," Allan Emery concludes, depicts the way that "science turned people into images of Franklin at his worst: the paranoid technician."[13] For a magazine so supportive of science that the word appeared in its title, *Putnam's* puts into odd juxtaposition Brewer's support for Joseph Henry's scientific mandate and Melville's critique, none of which appears particularly well disguised. As a paratext, Brewer's essay shows that Melville's pieces do not align with a fixed magazine position but present an alternative point of view on issues consonant with the magazine's broader interests. What made the pieces suitable for *Putnam's* was Melville's use of magazine conventions to express his ideas.

"The Lightning-Rod Man" and chapter VII of "Israel Potter" converse with history and the history of science as their effects are felt in more mundane domesticated conflicts. The authoritative footnotes Brewer includes in his essay extend the conversation to other voices outside the magazine; there are quotations from Senator James Pearce's report on the distribution of Smithson's fund and from a lecture delivered by Joseph Henry. Melville instead strikes up a dialogue with his magazine surroundings by enacting this dialogue in dialogue form. Brewer speaks to Joseph Henry's detractors by defending the right of the scientist of electromagnetism to implement Smithson's vision over that of the bureaucrats and financiers. Both of Melville pieces proceed by way of a battle of wits between two antagonists: the lightning-rod man and the narrator; Franklin and Israel Potter. In Melville's world, his fictional conversations say something about the nature of conversation itself.

Both scenes take place in a single room and proceed mainly by way of direct speech after introducing and describing the lightning-rod salesmen and Franklin. Melville's salesman is in the business—like Morse—of practical application, though the story says more about what happens when that application veers away from the optimism of invention and how such optimism itself is delusional. The lightning-rod man first intrudes on the narrator's hospitality; then zealously espouses the practical benefits of his conductor, now an object of commercial exchange rather than enlightenment experiment: "Hark! Quick," he says at another crash of thunder, "look at my specimen rod. Only one dollar a foot" (*PT* 121). And he maintains his blinkered pitch even as the narrator, refusing to be gulled by the sales patter, points out instances when rods fail. The same tension Brewer identifies between Smithson's expectations for the institution and the practicalities that result after the interventions of Congress are evident in the disparity between the thrill of scientific discovery and the degraded performance of Melville's commercial lightning-rod man.

The narrator of "The Lightning-Rod Man," on the other hand, is a benevolent figure happy to take in strangers to his house and comfortable with the art of conversation. Despite defying both his opening attempts—the thunderstorm is not "fine," says the stranger, but "awful"; "Not for worlds!" will he stand on the hearth as directed—the narrator continues by jokingly comparing the tripod-holding intruder to the classical figure of Jupiter Tonans (*PT* 118). The salesman quickly shows his sly aptitude in the conversational arts; his manner and what conversation he proffers are all part of his sales pitch. While the narrator takes exception to being ordered around in his own home, the salesman achieves his intention of turning the conversation to his business as he forces the narrator to ask of this rude intruder: "If you come on business, open it forthwith. Who are you?" (*PT* 120). Once he knows the stranger's business, the battle of wits commences.

If the salesman wins the opening gambit by forcing the narrator to engage him on matters of business, his mirage of pseudo-knowledge also contains the means by which the narrator sees through it. When the salesman explains in a patronizing tone—"Do you comprehend?"—that lightning passes from earth to the clouds in a "returning-stroke," the narrator is inspired with confidence rather than alarmed (*PT* 122). What the narrator understands by the "returning-stroke" he does not say. But this moment marks the point at which he feels confident enough to regain authority in his own home. He is, he says, content to place his trust in God and sends the "false negotiator" packing as the "scroll of the storm is rolled back" to show the house undamaged (*PT* 124).

Melville dismantles the hubris of science as it turns facts and principles into language and discourse. The language of science in the mouth of the lightning-rod salesman is piously didactic and illusory; the salesman commands and conjures at the same time. As the response to the call of Brewer's essay, "The Lightning-Rod Man" undercuts the suggestion that science leads benignly. Soliciting Putnam to publish the essay, having first warmed him up, shows Brewer's strategic craft. What Putnam or anybody else working for the magazine knew of the infighting at the Smithsonian is hard to tell, but the essay was part of a struggle for power that science was fighting in order to secure its own institutionalization. In that process the magazine was one location in which protagonists used the dark arts of persuasion. What Melville does in "The Lightning-Rod Man" is to take one step back and make conversation itself the object of study. Rather than the rights and wrongs of arguments, "The Lightning-Rod Man" asks on what grounds a listener or a reader should judge arguments trustworthy.

Chapter VII of "Israel Potter" continues this dialogue in paratextual relationship to "The Lightning-Rod Man." The stakes of the analysis are loftier, although the disparity between antagonists makes it a slightly different conversation. In place of the lightning-rod salesmen there is the horse's mouth: Franklin, the "sage" of legend for whom readers are well prepared by the chapter's subtitle. Israel, they are told, will find Dr. Franklin "right learnedly and multifariously employed" (*IP* 37). The vernacular "right" and the verbose "multifariously" create a greater distance between the subservient, uneducated Israel and Franklin the *philosophe* than between the narrator and the lightning-rod salesman. The sense of distance is reinforced as Melville describes the "presence" of the man in whose company Israel finds himself. Franklin is one part intellectual, two parts alchemist. He is surrounded by the trappings of science and knowledge—pamphlets, books, and printed documents spanning many different subjects—but is wearing a dressing-gown "embroidered with algebraic figures like a conjuror's robe" when Israel first meets him; he sits "at a huge claw-footed old table, round as the zodiac," and the walls of his room have "a necromantic look" (*IP* 38). This was the first chapter of the serial Melville composed from his own imagination. The earlier chapters he based largely on the original source for the story, Henry Trumbull's *The Life and Remarkable Adventures of Israel R. Potter.* In imagining Franklin, Melville layers the trappings of wisdom from different ages; the modern man of science is the occultist of yore. As responsibility for knowledge of the world passes from one perspective to another, the depiction of Franklin suggests that current advancers of knowledge are prone to inherit the deficiencies of their predecessors.

As soon as Israel enters his company Franklin becomes the "grave man of utility" who suggests writing a pamphlet on the dangers of boots with high heels when he sees Israel's footwear, warns of the irrationality of tight shoes, and reels off aphorisms at every opportunity. Before Israel has managed two whole sentences, Franklin has told him two ineluctable truths: "Had nature intended rational creatures [to wear tight shoes] . . . she would have made the foot of solid bone, or perhaps of solid iron, instead of bone, muscle, and flesh"; and "Always get a new word right in the first place, my friend, and you will never get it wrong afterwards" (*IP* 40). More quickly follow, and Israel is trapped like a fly in the web of Franklin's linguistic dexterity; each effort he makes at conversation is pulled apart and thrown back at him with some accompanying nugget of wisdom. In "The Lightning-Rod Man" the narrator can more than stand up for himself, but Israel is not in a fair fight in this chapter. He is sent off to bed with *Poor Richard's Almanack* to read after dinner, which "in view of our late conversation," Franklin tells him, "I commend to your earnest perusal" (*IP* 45). There is in truth little conversation; Franklin simply dispenses language.

Chapter VIII of "Israel Potter" in the September issue reintroduced readers of *Putnam's* to Franklin and offered a fuller appraisal of Franklin the sage. The narrator is more respectful of his achievements, but the Franklin who seeks the company of the Parisian literati—"a soul with many qualities, forming of itself a sort of handy index and pocket congress of all humanity"—also "needs the contact of just as many different men, or subjects, in order to the exhibition of its totality." When conversing outside of this network such "exhibition" loses its luster. The narrator notes how Franklin's "casual private intercourse with Israel, but served to manifest him in his far lesser lights; thrifty, domestic, dietarian, and, it may be, didactically waggish" (*IP* 48). The showman becomes the dogmatist.

Melville's lightning-rod man is the redacted Franklin, one without the articulacy, the knowledge, or the wit, who tramps New England evading the "dissuasive" communal conversation the narrator undertakes with his neighbors (*PT* 124). Intruding into people's homes for private conversations, he manifests those "lesser lights" in his sales pitch and his hectoring tone. Like the humble Israel, prospective customers are in danger of being mesmerized by a conjurer's tricks with words. What they need to repel intruders is the "returning-stroke" of their own conversation. For the narrator of "The Lightning-Rod Man" this is his trust in God's ordained fate; more generally it is the belief in one's own voice. Eventually Israel recognizes that every time Franklin enters the room "he robs me . . . with an air all the time, too, as if he were making me presents" (*IP* 53). Seeking help in his dilemma from *Poor Richard's Almanack,* Israel summons the confidence to see through Franklin's talk: "'Oh, confound all this wisdom! It's a sort of insulting to talk wisdom to a man like me. It's wisdom that's cheap, and it's fortune that's dear. That ain't in Poor Richard; but it ought to be,' concluded Israel, suddenly slamming down the pamphlet" (*IP* 54).

The problem with both Franklin and the lightning-rod man is that they are men who want to talk but who brook no dialogue. Heard from their own position their ideas sound authoritative; heard from the position of an interlocutor the same ideas control and deceive. Though written separately and contingently juxtaposed in the August issue of *Putnam's,* Melville's two pieces introduce this interlocutory party to the conversation. Read forward and backward as each other's paratexts, and as paratexts of Brewer's essay on the Smithsonian, Melville's pieces foreground dialogue as a form that pulls the rug from under monologue. "The Lightning-Rod Man" converses with Brewer's certainties about science; through conversation the piece unpicks the debased offspring that follow from even the most important scientific ideas. Chapter VII of "Israel Potter" mirrors the dialogic structure of "The Lightning-Rod Man" but puts different personalities in dialogue. The stories speak across each other's borders so that one is able to imagine how the narrator of "The Lightning-Rod Man" might react differently to humble Israel—both hail from the Berkshire Hills—when faced with Franklin's aphorisms and gobbets of wisdom. His treatment of the salesman suggests he would give them short shrift. And that poor Israel might, in turn, be the kind of customer gulled by the salesmen.

Melville's two pieces remind the *Putnam's* reader that if science is to manage the way the world is known then skeptics still have a role to play in holding science's image of itself to account. With its multi-author format, incessant production cycle, and juxtaposition of nonfiction and fictional forms, a magazine like *Putnam's* allows that accounting to take place because it is dialogue in action. Melville takes the structure of a form whose contents speak to each other and internalizes it in "The Lightning-Rod Man" and chapter VII of "Israel Potter." As a result, characters are in dialogue with other characters in the same piece and also with their magazine bedfellows. These conversations are easy to miss when one reads writing that appeared first in magazines as stand-alone stories with firm borders. A story like "The Lightning-Rod Man" looks less like a discrete allegory of rebellion or religious revivalism when one thinks about it as magazine writing; it looks instead, to use George William Curtis's phrase, "thoroughly magazinish."

The Gentle Oscillations of "The Apple-Tree Table"

In the same issue of *Putnam's* as "The Lightning-Rod Man" and Chapter VII of "Israel Potter," a review essay appeared that carried on the magazine's conversation with science and provided a paratext for the final piece of magazine writing Melville published for Curtis in May 1856. Both the unattributed essay, titled "Spiritual Materialism," and Melville's story, "The Apple-Tree Table; or, Original Spiritual Manifestations," took up the conversation in the context of a cultural staple of the 1850s: the rise of the spiritualist movement following the revelations first of Shakers in the 1830s and early 1840s and then, more publicly and sensationally, of the Fox sisters in 1848, who claimed to be witnesses of spirit rappings.[14] Itself a form of conversation between the living and the dead, spiritualism proved a phenomenon that set advocates and naysayers talking incessantly. One part of that conversation took place in magazines. For Genette, the permeable borders of a text create a zone of transaction that works as "an influence on the public, an influence that—whether well or poorly understood and achieved—is at the service of a better reception for the text and a more pertinent reading of it."[15] When Melville intervened in the discussion of spiritualism in the pages of *Putnam's,* the voices he set chattering operated in just such a transaction zone.

Although "Spiritual Materialism" and "The Apple-Tree Table" appeared in different issues of *Putnam's,* and more than eighteen months apart, Melville conceived and wrote his story well in advance of its publication. "The Apple-Tree Table" tells the story of a narrator and his wife and two daughters—the same family who appear in "Jimmy Rose" and "I and My Chimney"—as their lives are overtaken by mysterious ticking sounds coming from a small table the narrator retrieves, along with a copy of Cotton Mather's *Magnalia Christi Americana,* from a dusty and insect-infected garret. The daughters are convinced the ticking is evidence of spirits. Eventually two bugs eat their way out of the table and the ticking is explained. A version of a similar story appears at the end of Thoreau's *Walden,* though Melville likely read about other instances in two sources: Timothy Dwight's *Travels in New England and New York* (1821) and D. D. Field's edited collection, *A History of the County of Berkshire, Massachusetts* (1829). A copy of the latter Melville read at the Berkshire Athenaeum in Pittsfield. He also used the book when writing *Israel Potter* and his annotations remain intact. On the back flyleaf he wrote: "Table-Bug—Block bug." He made the annotations between July 1850 and June 1854 (*PT* 722).

There is no extant correspondence between Melville and *Putnam's* about "The Apple-Tree Table," but Melville initially sent the story to *Harper's* in the autumn of 1855, so he likely wrote it in the summer of 1855 or earlier.

Several critics have proposed Mather's *Magnalia* as an additional source for "The Lightning-Rod Man."[16] All this suggests that "The Apple-Tree Table" comes out of the same ideas and sources as the two pieces discussed above that appear with "Spiritual Materialism" in August 1854. The review essay is, then, an odd kind of hybrid paratext to "The Apple-Tree Table": epitextual in the sense that it appears in a different issue (and volume); peritextual because it appears within that larger entity of *Putnam's Monthly*—like Melville's writing—and within the same issue to which "The Apple-Tree Table" is connected by its sources.

The substance of "Spiritual Materialism" is a skeptical account of the first volume of *Spiritualism,* by John Worth Edmonds and Dr. George T. Dexter, published in New York in 1853. The review opens with an epigraph from Act II, Scene 3 of *Macbeth* in which a hungover porter, stirred from his slumbers by the sound of MacDuff and Lennox knocking at the gates of Macbeth's castle, makes comic asides about guests he imagines might be doing the knocking. The epigraph sets the mocking tone of the relentlessly logical consideration of the knockings heard by the Fox sisters in Rochester, New York, which are now, the reviewer claims, "echoing through all the limits of Christendom" and "*turning the tables* upon all unbelievers." Tables in one form or another preoccupy the review. The object around which spiritualists sit and on which rappings are heard, the table is also the object that "takes to its legs and perambulates" according to some spiritualist accounts. But the reviewer's position is that immaterial spirits cannot manifest themselves materially: "If a spirit finds no obstacle in high walls, and closed doors, and stopped cracks and keyholes hermetically sealed," then "a table cannot by any possibility stand in his way, he cannot by any possibility personally push it, or maul it, or upset it." Thus the argument is sealed. "The duty of a true man," the reviewer says, is to "unveil the imposture—to make head against its encroachments, by fairly *proving* it unreasonable and dangerous," a phenomenon that "strikes at the root of the ancient creeds of Christendom," whose status the rest of the review defends.[17]

The events of "The Apple-Tree Table," the narrator tells the reader, "happened long before the time of the 'Fox girls,'" but the story is written in their shadow. And neither was this the first time Melville and the spiritualist sisters from western New York State shared magazine space. The March 16, 1850, edition of *The Literary World* carried a review of the recently published *Explanation and History of the Mysterious Communion with Spirits*. In this short book, Eliab Capron and Henry Barron relate the spirit-rapping experiences of John Fox and his daughters that follow them from their home village of Hydesville to nearby Rochester. The review is belittling and skeptical and ends with a joke at the Foxes' expense: "If the spirit has any self-respect he will visit with indignation the Christy Minstrels, who have impiously lampooned his memory in the following conundrum:—'Why is Rochester like a threepenny grocery?' 'Because it keeps bad spirits on the tap.'"[18] The review does, however, disclose that the first spirit who contacted the sisters was a murdered peddler, though what he peddled—one hopes, of course, for lightning-rods—is not made clear. Only five pages earlier in the magazine there appeared a glowing review of Melville's *White-Jacket*; immediately following the review of Capron and Barron's book was Melville's own review of Cooper's *The Red Rover*, "A Thought on Book-Binding."

A pattern of paratextual recursiveness begins to emerge when one notices these juxtapositions. The review of a book on the Fox sisters appears beside Melville's entirely paratextual interpretation of Cooper; in a different magazine, the Fox sisters move from paratext to text as Melville incorporates them in "The Apple-Tree Table." The essay on "Spiritual Materialism" in the August 1854 issue of *Putnam's* is paratext to "The Lightning-Rod Man" and "Israel Potter" and its contents one part of the dialogue Melville engages in "The Apple-Tree Table" in a later issue of *Putnam's*. Stamped through these texts, paratexts, and intertexts like a vein of quartz through a rock seam is the subject of Franklin's scientific inheritance.

Franklin featured regularly as a communicant in séances because spiritualism, whatever its religious and supernatural dimensions, was also a product of the machine age. Rappings were a crude form of the code Morse invented for the telegraph. Where the telegraph enabled communication across geographical space, spiritualism claimed to enable communication across metaphysical space and time; the spiritualist body, in line with Franz Mesmer's ideas about animal magnetism, became a telegraph machine transmitting words from one realm to another. The reviewer in "Spiritual Materialism" debunks the idea that spirits "possess something like the substance of electricity." Because spirits are less dense than the force they are supposed to permeate, "they can no more affect such a force, or receive impressions from such a force, than they can directly affect or be influenced by objects visible and tangible to mortal senses."[19] But such arguments did not stop spiritualists from believing they could use magnetism and electricity to measure the invisible spirit world and thus legitimate their claims. One part of the spiritualist enterprise was to build and describe machines; in communications with the spirit world Franklin appeared carrying out his scientific experiments from beyond the grave.[20]

Science and spiritualism were not opposite poles of experience, then, nor mutually exclusive ways of perceiving and explaining the world. The language Melville uses to describe Franklin in "Israel Potter" already identifies something of the shaman in the scientist, and the proximate nature of these two roles continues in "The Apple-Tree Table." In the garret, along with "broken-down old chairs, with strange carvings, which seemed fit to seat an enclave of conjurors," the narrator finds markers of scientific experiment and discovery like those surrounding Franklin in his Parisian study: old documents, "a broken telescope, and a celestial globe staved in," and "old vials and flasks" (*PT* 380). The "necromantic little old table" the narrator retrieves has two features "significant of conjurations and charms—the circle and the tripod" (*PT* 378). The table's "three cloven feet" make it look like Franklin's claw-footed table and an inverted version of the "tri-forked thing" the salesman carries in "The Lightning-Rod Man." Melville then puts at the heart of his story a narrator confronted by a mystery—the ticking table—and the possible explanations that might solve the mystery for him as they find expression through his wife and daughters. Unlike other magazine pieces about spiritualism, where opinions were not always so carefully considered, Melville's "The Apple-Tree Table" treads light-footedly between skepticism of the spiritualists and skepticism of the logicians and scientists.

Melville choreographs this dance through a narrator who is unsure of his own mind and prone to suggestion. Much of the story's comic effect proceeds from these character traits; they also place the narrator in the same relation as 1850s magazine readers to the more strident discourses on spiritualism. The narrator is forced into conversation with these discourses as he talks with his wife and daughters and through his reading. If tables were for spiritualists the site of communion with each other and the dead, the table he brings down from the garret is for the narrator the place where he sits reading in his cedar-parlor, where the family eat breakfast and play cards, and over which they squabble.

On one side, the narrator is father to two daughters, Julia and Anna, liable to see spirits everywhere. On the other side is the narrator's "matter-of-fact wife" to whom "the prejudices of Julia and Anna were simply ridiculous" (*PT* 381). The narrator is less harsh on his daughters than his wife, but once he starts reading Cotton Mather one evening he finds himself "starting at the least chance sound." What perturbs him is that notwithstanding Mather's "practical, earnest, upright" reputation, here is a man who can put forward convincing accounts of witchcraft and, what's more, each case is "corroborated by respectable townsfolk, and, of not a few of the most surprising, he himself has been eye-witness" (*PT* 382). When the table begins ticking and he can find no explanation, Mather plays on his mind; of his daughters he confesses that "their example was catching." He recovers equilibrium only by letting different people influence him: "Towards noon," he says, "this sort of feeling began to wear off. The continual rubbing against so many practical people in the street, brushed such chimeras away from me" (*PT* 387). What the narrator thinks and feels, then, comes readily from outside himself, and like a spiritualist clairvoyant he is easily moved by external influences.

Invoking the Greek rationalist and materialist Democritus as comfort, the narrator repeats the kind of phrases one finds in "Spiritual Materialism"—"any possible investigation of any possible spiritual phenomena was absurd" (*PT* 388)—but quickly allows his eye to be distracted by his ear. Finding he can't concentrate on reading, he once more hears the ticking table and finds that "the contest between panic and philosophy remained not wholly decided" (*PT* 388). When the first bug finally emerges from the table, Julia is convinced the insect is evidence of "witch-work" and both sisters persist in cries of "Spirits! spirits!" (*PT* 391). His wife's reaction is "scornful incredulity"; she is "business-like" in sealing the hole in the table (*PT* 392). But the narrator finds himself with "feelings of a mixed sort" and in "a strange and unpleasing way," he says, "I gently oscillated between Democritus and Cotton Mather," though to wife and daughters he professes to be "a jeerer at all tea-table spirits" (*PT* 394).

When the second bug emerges the family tries to settle the cause of the matter by bringing in the naturalist Professor Johnson, who offers an entirely rational explanation: the bugs are the result of eggs laid in the wood many decades ago and have only now hatched and eaten themselves free. The professor, who sneers at Julia's "spiritual hypothesis," claims that some bug laid the eggs ninety years before the tree was felled and, given that the table is estimated to be eighty years old, this "would make one hundred and fifty years that the bug had laid in the egg. Such, at least," the narrator says, "was Professor Johnson's computation" (*PT* 397). When science is called in for proof, then, it can't even be trusted to add up correctly. No wonder Julia still believes in spirits, though now in delight rather than terror.

Whereas the narrator never does say whether he comes down in favor of Democritus or Mather, his wife's unfaltering skepticism and dismissal of anything but matter-of-fact explanations make her a static character who exerts little influence over the story or the reader. Like Franklin in "Israel Potter" and the peddler in "The Lightning-Rod Man," she has a monologic view of the world and is quick to dispense her wisdom at the expense of others. Melville's narrator lingers instead over his daughters. Julia and Anna show the capacity for change, and the final sentences of the story read like a defense of their position, for all they clutch at spiritualist explanation. Science and rationality offer only bad math and graceless sneering. The second bug may only live for a day, "but my girls have preserved it," the narrator says. "And," he continues proudly, just in case we disregard the girls too quickly, "whatever lady doubts this story, my daughters will be happy to show her both the bug and the table" (*PT* 397). It is the daughters who turn the events of the bug's emergence into narrative and dialogue in their willingness to try to convince skeptics. What price Democritus and sneering in the face of wonder and conversation?

"The Apple-Tree Table" is another of Melville's pieces of magazine writing that raises an epistemological dilemma. In "Cock-a-Doodle-Doo!" the narrator searches for the cockerel whose voice he can clearly hear. In "Bartleby, the Scrivener" there is the mystery of why Bartleby behaves the way he does. In "The Encantadas" the multiplication of perspective dislodges the security of any one of those perspectives. In "The Apple-Tree Table" the claims of science and the supernatural to explain the world are put into dialogue. The daughters rely on the evidence of "two sealing-wax drops designating the exact place of the two holes made by the two bugs" (*PT* 397), but this evidence is really only circumstantial. The holes and the preserved bugs do not explain. They are metonyms of a process in which, despite the same evidence, explanation works by argument and belief, expression and conviction: Professor Johnson's account that the narrator finds "lucid" but "a little prosy"; and the daughters' account of the "spiritual lesson" they have witnessed (*PT* 397).

The narrator finishes his story by likening the two holes made by the bugs to the spots "where the cannon balls struck Brattle street church" (*PT* 397), a reference to the siege of Boston at the beginning of the Revolutionary War. Like the bugs, the cannonballs are effects whose cause remains arguable. How the cannonballs are propelled at the church is a simple enough question to answer, as is how the bugs free themselves from the table. The whys and wherefores of how these events come to pass and what significance they carry require a different order of speculation. The church, like Brattle Street itself, was named after Thomas Brattle, a businessman more hostile than Cotton Mather to the Salem witch trials; his church subsequently attracted the ire of Mather by rejecting Calvinism for more tolerant and liberal forms of worship. These battles over belief and how religious men differently account for earthly phenomena prepare the ground for men like Franklin, whose sister was married by the minister of Brattle Street Church, and who corresponded regularly with Samuel Cooper during his time as minister at the church from 1743 to 1783. Overlapping with the liberalization of religious belief, the emergence of enlightenment science added new arguments and voices to the search for causes. Spiritualism was a subplot in the larger story of science's gradual usurpation of religion. The odd intrusion of history at the end of "The Apple-Tree Table"—the link the narrator makes between bugs and cannonballs—brings into juxtaposition these shifting intellectual undercurrents; they are the paratexts Melville's magazine writing engages in conversation.

Scientific Racism in "The 'Gees" and "Benito Cereno"

Science and religion were also the evidential ground on which Americans and American magazines fought intellectual battles about race. The burgeoning fields of ethnology and ethnography gathered new archives that eventually found their way into public institutions like the Smithsonian; the interpretation of these archives provoked controversies about human origins and distinctions distorted by the sectionalism that would lead to the Civil War. Melville intruded directly into these controversies in "The 'Gees," a short piece *Harper's* published in March 1856.[21]

Like the narrators of "Bartleby, the Scrivener" and "The Fiddler" before him, the narrator of "The 'Gees" is also a writer, and he begins by observing the origins of his work: "In relating to my friends various passages of my sea-goings," he says in a short introduction, many interlocutors express incomprehension when he uses the word *'Gee.* On hearing this word, the narrator must interrupt himself—"and not without detriment to my stories"—to offer his listeners enlightenment. As a result, he goes on, "a friend hinted the advisability of writing out some account of the 'Gees, and having it published. Such as they are, the following memoranda spring from that happy suggestion" (*PT* 346). Melville's own entry into print similarly resulted from relating stories about his time at sea to friends and family.[22] But in "The 'Gees" the information the narrator passes on in the magazine is much more specialized: not tales and experiences but idiomatic language and local knowledge about a group of people set down in "memoranda" rather than in "A Peep" or "A Narrative" as in *Typee* and *Omoo.* Through the narrator's claim that what follows results from conversation and dialogue with friends, "The 'Gees" enters the pages of the magazine to engage in conversation a different audience the narrator thinks might benefit from his understanding of the world. At the same time, and at a different level of knowingness, "The 'Gees" also opens up a dialogue with those who sought to apply a scientific method to the study of race and culture, the ethnologists and ethnographers whose work magazines advertised and reviewed and in whose shadow the magazines themselves published many pieces of writing about unfamiliar climes and their inhabitants.

Written in the register of instruction, then, at the same time as it instructs about Portuguese inhabitants of the Cape Verde Islands, "The 'Gees" instructs about the supply of other ethnological and ethnographic instruction magazine audiences consumed in the 1850s. As Carolyn Karcher notes, "The 'Gees" is a satire on ethnology and particularly the brand of ethnology practiced by Josiah Nott and George Gliddon in their much reprinted and popularized *Types of Mankind* (1854). *Putnam's* considered *Types of Mankind* significant enough to make a long review of the book the first piece of their July 1854 issue.[23] Karcher suggests that Melville wrote "The 'Gees" after reading it. She imagines that Melville "must have closed this number of *Putnam's* with the foreboding that *Types of Mankind* . . . threatened to exert an influence as profound as it was pernicious." "The 'Gees," she argues, is his attempt "to beard the ethnologists in their laboratory."[24] The chronology certainly works: "The 'Gees" was one of the "brace of fowl" Melville sent *Harper's* on September 18, 1854, though the piece remained unpublished for eighteen months (*PT* 714). And Karcher's razor-sharp reading of "The 'Gees" shows how Melville establishes an analogy between 'Gees and African Americans and then parodies the language of ethnology, whose vocabulary creates and sustains racial hierarchies. Ultimately, she argues, "Melville undertook nothing less than to undermine the very basis of ethnology as a science classifying men according to observable criteria. In its place he advanced a unitary view of mankind."[25]

That would be a heady achievement for any three-page magazine piece. Plucking "The 'Gees" out of *Harper's* and only allowing it to talk to the *Putnam's* review belies the nature of the ongoing conversation in both magazines about Nott and Gliddon's book and the ideas *Types of Mankind* promoted. Continuing this chapter's emphasis on paratexts and the dialogue in which magazines pieces engage, "The 'Gees" worked as a piece of magazine writing because it allowed *Harper's* to continue its own skeptical attack on *Types of Mankind,* a position driven not by anti-racism but a religious skepticism about the pseudoscience of ethnology Nott and Gliddon practiced. During the eighteen months "The 'Gees" spent loitering in *Harper's* offices, the conversation about human origins and distinctions continued; like an early guest at a party who ends up stuck at the side of the room away from the main action, "The 'Gees" relied on *Harper's* to eventually shepherd it into a conversation in which the *Putnam's* review was only one voice.

At the heart of the intemperate conversations about race in the 1850s were conflicting ideas about whether different races developed from a single point of origin or from multiple points. *Types of Mankind* does not stand in for a single ethnological view on this matter. There were ethnologists who disagreed with the arguments of the book, and many others who objected to conclusions the authors drew from scientific evidence. Even though the *Putnam's* reviewer of Nott and Gliddon's book was not one of them, many ethnologists, natural scientists, and educated commentators used the pages of magazines to make the unitary case for human origins that Karcher sees in "The 'Gees."

The belief that races developed from multiple origins—polygenesis—flourished in the work of some influential American natural scientists and ethnologists, most notably Samuel Morton's *Crania Americana* (1839). Morton argued that differences in skull sizes between races were too significant to be the result of common ancestry; the result of design instead, he argued, they indicated the long-standing separation of the races. Sharing the same classificatory impulse with many nineteenth-century attempts to better understand the human body, Morton's work was similarly influential beyond the scientific domain and had social and ideological consequences. The history of these consequences—through social Darwinism, eugenics, and biological racism—is still with us; in 1854 it resulted in *Types of Mankind,* whose frontispiece carried an engraving of Morton in dedication.

The long *Putnam's* review of this seven-hundred-page work followed up an earlier report on the impending publication of Nott and Gliddon's book in March 1853. Just before a brief, disparaging comment about E. D. E. N. Southworth's "ponderous" *The Curse of Clifton,* the magazine gave notice of "a work on the *Types of Mankind*" and expressed confidence "that it will be a book of great utility."[26] The full review first lays out the idea of monogenesis—racial development from a single point of origin—as supported by the Bible and existing science, and then goes on to defend polygenesis and the validity of the science Nott and Gliddon use to make their case. Literal readings of the Bible, the reviewer argues, are mistaken and scripture makes for poor evidence. Humans of all races certainly share more in common than they do with any other species: "A man is . . . entitled to every consideration that properly pertains to man, as separated from ape, baboon, bat, or any other creature." But the reviewer is also clear that "so far as scientific and archaeological inquiries go, the preponderance of evidence is on the side of fixed and primordial distinctions among the races."[27] While Gliddon was primarily an Egyptologist, Nott was a trained physician, a slave owner, and an apologist for southern slavery. The review appeared as Godwin and Curtis stepped away from the magazine, but the appointment of Frederick Beecher Perkins hardly damaged the magazine's antislavery sympathies. If the nature of the review is surprising for a progressive magazine, then it is a reminder that *Putnam's* took no fixed progressively political line through the course of its brief history and that the magazine's faith in science could lead it into dangerous territory when ethnologists like Nott and Gliddon used science to justify their political prejudices.

Frederick Douglass certainly understood the motives of those making the polygenist case. In "The Claims of the Negro Ethnologically Considered," first a speech delivered at Western Reserve College in Ohio in July 1854, Douglass described Nott and Gliddon's book as the "most compendious and barefaced" of attempts "to disprove the unity of the human family, and to brand the negro with natural inferiority." Furthermore, he argued, "slaveholders have availed themselves of this doctrine in support of slaveholding. There is no doubt that Messrs. Nott, Gliddon, Morton, Smith and Agassiz were duly consulted by our slavery propagating statesmen."[28] And *Putnam's* soon changed its mind about *Types of Mankind* with another essay, in January 1855, whose title, framed as a question—"Are all Men Descended from Adam?"—appears self-consciously to engage and rewrite the earlier title, "Is Man One or Many?" While the argument of this later piece is tortuous, especially without the sense of geological time or Darwinian evolution familiar to any present-day understanding of biological development, the conclusion is clear enough: "The various converging arguments from science, history, and tradition, as well as the deeper moral consciousness of the race, are, we conceive, conclusive of the unity of mankind."[29] The emphasis on religion in both the title and the argument of this essay addresses the larger battle between science and Christianity for intellectual priority. In the conversations about human origins, science and religion twisted around one another in odd shapes. Polygenists like Nott and Gliddon disparaged religion, but Christians could be polygenists, like the Unitarian Louis Aggasiz; monogenists defended their beliefs on scriptural grounds, or they could take on the polygenists on scientific grounds, like the Reverend John Bachman.[30]

So exercised was *Harper's* by the arguments and implications of *Types of Mankind* that two consecutive editorials in September and October 1854 attempted to dispute the book and its findings. In tenor, as one might expect, these pieces lack the sharpness of Melville's satire in "The 'Gees"; they operate not through punning and parody but direct hostility and aim to undermine polygenist arguments on first principles. Nonetheless, they show that *Harper's* thought as little of ethnologists as did Melville. The first editorial mocks the presumption of scientists to know more than God, and of ethnologists it notes dismissively that "no show of second-hand learning in Egyptian antiquities, . . . no amount of facts even, or phenomena, in natural history, however soberly collected and carefully classified, can avail to decide the great question of origin while this higher law remains undiscovered and unrevealed." There are, *Harper's* argues, moral, logical, and metaphysical laws that are beyond the naturalist and that cannot "be reached by sense or observation."[31] There is something of the "The Apple-Tree Table" narrator's residual trust in explanations beyond science here: a faith that material facts contain more than one can explain through science. For *Harper's* this is true especially of Josiah Nott, who, it argues, is much less qualified to pass judgment on the physical world than the early British empiricist Francis Bacon. The second *Harper's* editorial restates the monogenist argument, but faced with scientific and Christian defenses of slavery prefers the latter because the former is potentially much more destabilizing. The Christian position "will be found in the end to be the true conservatism."[32] The implicit thrust of this view in *Harper's* is that science, and certainly the pseudoscience of ethnology, cannot sustain the claims it professes.

Given such hostility, it seems more likely that the magazine understood full well the satire of "The 'Gees." The surprise is that they held back the piece for so long when it made excellent company for these "Editor's Table" columns. When finally published, though, Melville's piece also sat comfortably in the March 1856 issue, which continued a fascination with overseas spaces and races that the magazine treated with a casual orientalism common to both *Putnam's* and *Harper's*. The issue's gateway to foreign exploration was an opening essay in which the landscape artist T. Addison Richards guided the reader on a richly illustrated tour of the Juniata River area of Pennsylvania. Noting the importance of Pennsylvania as a thoroughfare for immigrants, the piece ends by registering the arrival of the railways and the telegraph and the changes effected by modernization: "Steam and electricity must stir up the Juniata folk, as they are rattling the dry bones of all other communities."[33] Steam was the motor that took Commodore Matthew Perry on his expeditions to Japan in 1853 and 1854. The first of these trips forms the subject of the second article in the March 1856 issue. The essay describes the customs and appearance of Perry's Japanese hosts, distinguishing between "the people generally," who "are not remarkable for their good looks," and the "higher classes," who are "somewhat better looking."[34] After a piece on whaling on the high seas, which marks in passing the story of "Mocha Dick" and the whaleship *Essex,* the reader of *Harper's* then embarks on "Passages of Eastern Travel," where the narrator frames his account in the nostalgic and orientalizing discourse of a civilization in decline. "This worship, this creed," he writes of Islam, "is approaching its end," and the two hundred thousand people lying around him at night "are not worth the counting among the races of men" because "the end is coming."[35]

All of these pieces deal with modernity's futures in one form or another. Whether it is the extension of steam and electricity to rural Pennsylvania, Perry's aggrandizing steam-powered trips to Japan, a whaling industry whose products would soon become obsolete, or the American perception of an ancient civilization supposedly in decline, *Harper's* registers for its readers the friction of emergent and residual cultures and creeds and the peoples and races caught up in the structural shifts of power. *Harper's* signaled its faith in industrial progress by printing and reprinting many articles about new industrial techniques and projects, in the United States and elsewhere.[36] The magazine's forward-looking approach to manufacturing and industry based on new scientific methods was entirely consistent with its orientalizing depiction of other races and its dismissal of the science ethnologists used to support their views on race and human distinctions. Dominion of man over man was the result of political forces; the question of human origin is a matter for a higher authority than science: "In the domain of mere facts, or observation," the first "Editor's Table" article on ethnology declares, "we will give all credit to the naturalist. But this inquiry stretches far away beyond his narrow sphere. It involves logical questions, moral questions, metaphysical questions. . . . Now science, *commonly so called,* can not settle these questions."[37] In the practical world of mechanical application, science has its place; beyond this practical arena science overreaches. "The 'Gees" makes a similar distinction while supporting the magazine's antipathy toward ethnology.

Science first makes an appearance in "The 'Gees" when the narrator passes comment on the hardiness of the 'Gee. "Upon a scientific view," he claims, "there would seem a natural adaptability in the 'Gee to hard times generally." But the basis for such a scientific view remains undeveloped; to support his judgment the narrator reaches instead for religious analogy: "the kindly care of Nature in fitting him" for harsh experiences, "as for his hard rubs with a hardened world Fox the Quaker fitted himself, namely, in a tough leather suit from top to toe" (*PT* 347). To compare the skin of the 'Gee to the apocryphal suit George Fox stitched for himself means the narrator mixes up the natural and the man-made. If the suit for the shoesmith Fox was a practical garment he could make using his skills with a needle, to later admirers it symbolized his strength of character to withstand his spiritual battles with established religion. But science prided itself on empirical discovery, not on analogy and symbolism. The narrator's choice of evidence lacks any scientific credibility. The scientific "view" is subjective and, as the narrator continues to dispense his judgments, "The 'Gees" knowingly unpicks the narrator's own narrative of how one comes to know the 'Gee.

When he compares the 'Gee to livestock, the narrator dismisses the possibility that one can know either creature through intuition. To understand the 'Gee one must examine him like one examines a horse. After measuring and assessing physical attributes there is one other check to perform: "draw close to, and put the centre of the pupil of your eye—put it, as it were, right into the 'Gee's eye; even as an eye-stone, gently, but firmly slip it in there, and then note what speck or beam of viciousness, if any, will be floated out" (*PT* 349). Physicians used eyestones—small stones with one flat and one convex side—to remove dirt and other particles from under the eyelid. Using one's own eye as an eyestone, the narrator suggests here, finds no physical attributes and only imputes moral ones. Science, or the literal "scientific view," is partial; as the narrator demonstrates, it is put to use diagnosing moral, not physical or biological, qualities.

Even after all manner of examination, the narrator readily admits "the best judge may be deceived." So ship captains looking for deckhands should never negotiate with a 'Gee as a middleman, "because such an one must be a knowing 'Gee, who will be sure to advise the green 'Gee what things to hide and what to display, to hit the skipper's fancy" (*PT* 349). Searching for knowledge, sailors are so easily deceived they must invent ever more cunning ways of preventing deception. One captain, Hosea Kean, goes ashore and surprises 'Gees in their homes to see them as they truly are: "By this means, more than once," the narrator claims, "unexpected revelations have been made. . . . In the stall, not the street, he says, resides the real nag" (*PT* 350). Ethnologists keen to see a 'Gee for themselves should show caution when looking at those ashore in Nantucket or

New Bedford; these are "sophisticated" not "green 'Gees" and "liable to be taken for naturalized citizens badly sunburnt." The narrator cautions that "a stranger need have a sharp eye to know a 'Gee, even if he see him" (*PT* 351). To the ethnologist, one might object, sophistication and greenness should be irrelevant; the scientific study of race is concerned with the physical and biological qualities of the 'Gees as a group, not with their cultural performance. But the narrator of these "memoranda" demonstrates that ethnology always returns to ethnography. Relying on analogy and symbolism, cultural reference and moral distinction, the "scientific view" seeks evidence and truth only to find the sharpness of its own eye's failings. In "The 'Gees," the distinction the narrator makes between seeing and knowing means this satire on ethnology is also a satire on the epistemology of science and its failure to know even as it tries to establish the means of seeing by which it generates knowledge.

Melville trains his literary attention most vividly on race and disparities between seeing and knowing in "Benito Cereno," written during the winter of 1854–55 and beside which "The 'Gees" looks like an apprentice piece. The later story takes the risk of forgoing topical references and allusions to science of the kind one finds in "The Lightning-Rod Man," "Israel Potter," "The Apple-Tree Table," and "The 'Gees." Much more important than race to one contemporary reviewer of *The Piazza Tales* was the story's "thrilling, weird-like narrative."[38] The weirdness comes from the transfer of content to form; Melville wrote about race in his story at the level of narration, perspective, and literary language. Readers engaged in dialogue with their magazines, and other writers providing material for magazines, did not always want such boldness. Writing a story in such a manner produced something less beholden to magazine paratexts than some of Melville's other work, even while the story relies on Amasa Delano's account of his voyages published in 1817. George William Curtis's declining opinion of "Benito Cereno" registers from an editorial perspective what Melville's story tells from a literary perspective: that the mechanisms of racial dominion are embedded at a level more abstract than the public opinions of magazine book reviews, essays, and scientific pronouncements. The setting of the "blank ocean" against which Captain Delano finds the *San Dominick* appearing with "something of the effect of enchantment" loosens the story's attachment to the world of New York so precious to *Putnam's* and to the domestic scenes Melville populated in his other pieces

(*PT* 50). Adrift in the South Pacific, "Benito Cereno" works its magic at a tangent to magazine paratexts.

One such paratext was "About Niggers," a piece in the December 1855 issue of *Putnam's* in which the final installment of "Benito Cereno" appeared. The essay covers ethnological ground once more and works ironically through a conversation between an unnamed editorial "I" representing *Putnam's* and the figurative prig and naysayer Mrs. Grundy. Stereotypical black characters are introduced in order to undermine the bogus claims on which stereotypes rely. The piece deals with chattel and wage slavery, slave revolt, especially the Haitian Revolution and the role of Toussaint L'Ouverture, and concludes that black men are men who happen to be black and whose capacity for all manner of acts—passive and violent—confirms their human status. Though Delano's encounter with the *San Dominick* took place in 1805, Melville set "Benito Cereno" in 1799, right in the middle of the Haitian Revolution, and the juxtaposition of the revelation of the slave revolt in the final episode of "Benito Cereno" alongside "About Niggers" is therefore notable both contextually and paratextually; the essay is of a piece with the increasing antislavery message *Putnam's* published after 1854. Yet "Benito Cereno" surpasses at every turn the simplistic ironic form offered in "About Niggers," which plays to the crowd like a politician on the stump in front of a captive audience. Like the satire of "The 'Gees" once we recognize it, the irony reinforces the opinions of those who already know better rather than changing the minds of those who do not. Melville tries a different form in "Benito Cereno."

In the next chapter I look more closely at the power of story rewriting in "Benito Cereno" and *Israel Potter*, but in brief, what these cases both allow is for the distance of a minor historical drama to supplant the immediacy of more contemporary dramas whose intricacies exercise the pens of magazine writers, editors, and publishers in the mid-1850s. The cover of a real-life story frees rather than inhibits Melville, and "Benito Cereno" determinedly refuses to take the reader by the nose. The third-person narrator's careful staging of Delano's experience intervenes between author and reader; it withholds from, and discloses to, the reader crucial information in a way that the narrators of Melville's other pieces do not. As Melville stares back defiantly from Rodney Dewey's photograph, so his best narrators stoically resist the easy pleasures of the storyteller's quick win: the hastily revealed piece of information with which to settle matters or the key that unlocks a mystery. The topical in the magazine world is soon last month's topic. A story resists consignment to a back catalog in the degree to which it enables the means of its own rereading and later contemplation and transcends the paratext of publication.

The longevity of "Benito Cereno" results because the science in scientific racism is expunged as an object of debate by the narrative and the reader is left facing a conceptual problem much more unsettling than a quickly drawn satire of ethnology. Melville suffocates the ethnologists by removing from them the oxygen of ridicule. The seeing and knowing integral to questions of racial distinction become formal qualities of the text rather than subjects on which the narrative exercises opinions. This is immediately apparent as the story begins and works in the early pages in two ways: the construction of impossible spatial perspectives, and early examples of Delano's inability to see staring him in the face the slave revolt under whose influence the whole story unfolds. Delano's efforts to know what afflicts the "strange sail" in the harbor of St. Maria require him to swap "the glass" of his telescope, through which he first examines the *San Dominick,* for something more forensic (*PT* 46). The narrative elements are like the mechanical parts of a microscope; they are the lenses, the light source, and the calibrating wheels that help bring the specimen plate into focus.

The narrative moves forward through Delano's attempts to modify his angle of vision. He readjusts first by looking at the strange vessel through his glass. He continues to observe the ship's movements, though his vision is obscured by "the vapors partly mantling the hull," but "it seemed hard to decide whether she meant to come in or no—what she wanted, or what she was about" (*PT* 47). The next turn of the calibrating wheel comes when Delano lowers one of his whaleboats in order to gain "a less remote view" (*PT* 48). And "a still nigher approach" leads to a view "modified" that makes clear the "true character of the vessel." As he closes in still further, Delano sees the disrepair into which the ship has fallen and assesses the component parts of the vessel in detail: the spars, the ropes, the bulwarks, the forecastle, the quarter galleries, and the coat of arms on the sternpiece. The structure of the vessel comes into view like the fibers in a piece of cloth closely examined. Still, though, there is obfuscation: the canvas wrapped around the prow, the "copper-spike rust" and "dark festoons of sea-grass" shrouding the ship's name (*PT* 49). Once aboard the *San Dominick,* Delano is then faced with yet more difficulties in turning what he sees into knowledge.

At this point, the narrative management of perspective begins to overwhelm the capacity of Delano's observation. Boarding the ship reveals another level to the structure of the specimen. Going past the cloth's fibers, what now comes into view is the molecular structure of the fibers themselves. Now Delano, the subject of "all eager tongues," with "one eager glance took in all the faces, with every other object about him" (*PT* 49). This panoptic or omniscient perspective, what the narrator describes later as "that first comprehensive glance," is impossible. Glances are never comprehensive. Somehow, the glance takes in both ten particular figures—the "four elderly grizzled negroes" picking oakum and the half dozen "hatchet-polishers"—as well as the "scores less conspicuous" who populate the ship (*PT* 50). Somehow the glance is simultaneously varifocal, looking at the same time in several places and through several focal lengths, while also anticipating the one absentee from this "hubbub of voices" of most significance to Delano: the ship's commander, Don Benito, who returns "an unhappy glance" to his visitor (*PT* 51). Delano now embarks on that process of trying to read the Spaniard and his relationship with the ship's other occupants. This reaches a false summit at the end of the first part of "Benito Cereno" as *Putnam's* published it in the October 1855 issue.

The impossible perspectives the story uses in these early sections contribute to that larger problem of perception that affects Delano as he nears and boards the *San Dominick.* Delano is "a person of a singularly undistrustful good nature," and this makes him easier to deceive (*PT* 47). But so does his failure to know what lies behind what he sees in front of him. When Don Benito tells Delano that his friend, Alexandro Aranda, has died of the fever, Delano suggests to the quivering Spaniard that he knows "what it is that gives the keener edge to your grief" and thinks it must be something similar to the grief he himself experienced when consigning to the sharks one of his friends who died at sea (*PT* 61). Delano thus responds with an empathy in which knowledge comes from looking at oneself rather than at what is before one's eyes.[39] Having already "witnessed the steady good conduct of Babo" (*PT* 52), when Don Benito faints and falls into Babo's arms Delano sees only an obedient servant making "a silent appeal . . . to his master" (*PT* 61). Delano cannot see through the performance of Atufal's submission that quickly follows, and he does not know that while he is right when noting that "padlock and key" are "significant symbols, truly," their significance is not in what he sees—Don Benito with the key, Atufal in chains and padlock—but the inverse: Babo and Atufal are in charge of the key (*PT* 63).

Delano also fails to know the real state of the *San Dominick* because of a willingness to make assumptions or inferences that he bases on his own codes of behavior. Don Benito's reserve, for instance, displeases him; he explains it away as "conscious imbecility—not deep policy, but shallow device" that in any case Delano does not take personally (*PT* 54). The lack of discipline aboard ship, "the noisy confusion" that "repeatedly challenged his eye," Delano puts down to the absence of senior officers. On decks where "not so much as a fourth officer was to be seen," Delano's eye is distracted by what he does not see because he has no other explanation for the disorderliness. When Don Benito moves from Delano's side to whisper with Babo, Delano is embarrassed at Benito's discourtesy while the "menial familiarity of the servant lost its original charm of simple-hearted attachment" (*PT* 64). He catches a Spanish sailor who "kept his eye fixed on Captain Delano" and then moved to look at "the two whisperers." Delano thinks himself the subject of the whispering. From these actions—his looking at someone else looking—Delano assumes Don Benito an impostor: "some low-born adventurer, masquerading as an oceanic grandee; yet so ignorant of the first requisites of mere gentlemanhood as to be betrayed into the present remarkable indecorum" (*PT* 64). So important to Delano are these markers of distinction that he is incapable of recognizing the possibility of other kinds of impostors: the slaves who are now commanders but who are "masquerading" as dutiful and submissive servants.

In the final pages of the first part of "Benito Cereno" a crescendo of interpretation comes over Delano. Fearing for his ship rather than himself, he reads the "gloomy hesitancy and subterfuge" of Don Benito's account of events as "just the manner of one making up his tale for evil purposes" (*PT* 68). But Delano draws back from this explanation because he cannot believe it possible to "counterfeit" what he observes: "the very expression and play of every human feature." It is "incredible" that every person aboard the *San Dominick* is "a carefully drilled recruit in the plot."

And the questions Don Benito asks Delano about his ship that give rise to Delano's suspicions are the same questions that prove to him the questions are innocent: "The same conduct, which, in this instance, had raised the alarm, served to dispel it" (*PT* 69). Finding these thoughts "tranquilizing," Delano looks in the eye subterfuge of a different kind and cannot even see it (*PT* 70).

We can be too hard on Delano. What, after all, does rebellion look like? If we assume we know, then neither would we be able to identify it should it appear in different guise. Readers with the benefit of hindsight can see what Delano misses. But this was a benefit the pioneer readers who sat down with the first part of "Benito Cereno" as it appeared in *Putnam's* did not possess. As a serial, "Benito Cereno" mirrors Delano's own inability to know the true state of affairs aboard the *San Dominick* and what fate awaits him. The reader, like Delano, knows the truth of the matter only retrospectively; the narrator sees on the reader's behalf what Delano cannot see, but the reader becomes aware of this and knows Delano's faults only after reaching the December issue of *Putnam's.* What Delano cannot see is that Don Benito is scared for his life; that African slaves are capable of the kind of intelligent subversion whose preparation, execution, and perpetuation requires sophisticated acts of disguise and manipulation. Important as it is that the reader eventually recognizes Delano's blind spots and the racist assumptions from which they stem, the achievement of "Benito Cereno"—enhanced by serial magazine publication—is to show that seeing and knowing are unreliable companions because they are embedded in the narrative forms by which readers assimilate them.

Like "Bartleby, the Scrivener" and "The Encantadas" before it, "Benito Cereno" asks fascinating epistemological questions about observation and knowledge that expanded the horizons of magazine writing in the 1850s. With the exception of brief references to sophisticated and raw Africans that reprise the language of "The 'Gees," "Benito Cereno" gains philosophical and historical traction from the deletion of topical specificities; Melville moved the historical specificities into what Curtis called the "dreary documents" at the end. There is little doubt that "Benito Cereno," like "The 'Gees," is embedded in the magazine paratexts of *Harper's* and *Putnam's* and that these paratexts, like the ironic sketch "About Niggers," are important contexts and counterpoints for understanding the representation of race in "Benito Cereno." They are also important paratexts and contexts for understanding how some writing goes beyond them. As I noted in the introduction, part of the reason for examining the embeddedness of Melville's authorship in magazine writing more generally is to understand what qualities separate the memorable from the forgettable. The irony of "About Niggers" and the satire of "The 'Gees" are blunt instruments that certainly leave their mark; by comparison, "Benito Cereno" is a scalpel that dissects the body of American racism.

When Melville wrote about the Galapagos Islands in "The Encantadas" he created a world at odds with Darwin's version of the same islands. On the subject of human origins, it was Darwin who eventually settled the scientific argument in favor of monogenesis with *The Origin of Species* (1859), a victory even Nott accepted, though he did not change his views about slavery. Like magazines quickly replaced by the next month's issue, some ideas have a shelf-life even if they do not have a sell-by date. Ethnologists of the "American School" are now themselves specimens. The historical occasion in whose context they were caught up was a scientific revolution in the study of human biology. From Darwin to DNA and the human genome project, this revolution was more thoroughgoing than probably anyone in the nineteenth century could foretell. But the failure of American ethnologists like Nott and Gliddon was to mistake evidence for fact, opinion for truth, and their historical moment for universal experience. "Benito Cereno" transcends the paratexts and contexts of magazine writing because its narrative form anticipates the problems of such category errors. Against pseudoscientific hubris "Benito Cereno" shows that seeing is not knowing. When the narrator of "The 'Gees" notes that stopping to enlighten his listeners with facts about Cape Verdean sailors is "not without detriment to my stories," he articulates what Melville's best magazine stories communicate implicitly: that in stories, not facts, should a writer trade.

5

Melville's "Pilfering Disposition"

In Washington Irving's "The Art of Book-Making," one summer afternoon Geoffrey Crayon wanders into the British Museum. Briefly distracted by minerals, mummies, and hieroglyphics, Crayon sneaks through a door and finds himself in the museum's reading room watching "studious personages, poring intently over dusty volumes, rummaging among mouldy manuscripts, and taking copious notes of their contents." Call slips deliver to the desks the books from whose "sequestered pools" writers draw "to swell their own scanty rills of thought." Books, Crayon concludes, are made from other books. Drifting off to sleep in the soporific atmosphere, he dreams of authors donning books like clothes and fitting themselves out by mixing and matching periods and styles. In his review of *The Red Rover,* Melville suggested a book should be "appropriately apparelled" and that in their bindings books "should indicate and distinguish their various characters" (*PT* 238). For Crayon, the contents of books are clothes an author wears. Eventually evicted as a poacher on this literary estate, he asks himself, "May not this pilfering disposition be implanted in authors for wise purposes; may it not be the way in which Providence has taken care that the seeds of knowledge and wisdom shall be preserved from age to age, in spite of the inevitable decay of the works in which they were first produced?"[1] If the art of making books required such a "pilfering disposition," then Melville was the Michelangelo of his age; a long-standing user and borrower of literary sources, he perfected the art in his magazine writing.

This chapter focuses on *Israel Potter* and "Benito Cereno," where

Melville's literary pilfering took a new turn. We have long known that canonized mid-nineteenth-century writers dipped their buckets in the wells of popular literature and culture to hydrate their stories and characters. Like his contemporaries, Melville assimilated and transformed "key images and devices" from his social and literary milieu in a process David Reynolds describes as "the arrival at literariness after an immersion in the popular."[2] Melville's pilfering of James Maitland's *A Lawyer's Story* for "Bartleby" is a case in point. And in his early novels he supplemented semi-autobiographical or original stories with other sources he consulted. But in his magazine writing, Melville did not just adapt "images and devices"; he rewrote already published narratives of real-life experiences: Henry Trumbull's *Life and Remarkable Adventures of Israel R. Potter* (1824) and chapter 18 of Amasa Delano's *Narrative of Voyages and Travels in the Northern and Southern Hemispheres* (1817). A writer's job is always an epistemological labor that builds knowledge of the world in which he or she lives; Melville now added a metafictional copestone. *Israel Potter* and "Benito Cereno" are writing about the process of writing and publishing.

In this chapter I make several original claims: that with *Israel Potter* Melville showed himself the consummate editor of second-rate raw material; that in "Benito Cereno" he edited Delano's original account into a prototype for the American psychological thriller; and that both texts are better understood as examples not of Melville's immersion in the prosaic terrain of popular literary culture but of an embeddedness in which he was an editor and surrogate reprinter. Melville did not just rework generic characters or ideas; in *Israel Potter* and "Benito Cereno" his rewriting of existing narratives extends our understanding of what magazine writing involved to include the processes of editing and reprinting. Working and shaping material rather than inventing from nothing lies at the core of Melville's art in this late magazine period. *Israel Potter* and "Benito Cereno" turn two-dimensional originals into three-dimensional copies. If, in the rush to interpret what their writings mean, we sometimes forget what writers do when writing and rewriting, one can say of "Benito Cereno," for example, that only from Melville passing Delano's account through his imagination do the meanings of that story follow. The important issue this chapter addresses, then, is not the distinction between high and low culture, but between writing and editing, plagiarism and innovation, and the unique and the generic text.

"The unvarnished truth": Sources, Plagiarism, Reprinting, and Editing

Identifying the sources Melville used in his writing and how he used them is an industry whose development began as soon as Melville published *Typee* in 1846 and matured with his recovery in the twentieth century. Melville's first reviewers noted not just the obvious thematic resemblance of *Typee* to *Robinson Crusoe* but more specific affinities with nonfiction sea narratives such as David Porter's *Journal of a Cruise Made to the Pacific Ocean* (1815) and Philip Carteret's *Account of a Voyage Round the World* (1773). Mary Bercaw Edwards's ledger of the first 140 years of this activity for all of Melville's work is a model of broad and deep reading. She shows where Melville acquired his material: books he bought purposely to help him with his writing; books he chanced upon, such as Trumbull's tale of Israel Potter; books friends and family lent him; and books read aloud in his family circle. Melville then used these sources in two ways: by incorporating old facts in new narratives, and by editing and adapting already published narratives.[3] The only instances of this second approach are *Israel Potter*, "Benito Cereno," and the Indian-hater chapters of *The Confidence-Man,* which adapted part of James Hall's *Sketches of History, Life, and Manners in the West* (1835). All, that is, come from the end of Melville's fiction-publishing career.

The difference between Melville's working method for his earlier work and for *Israel Potter* and "Benito Cereno" is evident when one compares these later narratives with *Typee.* John Bryant's forensic analysis of that novel's composition puts to rest the idea that Melville sat with sources open before him as he started writing. Bryant shows that Melville wrote an initial, much shorter, version of *Typee* and then expanded it with additional material he foraged from David Porter and another key source, Charles Stewart's *Visit to the South Seas, in the U.S. Ship Vincennes, during the Years 1829 and 1830* (1831). So the use of his sources "most certainly occurred late in the compositional process" once Melville ran out of his own anecdotes.[4] *Moby-Dick* followed the pattern of *Typee*: a core narrative supplemented by the sources Melville had read or was still reading until quite late in the writing cycle.[5] *Israel Potter* and "Benito Cereno" reversed this method. Rather than supplementing his own work with sources, Melville supplemented sources with his own work.[6] Here he returned to a method that occupied him immediately before he started writing for magazines. *The Isle of the Cross* reworked a story Melville heard from his father-in-law's colleague John Clifford, and which Clifford then wrote down in a letter to Melville on July 14, 1852 (*C* 621–25). That novel does not survive to show how Melville imagined and fictionalized the story of Agatha Hatch and James Robertson. *Israel Potter* and "Benito Cereno" suggest that Melville understood how he could edit and rewrite narratives to enhance, enliven, and deepen the original kernel of stories contained in these sources.

In either of the modes in which Melville used sources, the specter of plagiarism is never far away. But copyright legislation was in its infancy in the 1840s and 1850s, and the idea of ex nihilo creativity was not universal. Writers and thinkers, Robert Macfarlane argues, "began to speak out against the overvaluation of originality as difference"; other models "envisaged creativity as a function of the selection and recombination of pre-existing words and concepts."[7] With Melville, the relativist position on plagiarism holds sway.[8] John Bryant makes a convincing case for *Typee* that plagiarism and appropriation are forms of textual version or revision. Manifesting itself as "a kind of problematic quotation," such plagiarism becomes "one writer's synecdochal version of another writer's writing." Melville used this method strategically to make the "canny observation that the media through which readers learn of distant places distort rather than illuminate the reality of colonial Pacific life" and "to awaken his readers to their unacknowledged complicity in that process."[9] Revising one's literary borrowings, then, becomes part of Melville's creative process; recasting pilfered material is a form of intertextual monkey-wrenching that realigns the cogs and rods that make up the machinery of meaning.[10]

With *Israel Potter* and "Benito Cereno" Melville faced a new challenge. "Bartleby" soon abandoned Maitland's *The Lawyer's Story,* and there is no evidence Melville owned or read Maitland's book beyond the initial chapter published in the New York City press. Never before had Melville taken a self-contained, published work and made it the basis for one of his own narratives. We can only speculate why he decided to try this literary formula. Perhaps the experience of hearing Clifford's tale of Agatha Hatch and his writing of *The Isle of the Cross* alerted him to the compelling nature of everyday stories circulating in the shadows of American culture. We know the story of Israel Potter's life had been exercising Melville since at least 1849, when he travelled to Britain and France. In his journal, he notes buying a London map of 1766: "I want to use it," Melville wrote, "in case I serve up the Revolutionary narrative of the beggar" (*J* 43). That both *Israel Potter* and "Benito Cereno" are historical stories based on real events also gave Melville the opportunity to reflect on the way those events filter into the world in which they occur and into the narratives by which the past is understood in the present.

Israel Potter and "Benito Cereno" may also mark the waning of Melville's faith in his capacity to generate original fiction. Only *The Confidence-Man* would appear after the end of his career at *Putnam's* and *Harper's*, one last hurrah in the face of declining health, sales, and public recognition. Nina Baym makes the bold but compelling claim that even from the beginning of his writing career Melville "had no great respect for fiction" and moved from "impatience with its demands to a clear sense that fiction and truth telling are opposed activities." The provisional and constricted short form of magazine writing suited Melville better because the guiding principle of the short form was "limitation rather than freedom."[11] The caveat here is that *Israel Potter* is a long form in the guise of a short form: a novel written in serial. Neither by magazine standards was "Benito Cereno" short. Magazines serialized some stories that were not full-length novels, but by far the majority appeared in a single installment. The limitation *Israel Potter* and "Benito Cereno" work within is not length but their conspicuous reliance on a source story.

For this reason, I treat *Israel Potter* and "Benito Cereno" as angular inhabitants of what Meredith McGill calls the "culture of reprinting." The 1790 U.S. Copyright Act granted copyright for a term of fourteen years, with a right of renewal for another fourteen years if the author survived to the end of the first term. The case of *Wheaton v. Peters* (1834) muddied the waters, however, by ruling that an author controlled the first but not subsequent publications of a work. This legal case helped maintain the ready and cheap supply of imported literature and hindered for a time the publication of American-authored books. Reprinting was not plagiarism, since works were usually published under the name of the original author. Neither was reprinting a form of piracy; without copyright laws, the republication of works was legal and commonplace, particularly in the 1830s and 1840s. And with reprinting came editing. Melville carried out root-and-branch editing work in *Israel Potter* and "Benito Cereno" rather than subtle variation. Authors are not usually thought of as reprinters, partly because, as McGill writes, "the subject of reprinting is significantly larger than the question of how authors are situated or how literary texts circulate and signify within this system."[12] As should be clear by now, however, in this book I am more interested in what authors do within systems than with what systems do with authors, and in what specific ways the culture of reprinting leeched into authorial activity still remains unclear.

Seeing Melville as a reprinter is certainly to broaden and rework McGill's concept, but like all great enabling ideas the "culture of reprinting" works best when seen as a continuum rather than a specific condition. With *Israel Potter* and "Benito Cereno" Melville took an original text, edited it, and republished it for profit in a different format. This was not the same as a New York City printer taking a British book recently arrived by ship from London, setting it in new type, and selling the resulting book to an American public without recompense to the original author. But the two acts share a family resemblance. Nor was Melville's example simply an editorial reworking. Editors help change and shape the work of others. All writers edit themselves, but Melville was editing other texts and then publishing them, at least when they appeared in book form, under his own name. Neither plagiarism nor invention, what Melville does to Trumbull's or Delano's narrative seems closer to McGill's idea of reprinting than to Reynolds's understanding of a work's "arrival at literariness after an immersion in the popular." Although not themselves responsible for the physical reprinting of other texts, authors can be surrogate reprinters when, as in Melville's case, they pass on these texts in reworked form to physical publishers. Surrogate reprinting is one more example of Melville's embeddedness in the material creation of magazines.

Magazines themselves were apt vehicles for editing and reprinting because of their composite nature. Magazines recycled and reprinted at will and with varying commitment to attribution. Even a magazine like *Putnam's,* which prided itself on origination, relied on a conceit: that the magazine had a continuous identity beyond the monthly production schedule and the collective of writers who provided content. But the *Putnam's* name, as I noted in chapter 3, continued through various changes in editorship and ownership. The job of these editors and owners was to condense into a serene title the hidden activity of production. Magazines were ultimately wrappers that sold themselves by absorbing writers' labor into the owner's brand. Faith in anonymity meant that *Putnam's* more than other magazines worked hard to maintain this conceit. Melville inhabited the conceit and embedded himself within it. He made himself into a magazine editor when he took on the job of altering Trumbull's and Delano's work in his rewriting of *Israel Potter* and "Benito Cereno" for the pages of *Putnam's.* Stretching the parameters of the conceit to edit dead writers and forgotten writing rather than new and contemporary work, Melville upcycled his sources with a flair Briggs and Curtis might have envied.

During his British Museum reveries about how books are made from other books, Geoffrey Crayon extends the metaphor of reuse: "Thus it is in the clearing of our American woodlands; where we burn down a forest of stately pines, a progeny of dwarf oaks start up in their place: and we never see the prostrate trunk of a tree mouldering into soil, but it gives birth to a whole tribe of fungi."[13] The kind of replenishment envisaged here—turning pine into oak, rotting into living matter—occurs in literature not organically but in the minds and hands of embedded authors when they work with the materials at their disposal. As I noted in the introduction, the centralization of publishing from the 1850s on meant that Melville was writing in a magazine world in which origination and iteration were unevenly changing positions. Editing and reprinting old narratives, he had one eye on each of the waxing and waning worlds of print. *Israel Potter* and "Benito Cereno" were both iteration and origination.

Israel Potter: "A silk purse come out of a beggar's pocket!"

What attracted Melville to the serial form is not clear, although the terms of his initial letter to Putnam on June 7, 1854, suggest money was a key motivation. Melville had already offered *Israel Potter* to *Harper's* but was met with silence because the magazine did not serialize American fiction at this time. In the United States and Britain, weekly and monthly magazine novels became increasingly popular beginning in the mid-1840s, after the initial success of pirated novels in story papers like *Brother Jonathan* and *The New World.* Harriet Beecher Stowe's *Uncle Tom's Cabin,* serialized in *The National Era* in forty weekly parts, indicated the potential of this mode of publication; Robert Bonner at the *New York Ledger* was soon adding tens of thousands of subscribers with popular serializations by Fanny Fern and E. D. E. N. Southworth.[14] With his letter Melville enclosed the first sixty pages of *Israel Potter.* He asked for an advance of $100 and agreement that "not less than the amount of ten printed pages (but as much more as may be usually convenient) [are] to be published in one number" (*C* 265). One can best judge Melville's negotiating skills, and his value to the magazine, by observing that Putnam offered neither the advance nor the guarantee of a ten-page minimum. Melville received five dollars a page as for all his work for the magazine; five of the nine installments were less than ten pages.

Only an incomplete transcription of Melville's letter to Putnam survives. The transcription breaks off just as Melville seems on the point of providing the "more particular understanding" of the manuscript he is enclosing (*C* 265). This is as close as he gets to explaining his reasons for basing his serial so closely, at least in the first part of the manuscript, on Trumbull's story. What he wrote we can only surmise. Walter Bezanson suggests that Melville felt obligated to explain his adaptation to Putnam, though quite why is not immediately clear given that Putnam had just rejected "The Two Temples." Melville's reassurances that the new serial contained "nothing of any sort to shock the fastidious" (*C* 265) more likely suggest a publishing relationship where power resides with the publisher. Putnam's refusal of Melville's terms suggests likewise. As for the reliance of *Israel Potter* on Trumbull's narrative, the time for Melville to tell Putnam that the serial "was to be basically a rewrite job," Bezanson argues, "was now rather than after the critical vultures could move in, and it is probable that in the passage omitted from the letter Melville explained his intentions" (*IP* 183). While this seems a reasonable assumption, Melville was rarely forthcoming with magazine editors and owners about the content of his writing. What is remarkable about much of Melville's professional magazine correspondence is precisely the lack of discussion. This one missing letter may, of course, be simply a departure from his usual practice. But there is no evidence that when submitting "Benito Cereno"—a piece just as reliant on Delano as *Israel Potter* is on Trumbull—that Melville felt it necessary to offer a similar explanation.

While the "particular understanding" Melville provided for Putnam remains a mystery, that Melville sent only the first sixty pages of *Israel Potter* offers some clue to the story's composition and Melville's conception of what he wanted to achieve with the work. A sensible assumption is that the sixty pages were all Melville had written to date. "It is quite possible," Bezanson notes, "that Melville did not know yet that he would abandon sustained use of the *Life* in the next batch of writing" (*IP* 183). The "next batch" were the chapters on Potter's meeting with Franklin in Paris, from which point Melville's narrative—before rehabilitating one or two incidents toward the end—dramatically diverges from Trumbull's. Sheila Post-Lauria argues that once *Putnam's* accepted the serial Melville changed his original intention to write a derivative, paraphrased biography of the sort favored by *Harper's* and instead wrote a challenging, evaluative biography better suited to *Putnam's* more demanding and intellectually discerning tastes.[15] Post-Lauria conveniently ignores the first chapter of Melville's *Israel Potter*, which adds entirely new material to the Trumbull version and would have been part of the first sixty pages sent to Putnam. Even leaving this aside, her argument seems to contradict Melville himself: what he pointed out to Putnam was that the new serial, as well as containing "nothing of any sort to shock the fastidious" also has "very little reflective writing in it; nothing weighty. It is adventure" (*C* 265). Either Melville was selling Putnam short or, more likely, he knew exactly how his narrative would develop and the adventures he would add as Potter moved from Franklin's company into the company of John Paul Jones.

What neither Bezanson nor Post-Lauria credits is what we know for sure: that Melville read Trumbull's book at some point in the 1840s and had been thinking of writing a narrative based on it for at least five years. It's certainly possible that Melville did not plan his own work chapter by chapter; much less likely is that he would embark on a long piece of writing after such a gestation period, and commit to the monthly cycle of writing, without a clear idea about how he would supplement and improve Trumbull's version. The best proof of Melville's preparedness comes from Trumbull's narrative itself. From the point at which Trumbull's Israel finds he can longer travel between London and Paris because "all intercourse between the two countries was prohibited"—on page 51 of the book's 108 pages—all thereafter becomes a sentimental tale of Israel's wretched life in London: bouts of poverty, imprisonment, the death of his wife and nine of his ten children, and his continual hard labor, either in a brick factory or as a chair mender. These are hardly the "Remarkable Adventures" promised in Trumbull's title. Melville even offers his own commentary on Trumbull's version of Potter's woes: "Best not enlarge upon them. . . .

The gloomiest and truthfulest dramatist seldom chooses for his theme the calamities, however extraordinary, of inferior and private persons; least of all, the pauper's" (*IP* 161). Melville does follow Israel to the brick factory and back to the United States, but the more likely reason he gave up on Trumbull's narrative after the Franklin encounter is that there was very little good material left to work with.

The declining adventurousness of Trumbull's narrative may itself have been intentional. Trumbull had few literary credentials; he was a hack writer of cheap popular books. He became a newspaperman when he took over the running of the *Connecticut Centinal* from his father and worked with Nathaniel Coverly in Boston on *The Idiot,* a weekly gossip sheet. Truth little bothered Trumbull. He was, according to David Chacko and Alexander Kulcsar, "one of our early and most prolific literary liars."[16] The purpose of Trumbull's narrative, which he freely admits in the preface, is to advertise Potter's plight in the hope that the Revolutionary War veteran might secure before dying the pension recently refused him by the American government. In light of this context, the aim of the sentimental second half of Trumbull's book seems best suited to generate a sympathetic response from the pension administrators. Melville may not have known the true events of Potter's life; he was a skilled enough reader to know when a story was treading water for sentimental effect. What Melville did, as he wrote to Putnam, was to provide the "adventure" that improves the second half of a narrative heading nowhere. The continuity of this adventure was also vital to the serial form in which Melville wrote *Israel Potter.*

Newspapers recognized Melville's authorship and his efforts as the serial began to appear, though none questioned, probably because they did not know, that they were reading a new version of an old story. The *New York Commercial Advertiser* of July 3, 1854, called "Israel Potter" the "greatest literary attraction" in the July issue of *Putnam's,* and praised Melville's "original American romance" as "much more interesting, and likely to be much more popular than even his admired narratives of South Sea adventures." In September, the *New York Citizen* claimed that "Melville is reaping fresh honors in his 'Israel Potter.'" In January the same paper described it as "a stirring narrative, and admirably written; so that if you begin you must finish it" (*IP* 209–10). Almost as soon as the serial ended in the March 1855 issue of *Putnam's* the book version appeared. Reviews were mainly positive, though often short; major magazines like *Harper's, Graham's,* and the

Southern Literary Messenger did not register their opinions. The reviewer in *Putnam's,* however, thought he had caught Melville out.

Melville's new preface to the book edition takes the form of a dedication. The figure of "The Editor," who poses as its author, admits that the following narrative is drawn from an earlier account—"forlornly published on sleazy gray paper"—a tattered copy of which he has "rescued by the merest chance from the rag-pickers" (*IP* vii). To the reader unfamiliar with Trumbull's version, this morsel of information works as a standard literary device, much like Irving's ruse of finding "Rip Van Winkle" and "The Legend of Sleepy Hollow" in the papers of Diedrich Knickerbocker, or Hawthorne's narrator finding in the custom-house Jonathan Pue's original that he rewrites in *The Scarlet Letter.* The *Putnam's* reviewer, however, notes that the original of *Israel Potter* "is not so rare as Mr. Melville seems to think. At any rate, we have a copy before us, as we write." While he points out that Melville "departs considerably from his original," the review finishes with a barb: "How far he is justified in the historical liberties he has taken, would be a curious case of literary casuistry."[17] Being thrown under the carriage by one's own publisher was certainly a novelty for Melville. Had he after all, Bezanson asks, "not forewarned Putnam? Or had Putnam not passed the word along? . . . Or did someone on the staff, feeling that the magazine, or the public, had been duped, take this means to even the score?" (*IP* 218).

The answer is that Putnam was no longer *Putnam's.* The founder from whom the magazine took and kept its name had relinquished his management and ownership of the magazine. The May 1855 issue in which the review of *Israel Potter* appeared was the first under the new ownership of Dix & Edwards and the editorial control of Curtis, Dana, and Olmsted. Melville may still have been a *Putnam's* author, but the magazine had nothing to gain from a positive review of a book published by G. P. Putnam & Co. Neither did Curtis have anything to do with the commissioning of the magazine version of "Israel Potter"; his furlough from the magazine began in July 1854, just as Melville proposed his serial to Putnam. Curtis's misgivings about "The Bell-Tower" and "Benito Cereno" would follow later in 1855. The review of *Israel Potter* in *Putnam's* is anonymous, but the likeliest reviewers are Curtis or Dana. Trumbull's book was originally published in Providence, Rhode Island, in 1824. Curtis was born in Providence that same year; although schooled for a short time in Jamaica

Plain, Massachusetts, he returned to Providence during the 1830s and was there through late March and April 1855, the time when someone wrote the *Israel Potter* review. It is very possible that Curtis wrote the review and that its spirit was to signal a new beginning for the magazine. He had already written to George William O'Connor in March indicating that he hoped the "new regime . . . is to be better than the old."[18] There was no better way to achieve this new regime than by separating the magazine from the work and the literary judgments of the old regime, especially in a review of a book too reliant for the reviewer on the old than the new.

Melville's interpretation of Trumbull's narrative, the transformation from book to serial, and the additions he makes are lost on Curtis (or whoever was the *Putnam's* reviewer), but these editing techniques transform the original story. The editor in Melville saw that the balance between narrative time and historical time, while workable at the beginning of Trumbull's book, are out of kilter thereafter; he rectified this limitation by working in the spirit of the first part of the narrative—placing an ordinary man into historic events and connecting him to heroic historical figures—and imagining the serial dramatic action that might ensue if an author was given license to invent. The resulting shift in the story's center of gravity means that while Potter spends as much time in penury in Melville's version as he does in Trumbull's, Melville condenses these forty-five years into a single short chapter. Melville did not need to appeal to the sympathy of Washington's pension bureaucrats; he was engaged in literary pursuits and his editing and rewriting of Trumbull's narrative produced several literary adjustments faithful to both the spirit of experimentation and the limitation of the magazine form. One key element was the addition of the preface to the published book. I deal with this last in part because it was the last change Melville instituted in his version but also because it suggests how he retrospectively imagined the narrative he had written for the pages of *Putnam's*. The preface is an addition to, and a revision of, Melville's own version of Potter's narrative as well as an addition to Trumbull's narrative.

The one editorial choice Melville made right from the very beginning was to prefer a third-person to a first-person narrator, a change he repeated when he rewrote Delano's narrative in "Benito Cereno." Freed from the necessity of personal appeal or pretensions to authenticity, Melville did not need Potter to make his own case. Neither did Melville require Potter, or Delano for that matter, to be a cerebral narrator like Ishmael. The events Potter experiences in Melville's narrative certainly affect him, but they are too reliant on fortune to bring about the kind of character development one finds in a bildungsroman. Potter is tossed about not so much on the currents but on the waves of history, where there is little opportunity for his character to develop to a point where it might determine his fate. By changing from a first-person to a third-person narration, Melville turns Potter's story from autobiography into fictionalized historical biography and creates the latitude to explore how a life intersects with history. In magazines like *Putnam's* or *Harper's*, which published nonfiction and fiction side by side, people were only a turn of the page away from national and international events, and Melville's narrative neatly embeds this principle into its dynamics.

The third-person narrator in *Israel Potter* starts to develop in the first chapter the theme that history is geographical as well as temporal in order to create Potter's historical presence. Where Trumbull's *Life* begins with facts, dates, and events in mundane sequential order, Melville's first chapter defamiliarizes the world out of which Potter appears in a manner well-suited to *Putnam's* cosmopolitanism, a trait I discussed in chapter 3. The narrative does not start with the individual—the "I was born" character of Trumbull's narrative—but with an anonymous traveler moving through space "in the good old Asiatic style" who finds a Berkshire, Massachusetts, that "remains almost as unknown to the general tourist as the interior of Bohemia"; a place where "you have the continual sensation of being upon some terrace in the moon. The feeling of the plain or the valley is never yours; scarcely the feeling of the earth" (*IP* 3). Spaces also change places with one another: what in summer are "wild, unfrequented roads . . . overgrown with high grass," in the winter are covered "with the white fleece from the sky. As if an ocean rolled between man and man" (*IP* 6).

Growing up in this strange world where the sky becomes the ground, the ocean the land, Potter is a boy of the New England hills who little thinks when "hunting after his father's stray cattle" that he will in turn "be hunted through half of Old England, as a runaway rebel" or that "worse bewilderments awaited him three thousand miles across the sea" (*IP* 6). Rooted and then uprooted, as time passes and history occurs, Potter will experience that history through his movement across space. The proleptic and catalyzing phrases of this first chapter add a scope and perspective in which the reader finds a character, "our hero" (*IP* 6), for whom history—the natural history of his environment, the cosmic history of the celestial landscape, the national history of New England settlement—is already set in motion. Having these passages told from the first-person perspective would equip Israel with too much knowledge of the world that awaits him; from the third-person perspective he is a character with a place in the scheme of larger things beyond his comprehension.

Melville uses the third person to similar effect in the battle between the *Bon Homme Richard* and the British warship *Serapis*. This was one of the major battles of the Revolutionary War, and the narrator registers the difficulty in following the events—"the intricacy of those incidents which defy the narrator's extrication"—as they play out in the waters off the east coast of Britain (*IP* 120). For a fuller version of the battle, the narrator points the reader elsewhere, "because he must needs follow, in all events, the fortunes of the humble adventurer whose life he records" (*IP* 120–21). And while omniscience should be able to focus on more than one place at the same time, the narrator also notes that following Potter "necessarily involves some general view of each conspicuous incident in which he shares" (*IP* 121). The "general view" is geological, of the "incessant decay" as the coast "succumbs to the Attila assaults of the deep" (*IP* 121); positional, as the ships maneuver into view of another; and celestial, as the harvest moon rises like a "great foot-light" to "cast a dubious half demoniac glare across the waters" (*IP* 123). As the narrator watches the scene developing, so now in the moonlight do spectators from cliffs on shore. What they see is obscured by mist and cloud; into this opacity only the narrator can venture, "to go and possess it, as a ghost may rush into a body" (*IP* 124). Here the general view gives way to a more specific view, not of Israel, who is entirely absent for the time being, but of John Paul Jones as he "flew hither and thither like the meteoric corposant-ball, which shiftingly dances on the tips and verges of ships' rigging in storms" (*IP* 126). Only as the battle commences in earnest does Israel reappear, at which point he responds to Jones's order to throw a grenade aboard the *Serapis*.

The narrator's awareness of perspective is one notable feature of the aesthetic tenor of this chapter, in which Melville's writing in *Israel Potter* reaches its apogee, as Robert Levine rightly notes. Levine also points out Melville's use of a wide range of allusions in the scene—to Milton, the Scottish poet James Macpherson, Mephistopheles, and the Guelphs and Ghibellines—that turn the battle into an aesthetic spectacle, one observed by the onlooking crowds. By transforming the revolutionary energies giving rise to the battle into the stuff of aesthetic contemplation, Levine argues, "the implication of this amazing scene, with its emphasis on crowds over nations, is that something further may follow from the battle between warships that would do justice to the battle's incipient democratic energies—but not in *Israel Potter*."[19]

But why not in *Israel Potter*? Why should a scene have an "implication" more important than what it achieves as a piece of writing? For Levine, Melville's writing is a lesson: "we are encouraged to imagine new stories from the 'mouldy rags' we have been bequeathed."[20] As Melville transforms Trumbull's "mouldy rags" into a new story, so democratic energies will follow if we learn this lesson. I prefer to see Melville's writing as an action embedded in the process of turning a past into a present narrative; it was Melville who in *Israel Potter* imagined a new story out of the "mouldy rags" of Trumbull's *Life*. What Melville does in the battle scene is to have his protagonist "share" the "conspicuous incidents" of which he is a part; the attention to narrative perspective, and the use of third-person narration, help achieve this end better than could a first-person narration. Rather than in an abstract aesthetic future, it is in this formal change, partly driven by the demands of appearing as a long-running serial in a miscellaneous magazine like *Putnam's*, that the democratic energy of *Israel Potter* resides. Melville acts now, not at some point in the future, by lifting Israel from the "mouldy rags" of Trumbull's narrative and having history share its events with him. Any democratic potential comes from not just observing aesthetic spectacle; Melville and *Israel Potter* make aesthetic spectacle out of the forms they use to create magazine writing.

Across the geographic spaces of his adventures, Potter develops an aesthetic presence befitting the status to which Melville raises him. Facts and details in Trumbull's narrative rarely resonate beyond their moment of expression; in Melville's hands they become the occasion of poignant connection or proleptic intent. In Trumbull's *Life,* Potter takes to hunting after working as a chain-bearer for His Majesty's Surveyors. Although skilled with his fowling-piece, Trumbull has him bluntly observe that General Putnam instructs Israel and his fellow soldiers at Bunker Hill to reserve fire "until the enemy approached so near as to enable us to see the white of their eyes."[21] Melville draws the line that links hunting animal and human prey: "It never entered his mind, that he was thus qualifying himself for a marksman of men. But thus were tutored those wonderful shots who did such execution at Bunker's Hill; these, the hunter-soldiers, whom Putnam bade wait till the white of the enemy's eye was seen" (*IP* 9). Melville also enhances Potter's preparedness for Bunker Hill by inventing for him a whaling career absent in Trumbull's narrative. Promoted to harpooner, Israel, "whose eye and arm had been so improved by practice with his gun in the wilderness, now further intensified his aim, by darting the whale-lance; still, unwittingly, preparing himself for the Bunker Hill rifle" (*IP* 10).

Melville sees in Trumbull's narrative a life unfolding in front of itself that, with some judicious editing, becomes a life with meaning rather than a ghostwritten list of facts and events. That a "little boy of the hills, born in sight of the sparkling Housatonic, was to linger out the best part of his life a prisoner or a pauper upon the grimy banks of the Thames" (*IP* 6) is a fabrication of Melville's making but nevertheless truer to the spirit if not the reality of the life of the Rhode Islander Israel Potter. Melville introduces the habitat of the Berkshires he knew so well to create a ligature between a life's opening and its unfurling. When Potter sets off to sell the skins that are the bounty from his hunting, Melville imagines him as "a peddler in the wilderness," much like the porters who "roll their barrows over the flagging of streets" (*IP* 9). Foreshadowing Israel's experience of wandering the flagged streets of London looking for chairs to mend, Melville adds and connects in the way an editor might suggest; he has the narrative refer backward and forward in a way Trumbull either could not imagine or could not execute. Melville's narrative has a shape, a sense of place, and a sense of character and personality. In Trumbull's account Potter's life simply happens; there are incidents but no character, actions but no thought. By embedding his writing in the writing of another author Melville edits Trumbull's *Potter* into a serial narrative suitable for the magazine form.

He also finds more ways to ornament his raw material. He ventriloquizes characters Trumbull leaves silent: the incompetent soldiers from whom Israel escapes before heading for London (*IP* 17); Sir John Millet, who guesses Israel's nationality and status as escaped prisoner of war but gives him work and wine nonetheless (*IP* 26–27); and, more memorably, George III when Israel gets a job at Kew Gardens. In Trumbull, Israel has "frequent opportunities to see his Royal Majesty in person" and is one day "unexpectedly accosted by his Majesty." Melville has Israel observe the king slyly before their first meeting: "Israel through intervening foliage would catch peeps in some private but parallel walk, of that lonely figure, not more shadowy with overhanging leaves than with the shade of royal meditations" (*IP* 29–30). Melville adds the thoughts these glimpses inspire in Israel—"unauthorized and abhorrent thoughts," "dim impulses" of regicide that "shoot balefully across the soul of the exile" (*IP* 30)—that then disperse following his conversation with the king. The voices Melville adds to Trumbull's narrative turn the two-dimensional into the three-dimensional and effect a similar transformation of Israel himself, who shows a capacity for thinking when he drops from Melville's pen. One of the things he lights upon is the paradox that "the very den of the British lion, the private grounds of the British King, should be commended to a refugee as his securest asylum" (*IP* 29). This is not the first time, and far from the last, that being hidden in plain sight features as a narrative conceit in Melville's rewriting of Potter's story.

Several of these incidents occur as Israel tries to find a way of being "appropriately apparelled." He discards old clothes that give away his identity for new ones that will deceive his pursuers and enemies even as they foretell his future. Changing his "prince-like" clothes for the "wretched rags" of a ditcher, he finds himself wearing an outfit "suitable to that long career of destitution before him." In the patchwork coat and stringless breeches, Israel "looked suddenly metamorphosed from youth to old age" in dress that "befitted the fate" (*IP* 19). When he is inadvertently separated from John Paul Jones during an encounter with a British frigate, Israel—having shuttlecocked between British, American, and again British vessels—understands that "some audacious parade of himself offers the only hope" of preserving his freedom (*IP* 133). Dropping his jacket overboard, he has to rely on his wits after finding himself "black-balled out of every club" aboard ship (*IP* 136). When an officer asks "who the deuce *are* you?" (*IP* 137)—a question he twice repeats during the ensuing conversation—Israel blusters, invents, and plays the fool in order to outlast his interrogators. Under the pseudonym of Peter Perkins he manages to see out the voyage, swims ashore one night from the ship, and finds "some mouldy old rags on the banks of a stagnant pond" to replace his seaman's clothes (*IP* 152). Israel makes his way once more to London, where he lives the rest of his days before eventually finding a way back home.

The geographic adventures during which Israel meets history rely, then, on a succession of costume disguises. The same is true for other characters engaged in their own adventures. The narrator struggles to portray Franklin's multifariousness in the language of clothing. Franklin "dressed his person as his periods" and with the biblical Jacob and the philosopher Hobbes forms a triumvirate of "practical magians in linsey woolsey" (*IP* 46–47). Given the variety of Franklin's pursuits, the narrator feels "more as if he were playing with one of the sage's worsted hose, than reverently handling the honored hat which once oracularly sat upon his brow" (*IP* 48). Clothes are the ornaments of character; as they do on Israel, clothes gesture toward, without defining, the individuals who wear them; and they hold identity at bay more than they are its incarnation. Who the deuce is Israel Potter, or Benjamin Franklin, or John Paul Jones? The history to which Melville returns Israel Potter and these other figures is one where not being what one seems is the lifeblood of narrative time. When Israel Potter is what he seems—a poverty-stricken chair mender scratching a living in a London—historical time and narrative time break apart and decades can pass in a single chapter. The London crowds may provide security for the persecuted man, but there is no place in history for the anonymous man those crowds create.

Finally, then, to the preface. It was not published in *Putnam's,* and it is likely Melville wrote the dedication "To His Highness the Bunker-Hill Monument" near the time *Israel Potter* appeared in book form in March 1855. Melville's brother Allan wrote to Augusta on March 1, 1855: "Herman's book will not be out for a week yet. I was in at Putnam yesterday to get a copy but none were ready. He has sent a dedication to Bunker Hill Monument." Because the dedication was news to Allan, who also assumed Augusta—Melville's transcriber—did not know about it either, for Hershel Parker the "implication is that Melville had provided it for the book recently."[22] Walter Bezanson makes the point that if Melville wrote the dedication at this later date, and backdated the signature lines at the end of the piece "for historical and ironic effect" to Bunker Hill Day the previous year—"June 17th, 1854"—then "he was being literary rather than literal" (*IP* 191). This is a shrewd assessment of a dedication that appears, when one reads it at the beginning of the novel, to be the frame in which Melville composed *Israel Potter.* But the contrary is true: *Israel Potter* was the frame in which Melville composed the dedication. This is not to suggest that Melville was not conscious of the art he was creating while publishing serially in *Putnam's,* but the post hoc dedication casts the person who pens it as an editor rather than a literary composer.

Melville wrote other prefaces to his novels, but never in the guise of an editor. Unlike Henry James's prefaces, the spirit of Melville's commentary on his own work is playful rather than analytical. Casting himself as editor rather than author, Melville did more than simply cover his tracks in case reviewers made the connection—as did *Putnam's*—between Trumbull's *Life* and Melville's version. Anyone familiar with Trumbull's narrative would know the editor is lying when he claims that what follows "preserves, almost as in a reprint, Israel Potter's autobiographical story." What the editor has done to Trumbull's version amounts to much more than the "expansions, and additions of historic and personal details, and one or two shiftings of scene" he passes off as "a dilapidated tombstone retouched" (*IP* vii). By using the dedication to pull his own narrative into the orbit of an earlier version, Robert Levine argues, "Melville seems intent on writing a novel about the American Revolution that refuses to rise above the level of a 'minor' work."[23] But the dedication is more afterthought than signal of intent, especially as the novel was virtually unchanged from the magazine version. The preface is not of a piece with the rest of the narrative; Melville is constructing that narrative retrospectively and reading his own work as a reader might read "Benito Cereno" the second time around: with hindsight.

The judgment Melville exercises at this moment shows how he understood the composition of *Israel Potter.* Rewriting a narrative from a specific source for the first time, rather than supplementing his own work with sources, Melville poses as an editor rather than an author. Melville is acting like the reprinters who added prefatory matter to their editions of reprinted stories and books. He recognizes the connection between editing and reprinting and his role as a reteller rather than an originator of stories. The close attention he pays to the material status of the object he is working with also indicates the value of these roles. The editor takes something first "forlornly published on sleazy gray paper" and picked up "by the merest chance from the rag-pickers" (*IP* vii). He then turns this cheap and worthless artifact into an object he considers fine enough to present to the Bunker Hill Monument. Melville's editor turns rags into fine writing "appropriately apparelled" in the pages of *Putnam's* and the cloth binding of G. P. Putnam & Co., whose edition of Cooper's *The Red Rover,* with horseshoe embossing, Melville so admired.

Melville's preface to *Israel Potter* nods to an earlier version of the protagonist's life to show that copying is never plagiarism in the hands of a writer or an editor. As in some of his other magazine works, Melville turns to the material in both senses of that word when he wishes to affirm his authorship: in his contemplation of the paper on which writing takes place he generates the content that amply fills new sheets, magazines, and books. In "The Paradise of Bachelors and the Tartarus of Maids" he focused on the process that produced the fine paper on which he set down his own words; in *Israel Potter* he trained his sights on how stories are made from other stories, books from other books. Somewhere amid these two processes is an idea that clothes and paper are never far apart and that neither, too, are clothes and books. Writers wear books like clothes in the way Geoffrey Crayon describes when he enters the British Library reading room.

What Melville would not have known when he edited and reprinted Trumbull's narrative was that Israel Potter already existed in the world of books. In 1819 John Thomas Smith, who trained at the Royal Academy and went on to be Keeper of Prints and Drawings in the British Museum, sketched a series of itinerant London traders for a work published posthumously in 1839 as *The Cries of London.* Alongside the rat-catcher and corpse-bearer, the bladder-man and the water-carrier, is the chair mender Israel Potter. Smith's engraving of "one of the oldest menders of chairs now living" shows a mournful-looking Israel in cropped, ragged trousers, with rushes across his back should his cries elicit any trade. Smith is skeptical that much work comes Israel's way. The matted mass of rushes go unused for months at a time; Israel is about the streets by 8 a.m. primarily to find "broken meat and subsistence . . . for his daily wants."[24]

And Potter lived on after Melville: in Routledge's unauthorized edition of Melville's book, number 113 in their Cheap Series; and as *The Refugee,* an edition printed by T. B. Peterson, who bought the printing plates from Putnam and attributed two false works, *The Two Captains* and *The Man of the World,* to Melville on the title page. More bizarrely, Melville's fiction about Potter became fact in *Appletons' Cyclopaedia of American Biography* (1888). This book repeats Melville's invention that Potter served under Colonel John Paterson, commander of a Berkshire regiment; the real Israel, of course, served in a Rhode Island regiment. Charles Edward Potter's *Genealogies of the Potter Families and Their Descendants in America* (1888) repeated these mistakes (*IP* 280–81). All of which goes to show that there is a world of difference between copying and editing, between duplication and reprinting. It may not have been hard for Melville to improve on Trumbull's *Life,* but none of the pilferers of Melville's work managed to improve the editing job he did for *Putnam's* when he created "a silk purse . . . out of a beggar's pocket!" (*IP* 80).

"Passing from one suspicious thing to another" in "Benito Cereno"

Melville was likely filtering for some time the events Amasa Delano relates in chapter 18 of his *Narrative* to produce "Benito Cereno." Where *Israel Potter* roamed across continents and oceans in breathless adventure and pulled in sources to enliven and extend the breadth of invention, "Benito Cereno" details a single event against whose narrating the deep waters of the Pacific seem to lap only gently until Melville unleashes their full force. During the winter of 1854–55, Melville finished a serialized adventure novel and moved on to write a groundbreaking short story that, although itself serialized, arrived in one piece in the offices of *Putnam's* in April 1855, its inspiration undeclared.

"Benito Cereno" equally demonstrates Melville's skill as an editor. Amasa Delano's achievement was to take thrilling experience and turn it into the dust of a sea captain's reflection; it could have been the evidence on which Tzvetan Todorov based his observation that "no thriller is presented in the form of memoirs."[25] Melville's achievement was to edit Delano's dust into the prototype of the American psychological thriller. Poe had explored the psychological recesses of the human mind more vividly than most writers in his magazine tales of the 1830s and '40s. He adapted the traditional gothic tale of mystery and terror for an urbanizing sensibility whose sedimented fears Poe crystallized. But these tales do not match the narrative ingenuity evident in the stories of ratiocination featuring Dupin, where the treatment of temporality patented a formula for later writers in the detective genre. The psychological thriller actually requires much less terror, torment, and sensation than Poe provided. Above all it requires a narrative mode in which patience and elongation are as important as disruption and revelation. This is what Melville provided in "Benito Cereno" when his authorship fused with a preexisting narrative.

In this fusion, the story's unfolding defiantly burst the banks of the magazine form. Even a magazine like *Putnam's,* which prided itself on publishing new and original work, could not help but manage the printing of "Benito Cereno" awkwardly. Quantitatively and qualitatively, there was only so much newness the magazine could cope with. Too long for the editors to consider publishing it in a single issue, "Benito Cereno" was also a story too unified in its effect to withstand serialization. Moreover, it has a complex array of iterative and original attributes. Literally iterating another text by reprinting Delano's original—although stripping out all the iterations that mark Delano's text—it also originates a new text by editing Delano to produce new effects, new insights, and a new form. Even if unintentionally, "Benito Cereno" pulls us back to that transition between a culture of iteration and a culture of origination that McGill suggests is occurring in the 1850s. The story does so by embedding iteration and origination in its own narrative formation.

What Melville first saw and valued in Delano's narrative must remain conjecture given the silence in which he composed his story. The only break in his silence occurred when he prepared his *Putnam's* work for publication as *The Piazza Tales.* Initially, when the provisional title of the collection was *Benito Cereno & Other Sketches,* he appended "a M.S. Note" to "Benito Cereno." He wrote to Dix & Edwards in February 1856 withdrawing the note, explaining that "as the book is now to be published as a collection of '*Tales,*' that note is unsuitable & had better be omitted" (*C* 286). The contents of the "note" are unknown, but the difference between the more factual sketch and the more fictional tale suggests Melville saw no need to offer a qualification if "Benito Cereno" was to count as fiction. Even when that fiction—presumably unbeknown to the publishers—was so closely based on a factual, published account.

Yet why was it Delano's narrative that Melville chose to edit and rewrite? The sea narrative is crucial. It returned Melville to an environment he understood better than most writers, and the Pacific location suited the cosmopolitan magazine environment of *Putnam's,* whose articles regularly roamed the globe. But the slave revolt was an uncommon feature of magazine writing, even if revolts at sea were not themselves unusual. With the exception of Frederick Douglass's fictionalization of Madison

Washington's *Creole* rebellion in *The Heroic Slave* (1853), such stories exercised nowhere near the same hold on the American imagination as the dozens of slave narratives circulating before the Civil War. Delano does not even make a particularly apt candidate for attack: at various points in his book he criticizes slavery and imperialism. Delano's attraction to Melville, Robert Levine argues, "lay less in his villainy than in his geniality and liberality."[26] As he showed in *White-Jacket* on the subject of flogging, Melville was not interested in merely exposing evil: "It is next to idle, at the present day," the narrator announces, "merely to denounce an iniquity. Be ours, then, a different task" (*WJ* 143). The "different task" he undertook in "Benito Cereno" involved accommodating a social position in which Melville was pulled in different directions.

He was not as compromised as his father-in-law, the antislavery judge Lemuel Shaw, whose support for the letter of the law twice saw him rule in favor of slave owners in Fugitive Slave Act trials. But Melville married into—and was himself a less august member of—a social class that had much to lose should political disorder affect the ship of state. The Astor Place riot of 1849, which erupted close to Melville's home in New York City, was another mutinous event that critics argue forced Melville to confront his class anxiety and complicity in "Bartleby" and "The Two Temples."[27] In "Benito Cereno" and in the orbit of race, Melville once more tested, according to Levine, the "conflict between his political sympathies and his social anxieties"; between his contempt for "enslaving sea captains" and his fear that mutinies disrupted the social order he himself, and sea captains, were eager to preserve. Levine suggests that "to plumb this complicity" with the established order, Melville assumed for the first time in his writing the perspective of a sea captain during just such a mutinous episode.[28]

From within rather than without, then, does "Benito Cereno" put flesh on the bones of the story it edits and rewrites. This also required a counterintuitive formal gambit from Melville that rejects the inside accounts from Delano's original narrative, which appear in three parts. The first is "an extract from the journal of the ship Perseverance, taken on board that ship at the time, by the officer who had care of the log book." Two pages later, the second part begins. This is Delano's own account: "some remarks of my own," he calls them, whose purpose is to give the reader "a correct understanding of the peculiar situation under which we were placed at the time this affair happened."[29] The final part consists of court documents and depositions from the principle characters—Delano, Benito Cereno, and the midshipman Nathaniel Luther, who served on Delano's ship—and letters between Delano and the King of Spain's envoy following Delano's return to Boston. These are all testimonies from within: reports and comments of the men who experienced and combated the slave revolt and those whose task it was to judge the rights and wrongs of "this affair." But Melville chose to shun the form, if not the content, of the log and Delano's personal account. And the only deposition he includes in his rewriting is Don Benito's. So why abandon these narrative positions?

The "complicity" Melville addressed was too important to be left in the hands of such calculatingly official forms and characters. If the log is matter-of-fact in stripping out, simplifying, and summarizing the events on which Delano elaborates, the captain's own account also displays from the beginning an air of defensive self-interest. Delano laments that he is "in a worse situation to effect any important enterprize than I had been in during the voyage," mainly as a result of losing "extraordinarily good men" at New Holland who were "inveigled away from me" by Botany Bay convicts. Men of this ilk now also compose a good number of his new crew, having come aboard without Delano's knowledge. Through "strict discipline" and "wholesome floggings" he maintains order across the South Pacific. At St. Maria, three of the Botany Bay men run from the boat once put ashore; the captain puts another five men ashore when they give reason to suggest they too might abscond. The captain keeps his whaleboat on deck to deter other would-be escapees. From this climate of suspicion Delano then commends his crew for their conduct in the events that follow: "In every part of the business of the Tryal, not one disaffected word was spoken by the men, but all flew to obey the commands they received; and to their credit it should be recorded, that no men ever behaved better than they, under such circumstances."[30] Delano combines the role of enforcer and benevolent defender.

No doubt Melville understood that these roles were part of the captain's job description; that in just such combination did power seek to maintain order aboard ship in the weeks and months away from land. But in moving from one position to another in his narrative, Delano also demonstrates that he knows how to manipulate his role: to flog and succor as he deems fit. Or to line up the three narrative strands so they each repeat the same story. But all are tacitly blind to the subjectivity on which their apparent objectivity relies. Rather than accounts from within, they are retrospective accounts whose perspective is always external to the events themselves. Although written at varying distances from the events—the log is nearest; the trial next; Delano's account on his return to America the last—like planets aligned the accounts manage to stand in harmony. But even an amateur astronomer knows that the planets never align; a writer like Melville forcedly attuned by his early reception to distinctions between fact and fiction, authenticity and romance, knew the perjury of alignment.

To write "Benito Cereno" from within, Melville cast the log and Delano's preamble overboard. Melville also found no space for the defensiveness Delano continues at the end of his account, before the official documents, where he bemoans Don Benito's attempt to injure his character. Melville also dispenses with an explanation of how the *Bachelor's Delight* comes to be in St. Maria and whence it came. To rewrite the story from within, Melville actually dispenses with Delano's voice and opinions, his justifications and defenses—all of which Delano offers after the fact—and instead takes up a narrative position that shows the events appearing and unfolding not as iteration but for the first time to Delano as they appear and unfold for the reader. The opening retrospection locating the reader in the year 1799 quickly gives way to a narrator who hovers impersonally alongside Delano rather than looking back at him. What lies ahead for the reader—on first reading at least—the narrative withholds. There are, then, no signs of the iteration that marked the original publication in Delano's narrative. As he reworks an already published narrative that was itself written retrospectively, Melville strips out all signs of iteration.

By withholding knowledge of the mutinous crime from his narrative in this way, Melville undertakes that formal maneuver whereby the story of detection and investigation metamorphoses into the thriller. Rather than the story of a crime already known, whose investigation the reader follows, the thriller "suppresses the first and vitalizes the second" of these stories. In the thriller, Todorov explains, "we are no longer told about a crime anterior to the moment of the narrative; the narrative coincides with the action."[31] Here is the formal conceit that Melville uses to edit and rewrite Delano's narrative from dry, self-defensive reflection into psychological thriller. Until the point when Don Benito leaps from the *San Dominick* into Delano's boat, retrospection more generally gives way to the interplay of two other temporal modes with formal consequences for "Benito Cereno" as a piece of magazine writing: prospection and stasis. The tenor of Melville's narrative suggests that while nothing is happening, something is on the verge of happening.

In the previous chapter I suggested the opening installment of "Benito Cereno" demonstrates that seeing is not knowing. The lack of clarity in Delano's perspective as he moves closer toward and then onto the *San Dominick* also works to enhance the prospective nature of the narrative. Delano's continued attempts to decipher what he sees introduce a narrative rhythm in which curiosity is paramount. On Delano's behalf the narrator does not stop observing and speculating, and the second installment immediately revisits this theme. The speck Delano sees advancing toward the *San Dominick* carries the supplies for which he has sent; the captain's eye, however, is taken by events on deck as "two blacks, to all appearances accidentally incommoded by one of the sailors, flew out against him with horrible curses" and "dashed him to the deck and jumped upon him." When Delano asks Don Benito, "Do you see what is going on there? Look!" the Spanish captain staggers onto Babo's supporting hand (*PT* 70). Don Benito sees exactly what is going on; in his own looking Delano does not.

Yet the question opens an interpretive gap that requires an answer not forthcoming. Babo's actions instead "wiped away, in the visitor's eyes, any blemish of impropriety," and Delano's glance is "thus called away from the spectacle of disorder to the more pleasing one before him" (*PT* 70). When Babo soon conducts Don Benito below deck, Delano is left rubbing his eyes when he thinks the Spanish sailors return his glance "with a sort of meaning." Delano looks once more, "but again seemed to see the same thing" and "the old suspicions recurred" (*PT* 71). He asks questions of the sailors but concludes that "these currents spin one's head round almost as much as they do the ship" (*PT* 73). Distracted by the "ribbon grass, trailing along the ship's water-line" Delano finds himself "becharmed anew"; looking at the main-chains he once more "rubbed his eyes, and looked hard" but what he thinks he sees "vanished into the recesses of hempen forest, like a poacher" (*PT* 74). About these and other questions Delano finds himself "lost in their mazes" (*PT* 75). During the electrifying shaving scene, Delano finds his imagination "not wholly at rest" and imagines Don Benito and Babo "acting out . . . some juggling play before him." In response, he can only ask himself another question: "What could be the object of enacting this play of the barber before him?" (*PT* 87). This and all the other unanswered questions, like the crescendo of interpretation that comes over Delano at the end of the first installment, are false summits. But rather than stopping one's ascent they spur one on to reach the real summit where the narrative will provide answers.

The prospective rhythm of "Benito Cereno" is part of a larger narrative polyrhythm in which stasis also plays an important role. If the repetition of charged looks and glances—emblems of detection worthy of Poe's ratiocinative hero Dupin—and asked and unanswered questions imply the prospect of future resolution, they also create a circular pattern where nothing seems to be happening except the same thing over and over again. The accumulation of repetition heightens a tension that ultimately needs resolving; each moment of irresolution leaves one no closer to that resolution.

The descriptive writing Melville adds to Delano's account reiterates stasis. Immediately marooned on "a small, desert, uninhabited island toward the southern extremity of the long coast of Chili," Delano finds that the measurements of geographic distance and time evaporate as grayness takes over: the "gray surtout of the cloud," the "gray fowl, kith and kin with flights of troubled gray vapors" (*PT* 46). Distinctions of time and space are less easy to discern in such colorlessness and in "the shreds of fog here and there raggedly furring" the *San Dominick* (*PT* 48). Unlike in *Israel Potter*, where the movement of ships about the ocean provides a dramatic backdrop for Israel's own movements, in "Benito Cereno"—at least until the slave revolt becomes known—neither the *San Dominick* nor the *Bachelor's Delight* undertake any dramatic maneuvers. The reader spends little narrative time on the whaleboat "darting over the interval" between the two larger vessels (*PT* 95). And Delano's piloting of the *San Dominick* to anchor beside the *Bachelor's Delight* introduces movement to presage the resolution that follows shortly thereafter. As they lie becalmed through most of the story, so does the narrative action as Delano slowly—exceedingly slowly—accumulates moments of prospection whose resolution Melville withholds and withholds.

The rhythms of prospection and stasis certainly create a narrative tension in "Benito Cereno," though whether this amounts to narrative suspense, if by suspense is meant excited expectation, is moot. The magazine context and the rewriting context offer some help in deciding the case. Trish Loughran notes of the story's first installment as it appeared in *Putnam's* that "quite remarkably (for a serial fiction meant to attract further consumption), almost nothing happens." Her fascinating discussion of disposable and durable reading that follows—where the form of "Benito Cereno" consoles Melville's dissatisfaction with present-tense readings by deferring its meaning for later readings—seems to rest on the assumption that Melville wrote the story with serialization in mind. But there is a difference between material written for serial publication—like the adventuring *Israel Potter*—and material only serialized at the point of publication. There is no evidence that Melville wrote "Benito Cereno" (nor "Bartleby" or "The Encantadas") in serial form; he likely wrote and sent "Benito Cereno" to *Putnam's* as a single manuscript. When Loughran suggests that "the narrative caesurae that interrupt each section would appear to be as purposefully staged by Melville as many of the *San Dominick*'s spectacles are staged by Babo," she misses the point that the separation of the story into three parts in *Putnam's* was the responsibility of the magazine's editors, not Melville.[32]

There are practical oddities about the serialization of "Benito Cereno" that suggest likewise. *Putnam's* serialized "Bartleby, the Scrivener" in two parts of eleven and six full pages; "The Encantadas" in three parts of nine, ten, and six full pages. These were much shorter installments than "Benito Cereno," whose three parts took up fourteen, fifteen, and eleven pages. If Melville was writing with serialization in mind, then his experience of writing for *Putnam's* would surely have led him to put possible installment breaks, even potentially disruptive ones, elsewhere. *Putnam's* rarely published anything the length of the first two installments of "Benito Cereno." Whoever sectioned "Benito Cereno" at *Putnam's* made the breaks fit with the comings and goings of the whaleboat between the two larger vessels and the anchoring of the two ships beside each other. Loughran is right that serialization might make "Benito Cereno" a painful and frustrating read for a magazine consumer who must wait for the next issue. The third part does seem rushed when it reveals the slave revolt after only a couple pages, leaving the rest of the narrative to drift into what Curtis called the "dreary documents." But does this make it more likely that Melville, not *Putnam's,* sectioned the narrative? Another way to put this question is to ask whether the deferral of interpretation is Melville's monkey-wrenching against the magazine form or whether the magazine form simply exposes its own constraints—miscellaneity, seriality—that in turn constrain the literary forms it can accommodate. Seriality, as Melville knew from writing *Israel Potter*, suits episodic narratives; the psychological thriller, however, is not an episodic form because tension must build continuously and iteratively.

This is the "almost nothing" that happens in the first part of "Benito Cereno." But it is not that nothing happens; rather, what happens does so only very slowly and, because of the narrative perspective, does so mainly in the mind of Delano. To judge whether almost nothing happens in a narrative one must first have a sense of what needs to happen. Suspense can take several forms and is not necessarily apparent as the hooks, cues, and cliffhangers traversing each published installment and the next. What is more important about "Benito Cereno," as Charles Swann points out, is that in "the original" on which Melville builds "there is no suspense, no narrative secret" because the story is told three times, and the first time within a few paragraphs.[33] "Benito Cereno" does not conform to our contemporary understandings of suspense honed by decades of masterful generic accretion, but suspense was the most dramatic formal change Melville added to Delano's narrative by stripping out its iterations. While we can speculate about whether Melville had serialization in mind when he wrote "Benito Cereno," there is no doubt that in editing and rewriting Delano's narrative he made formal decisions whose evidence is his version of the story.

The delay or anticipation of resolution is still suspense. The unfolding of Delano's cognitive processes may well be a "painful" experience, as Loughran notes, for book as well as magazine readers, but painfulness is another side of the same coin as suspense. The reviewer of *The Piazza Tales* she quotes who finds the story "most painfully interesting" and who "became nervously anxious for the solution" registers just such an effect. Suspense, by definition, induces anxiousness; pain is not necessarily physical but a discomfort of the mind experienced as annoyance, vexation, or impatience. The pain comes from wanting a resolution the story withholds. Suspense in Todorov's terms moves from cause to effect: the reader is shown the causes—Delano's observation and investigation of the *San Dominick*—and interest is sustained (however painfully) by the expectation that certain effects (however long they take) will occur. Judged against this standard, what happens in the first part of "Benito Cereno" is everything that needs to happen.

If Melville's intention, as the narrative perspective in the rewritten version suggests, was to inhabit the perspective of a sea captain during a mutinous episode he cannot see, then would anything other than a painstaking exploration of Delano's cognition reiterate his ideological shortsightedness? That the resolution occurs only when Delano is about to give up his investigation and leave the *San Dominick* suggests that Melville understood the principles of suspense: the resolution is delayed until the very last possible moment. "Benito Cereno" even anticipates Chekhov's dictum that if you say in the first chapter that there is a rifle hanging on the wall then later in the story it absolutely must go off. Instead of guns in "Benito Cereno" there are the hatchets Delano sees the former slaves polishing when he first boards the *San Dominick*; when the scales drop from Delano's eyes and he sees "the negroes, not in misrule, not in tumult, not as if frantically concerned for Don Benito, but with mask torn away," the blades return as he sees the blacks "flourishing hatchets and knives, in ferocious piratical revolt" (*PT* 99). The hatchets and the revolt for which they are the metonym have been there from the beginning waiting for the narrative to unite them.

Then there are the exquisite miniatures of suspense where the flesh Melville puts on the bones of Delano's "actual reality" is itself inked with elaborate figures like the ornate tattoos that repel and fascinate in *Typee* and *Moby-Dick.* Melville has Babo shave Don Benito with such meticulous precision that the suspense resides in the economy of the language as much as in Delano's reaction that "the scene was somewhat peculiar" (*PT* 85). At the beginning of the process, Melville patiently depicts the simple process of finding a blade and then even halts the action momentarily for added effect. Having found the sharpest razor, Babo "then made a gesture as if to begin, but midway stood suspended for an instant, one hand elevating the razor, the other professionally dabbling among the bubbling suds on the Spaniard's lank neck." Babo's reassurance that "I have never yet drawn blood" is quickly modified by a prospective warning: "though it's true, if master will shake so, I may some of these times" (*PT* 85). The intimation contained here makes better sense on rereading, but Don Benito does not shake from feeling the cold; when he shudders nervously it is not because he fears shaving itself.

Hermeneutic interpretations of "Benito Cereno" emphasize the importance of such rereading. The first-time reader likely occupies Delano's perspective and does not know what is happening; on rereading, he or she is more alert to the point of view of the African revolutionaries. The full implications of racial structures of power are clearer; the Africans' desire for freedom and how they try to effect that freedom come into focus. There is nothing unique about the temporal conceit in "Benito Cereno" that makes the story one reads different the second time around. One knows Dupin's method the second time one reads "The Purloined Letter," or on a second viewing that the murderer in *Psycho* is really Norman Bates and that the shark will end up exploding in *Jaws*. But rereading is also a form of iterative retrospection that acts on narratives themselves working with retrospective and prospective forms.

The hermeneutic power of the classic detective narrative to provide a solution to a crime follows this pattern: the investigation is the reconstruction of the time leading up to the crime about which the reader already knows. But when the time of the action becomes the time of the narrative, as it does in "Benito Cereno" and the thriller, retrospection gives way to prospection, whose effects are felt so forcefully—and even painfully—in Melville's story. In this instance, rereading and the narrative's prospection are like the two north or south poles of a pair of magnets that will not stick together. Because even rereading does not provide a hermeneutic solution to the questions "Benito Cereno" asks. No matter how many times one rereads the story, discovering the revolt is not the answer to the questions the prospective narrative asks of the rereader: Why does Delano not see in the effects of the revolt the cause that produces them? And how can the mastery of one race over another aboard the *San Dominick* appear as the mastery of the mastered over the masters?

As these questions affect how we understand the story's treatment of race, power, and hierarchy, critics have offered interpretations that more than do justice to Melville's story. But "Benito Cereno" is still unusual in that it so early deploys the thriller's prospective form in such a confined set-piece drama all the more charged by the geographical isolation in which Melville stages the scene. "Sappy Amasa" (*PT* 86) misses his cues in rhythm with the performance around him and even fails at first to understand why Don Benito jumps aboard the whaler. But Melville's attention to narrative time, and specifically the shift away from prospection, continues once Don Benito breaks ranks: "All this, with what preceded, and what followed, occurred with such involutions of rapidity, that past, present, and future seemed one" (*PT* 98). Action and elision follow; time speeds up and the time of the narrative no longer coincides with the time of the action. And with Don Benito's deposition, for the first time Melville embarks on a sustained piece of retrospection.

Melville rewrites the original deposition to fit the narrative he has created, but the importance of the "dreary document," lost on Curtis, is that it does not fulfill the retrospective function. The narrator hopes the deposition will "shed light on the preceding narrative" and explains that Don Benito's fantastic account passes muster when corroborated by surviving sailors. But even in retrospection there is prospection: "If the Deposition have served as the key to fit into the lock of the complications which precede it, then, as a vault whose door has been flung back, the San Dominick's hull lies open to-day" (*PT* 114). Whether the hull is open for all to see or whether it lies open today, still, because what lies within defies seeing, is not entirely clear. Yet another false summit.

The mountaineer moves on to the next peak, which is the final conversation between Delano and Don Benito, but not before the narrator intervenes once more: "Hitherto the nature of this narrative, besides rendering the intricacies in the beginning unavoidable, has more or less required that many things, instead of being set down in the order of occurrence, should be retrospectively, or irregularly given" (*PT* 114). By far the largest section of the narrative is actually given to events in "the order of occurrence." This is Delano's experience of seeing, boarding, and sailing the *San Dominick* until Don Benito leaps into the whaling boat; they account for over thirty of the forty-two magazine pages as the story appeared in *Putnam's*. Only the deposition is "retrospectively, or irregularly given." The "many things" provided in this form are clearly significant and amount to everything known of events before Delano sees the "strange sail coming into the bay" at St. Maria (*PT* 46). They may even be more significant to the overall story than the events that occur during Delano's time aboard the *San Dominick*. Nevertheless, the narrator's plot spends most time dealing with Delano's experience.

The narrator's commentary on his own selection and ordering of events is itself a retrospective intervention that attempts to resolve what the content of the narrative cannot—as though truth is in the order in which one speaks rather than what one speaks. The denouement of the one final "irregular" account that follows pits Delano's assurance that "the past is passed" against Don Benito's understanding of human memory that makes his past also his present. Babo's gaze, which for several days after his death meets the "gaze of the whites," continues to cast a shadow over Don Benito (*PT* 116). At the very beginning of the story the narrator of "Benito Cereno" warns of the "shadows present, foreshadowing deeper shadows to come" (*PT* 46). And so in the final attempt at retrospective resolution the narrator returns the reader to the start of the narrative. Somehow in this Escherian landscape the final summit is not just false but takes the reader back to the foot of the mountain. The polyrhythm of prospection and stasis absorbs and negates the retrospective impulse for resolution.

In these terms, "Benito Cereno" is a piece of defiant origination in the face of perpetual iteration. And it is all the more powerful because its own origination lies in the editing and reprinting of Delano's original. Delano's account of the time between first seeing the sail of the *Tryal* and watching Don Benito jump into his whaling boat takes three pages. By striking out other parts of Delano's narrative and extending this section fifteen-fold, Melville rebalances the time of plot and story with seemingly little regard for what the magazine form does with longer work when it hacks stories into parts. If the effects of serialization are felt less harshly in the reading of "Bartleby" or "The Encantadas," this is because neither are thrillers; both are retrospective, not prospective, narratives, "Bartleby" obsessively so, while "The Encantadas" is also a series of episodic sketches that withstand partition.

Judging from a letter to Putnam of October 31, Melville sent the final pages of *Israel Potter* to the magazine in November 1854 (*C* 270) and probably began "Benito Cereno" immediately after this and completed it during the winter of 1854–55, a remarkably empty period in the biographical record when his correspondence almost entirely dries up. When he sat down to write "Benito Cereno," with the aim of rewriting Delano's experience for reprinting in *Putnam's*, Melville was possibly more concerned with literary than with magazine forms. From the serial and episodic nature of *Israel Potter*'s adventuring he turns, perhaps in relief, to what Curtis described as the "spun out."[34] At the point of first publication in October through December 1855, *Putnam's* mangles the literary experiment of a story for whose formal defiance—its pedal tone of prospection and stasis—it has no place. For all the deserved renown *Putnam's* accumulated over its short life, it never did publish much literature that proved as durable as Melville's. And of all Melville's magazine writing, "Benito Cereno" is the least magazinish.

Melville's editing and rewriting reached its highest creative point in "Benito Cereno." But this generative act is not always how critics understand the story. Catherine Toal suggests that Aranda's skeleton symbolizes Melville's rejection of his advice that Hawthorne "build about with fulness & veins & beauty" the story of Agatha Hatch (*C* 237). "Benito Cereno," she argues, is "a self-demolishing fiction that overturns the teleology of plot and the protocols of allegory, simultaneously with the ideal of sympathetic, collaborative alliance undergirding the 'Agatha' project."[35] Writers can struggle with the writing process; they can find it painful, as Melville did increasingly during 1855 and 1856 when suffering bouts of rheumatism and sciatica; they can remain dissatisfied with the "botches" they create. But to see in Melville's "Benito Cereno" a "self-demolishing fiction" one has to look past a great deal of writerly and editorial construction. The results of the creative process one finds in "Benito Cereno" may fit uncomfortably in the bounds of *Putnam's,* but the work does not deny its own existence. The story breaks the conventions of the serial form with purpose. Melville combines the roles of writer, editor, and even literary critic, to create out of the DNA of an earlier narrative form a new genotype. "Benito Cereno" is not self-demolishing, then, but a piece of editing and surrogate reprinting that creates a work of art out of Melville's "pilfering disposition." It is also a narrative on whose helical structures other art builds.

Melville proved himself yet another kind of embedded author when writing *Israel Potter* and "Benito Cereno." In chapter 1 I showed how intimately Melville understood paper and the role it played in mediating his writing life, and how after writing novels he continued to affirm himself as a writer by further embedding himself in the economy of paper. In chapter 2 we saw that contingent circumstances brought Melville and the magazines together but that Melville responded in pragmatic style by embedding himself in magazine genres and then innovating his way beyond them. I explored the collective and personal judgments magazine editors exercised in chapter 3 to argue that Melville's writing was a material object embedded in the contingencies of publication and in the aesthetic distinctions magazines practiced. Looking at the paratextual magazine material among which it was embedded when first published, in chapter 4 I showed that Melville's writing reached for ideas that in the magazine world of the 1850s other writers did not engage so artfully. Finally, this chapter has demonstrated how Melville embedded himself in the magazine form by taking up the role of editor in a culture on the cusp of transitioning from iteration to origination; his editing and reprinting of old narratives resulted in magazine writing that originated as it iterated. At every point where it was possible for Melville to invest his embeddedness, he returned it with compound interest.

Conclusion

At the end of 2011 "Bartleby, the Scrivener" took on a new life. Suddenly people were reading the story out loud in public and turning the refrain "I would prefer not to" into a slogan for posters, billboards, and banners. "Bartleby" had become a story of Wall Street for those who witnessed new kinds of depredations on America's most symptomatic thoroughfare; a nineteenth-century magazine story was now lead soloist in the orchestration of Occupy protests across the United States. Occupy did not pick "Bartleby" at random. A permanent fixture on high school reading lists and in introductory surveys of nineteenth-century American literature, "Bartleby" always had the advantage of not being *Moby-Dick,* that great whale of a novel students struggle to read; in "Bartleby" one makes Melville's acquaintance without embarking on a long and perilous voyage with Ishmael, Queequeg, and Captain Ahab. The story also persists in American literary culture with a stubbornness of which Bartleby himself would have been proud; its golden ratio of density to length keeps critics busy as they test out new methods and approaches. The result is that "Bartleby" has become the most written-about short story in American literature. No other story but "Bartleby" has ever been described as having its own "industry."[1] If such a thing as a public literary consciousness exists, "Bartleby, the Scrivener" is embedded there. The 2008–9 financial crisis and the economic events that followed inspired people to start humming a familiar melody.

Longevity is a notable achievement for any story. But it is particularly rare for the ordinariness and anonymity with which "Bartleby" entered and exited print circulation to precede such recognition and acclamation. No reprintings other than in *The Piazza Tales* appeared during Melville's lifetime. Some of Hawthorne's most important tales—"Roger Malvin's Burial," "Wakefield," and "Rappaccini's Daughter"—were not reprinted beyond the *Twice-Told Tales* and *Mosses from an Old Manse*; "Young Goodman Brown" reappeared only once, in 1859 in the Portland, Maine, *Christian Intelligencer and Eastern Chronicle.* But Hawthorne published multiple editions of these two collections during his lifetime, and his other tales were subject to perpetual and widespread unauthorized reprinting.[2] Poe's employment as an editor on various newspapers and magazines in different cities meant that he constantly reprinted his own work in slightly altered form. Multi-volume collections of this work appeared regularly after his death for the rest of the century.

Melville's magazine work did enjoy an afterlife, but like the end of his tenure as a writer of magazine stories it was an afterlife marked by diminuendo rather than fanfare. As Melville embedded his writing in the everyday rhythms of literary life—its material economies, its genres, editorial practices, paratexts, and cast-off narratives—so the ordinary life of literary culture reciprocally embedded Melville in its material practices and its recycling and anthologizing impulses. In ways that make the contemporary pervasiveness of "Bartleby" gloriously and inexplicably unlikely, Melville continued to knock elbows with characters intimately connected to his magazine work and remained embedded to the last.

By the summer of 1855 he had turned his attention to a new project, *The Confidence-Man.* The evidence suggests Melville still considered himself a magazinist at this point but that his patrons at *Putnam's* did not. Toward the end of June, George William Curtis wrote another of his diligent business letters to Joshua Dix. Among his thoughts on William Douglas O'Connor and Longfellow, Curtis offered a one-sentence judgment on Melville: "Decline any novel from Melville that is not extremely good."[3] This was ten days after his change of heart about "The Bell-Tower." Dix's letter to which Curtis responded no longer exists. But working backward from the date of Curtis's letter we know that Melville wrote to Dix offering him *The Confidence-Man* for serialization in the hope that he could secure the same five dollars a page plus novel publication that he arranged for *Israel Potter.* After Curtis's advice, Dix proved indifferent to Melville's magazine ambitions. The break he took to concentrate on the unserialized

The Confidence-Man meant Melville lost his magazine momentum. "The 'Gees" was nearly two years old by the time it appeared in *Harper's* in March 1856. "I and My Chimney" and "The Apple-Tree Table" graced the March and May issues of *Putnam's* even though Melville composed both stories the previous year. Cut adrift and determined to go through with what was now a stand-alone novel, Melville faded from the green wrappers of *Putnam's* and the white wrappers of *Harper's* and made only a fleeting encore when *Harper's* published several poems from *Battle-Pieces* in 1866.

In financial terms Melville would have benefited from more, not less, magazine writing. In retrospect, *The Confidence-Man* gloriously caps a maverick novel-writing career, but a pragmatic word persuading Melville to churn out more stories would have been sage advice; it might have kept him going long enough to produce fictional gems other than just the posthumously published *Billy Budd.* In February 1856 he paused to complete "The Piazza," a new story Dix asked him to write to introduce *The Piazza Tales.* But through the May publication of this collection, and the summer that saw him finish *The Confidence-Man,* Melville suspended his cycle of magazine writing. He was embedded in his own career to the extent that he either missed or misjudged the next move. All the best fiction writers have the capacity to distance themselves from their own writing, to demarcate author from narrator so that the writer's thoughts appear in the third person. Melville was no exception. But he showed little capacity for thinking about himself in the third person long enough to forge a career in the same way he forged memorable narrators and ideas. Like someone learning to dance, Melville spent too long having to think where to put his feet; by the time they were in the right place the music had moved on. Dix & Edwards, and even Curtis, still had enough faith in him and his magazine output to see *The Piazza Tales* and *The Confidence-Man* into print, but whether or not Melville intended to resume his well-paid magazine career, events intervened to move him in a different direction.

Melville had agreed to pay back the loan from his friend Tertullus Stewart, which had enabled him to buy Arrowhead, by May 1, 1856. Even with his magazine work he could not afford the repayment. Instead he put part of the Arrowhead estate up for sale. The land sold quickly and Melville avoided financial insolvency, though mainly thanks to the beneficence of his always reliable father-in-law, who found a way to discharge his son-in-law's debts even though Melville received payment for the land only in installments, the last of which was not due until April 1, 1859. Rheumatism and sciatica, as well as another unidentified illness, also affected Melville's health. Melville and his family thought a prolonged trip abroad would effect a cure. The time to head off was on completion of *The Confidence-Man.* Melville left the manuscript with his brother Allan and shortly thereafter set sail for Europe and the Mediterranean on October 11. By the time he returned on May 20, 1857, Melville's go-to publisher and magazine were in the midst of a spiral of decline from which neither would recover.

The rot at *Putnam's* had already begun by the summer of 1856. In the Dix & Edwards partnership, Arthur Edwards took responsibility for financial affairs. To the cost of all others involved in the firm he proved no John Jacob Astor or J. P. Morgan. Dix eventually discovered that Edwards had disguised from the other partners that a promised investment from Edwards's brother had never arrived. With their assets dwindling, the partnership needed capital from elsewhere. George William Curtis came to the rescue. He invested $10,000 in May 1856 and signed over to the company the copyright for all his books. But circulation continued to decline—to seventeen thousand by August 1856—and the other investors eventually forced Edwards to give up operational control. Frederick Law Olmsted, who invested $5,500 in March 1855, was furious with Dix:

> I can't tell how ashamed I am of being involved in such a mess as you describe. You have always, even when most out of temper with him, spoken of Edwards as prodigiously excellent as a man of business—a financier, namely. I am a wretchedly poor man of business. . . . But with half the obligations upon me that he has, if I made such a mistake as you describe him to have made, I would not sleep till I had resigned my office & relieved myself of obligations for which I was so incompetent. . . . That you have known of such a state of things and have still allowed Edwards to manage our money affairs is—I must say more than extraordinary—incredible.[4]

The firm was losing $1,000 a month, and disharmony affected relations among the partners. Substantial further investment was needed to pay off Edwards and put the business on a sounder footing.

Curtis came to the rescue again. Now married, he persuaded his father-in-law, Francis Shaw, to invest $25,000 in February 1857. In April, new articles of agreement dissolved the existing partnership; the business and its debts were sold for one dollar to a new firm consisting of Curtis, Olmsted, and the magazine's printer, John Miller, who joined the others to protect his financial interests. To try to publish their way out of trouble, Miller & Co.—from June, Miller & Curtis—issued an American version of the *Gentlemen's Magazine,* the first U.S. edition of *The Dead Secret* by Wilkie Collins, and a selection of long-forgotten minor works. Though Curtis defended their record, none of this activity brought financial stability. The inevitable followed. "We failed today!" Curtis wrote Olmsted on August 6.[5] Treated as a general rather than a limited partner, Shaw was left with debts of $70,000; Curtis lost everything and had to support himself with his work at *Harper's* and a busy lecturing schedule; *Putnam's* ceased publication with the September issue, though *Emerson's United States Magazine* bought the remnants of the business and kept the famous name alive for another year as the subordinate partner in *Emerson's Magazine and Putnam's Monthly.*

By the time Melville returned to New York City, then, *Putnam's* was in its death throes. This book began with Melville traveling to Dalton to buy paper on which to write *Moby-Dick* and fortuitously stumbling on a mill he would later turn into the subject of his magazine fiction. The creditors who consigned his literary employers at *Putnam's* to the ignominy of insolvency were the paper merchants Charles Kendall and Alexander Rice, who published an injunction in Boston and New York City newspapers preventing the partners of Miller & Curtis from disposing of their assets.[6] Embedded in the material economy of paper even before he began his magazine career, the end of Melville's magazine career was itself embedded in the balance sheet of paper exchange.

Had he wanted to continue with magazine writing there were magazines enough beyond *Harper's* and *Putnam's* to support his endeavors. As *Godey's Lady's Book* promised Melville to its readers in 1851, so now the *Atlantic Monthly* advertised Melville as a future contributor on the back cover of the new magazine's first issue in November 1857. Melville had written enthusiastically to the magazine's publishers, "I shall be very happy to contribute, though I can not now name the day when I shall have any article ready" (*C* 310). He may have fully intended to resume his magazine career at this point. But there is also something permanent about Melville's deferral. He does not suggest he might send something next year, or in the next few months. If to the lawyer in "Bartleby" dead letters sound like dead men, then not being able to "name the day" sounds like not wanting to name the day and not wanting ever to "have any article ready." The *Atlantic Monthly*'s promise proved false. The trip to Europe and the Mediterranean produced no new tales Melville felt compelled to turn into magazine stories or novels. Whether he knew it or not at this stage, Melville's fiction writing career was over.

With the help of Curtis's influence and contacts Melville chose the lecture circuit instead, but his diminishment continued. He told Curtis on September 15, 1857, that he had been "scratching my brains for a Lecture" and ended the letter by asking: "What is a good, earnest subject? '*Daily progress of man towards a state of intellectual & moral perfection, as evidenced in history of 5th Avenue & 5 Points*'" (*C* 314). If the suggestion was ironic, it indicated Melville's skeptical attitude to the venture that would see him embark on three unsuccessful seasons as a lecturer. Invitations arrived on Curtis's prompting, and Melville was thankful in his last known letter to his former editor: "I have received two or three invitations to lecture,—invitations prompted by you—and have promptly accepted. I am ready for as many more as may come on" (*C* 316). In his first tour, between November 1857 and February 1858, Melville spoke on "Statues of Rome" in sixteen towns and cities; the following season he chose "The South Seas" as his talk in ten locations; and in his final season, speaking on "Traveling," he appeared only three times. Lecturing required that Melville the writer become Melville the speaker. No longer words on a page, he was now a voice and a person in a room full of other people. Neither the lectures nor the lecturer proved compelling.

Unsuited to this new interactive world, Melville remained embedded during what remained of his publishing career in the mediatory relationships of print. In September 1857 he corresponded with Curtis about the printing plates for *The Piazza Tales* and *The Confidence-Man.* While he initially showed some interest in acquiring the plates, later he wrote Curtis: "Sell them without remorse. To pot with them, & melt them down" (*C* 316). Fire had already destroyed Melville's words when the Harper firm's premises collapsed in flames four years earlier; now his words would dissolve in another cauldron of fire. Late in life Melville still liaised with printers as he had done with *Moby-Dick.* He hired Theodore Low De Vinne, the printer of *Century Illustrated Magazine,* to produce his penultimate collection of poems, *John Marr.* One of the most important nineteenth-century American printers, De Vinne wrote books on the history of printing and typography and cofounded the Grolier Club in New York City with other bibliophiles to promote the book arts. De Vinne also printed books for the Grolier, one of which was Curtis's *Washington Irving: A Sketch.* Published in 1891, the same year Melville died and a year before Curtis himself died, the book appeared in a limited edition of 344 copies printed on handmade paper in a red morocco leather binding with the Grolier Club insignia stamped in gilt on the center of the front cover. This was much like the cover Melville said he would have preferred for Cooper's *The Red Rover* when he reviewed a new edition in 1850 (*PT* 237). *John Marr* appeared in much less distinguished clothing. The "light creamy tan stiff paper" bore only the collection's title and not even Melville's name (*PP* 563).

For *Timoleon,* Melville engaged the Caxton Press to see his final work into print. A much less prestigious and meticulous printer than De Vinne, the Caxton firm compromised the layout of Melville's poems by squeezing more than one poem onto a page and awkwardly paginating the collection (*PP* 577). Again, Melville's name was nowhere to be found. After starting out as a named author with prestigious publishers, then becoming an anonymous author for prestigious magazine publishers, in his editions of poetry with print runs of only twenty-five copies each, Melville capped his writing life by achieving the dubious status of anonymous self-publication.

But Melville's name and magazine life also lived on and became embedded in the anthologizing impulse of the mid- and late nineteenth century. Three of his stories materialized again in print. "Poor Man's Pudding and Rich Man's Crumbs" twice reappeared relatively quickly after the June 1854 issue of *Harper's*: in the *Salem Register* of June 19, 1854, and the August 1854 issue of the Buffalo *Western Literary Messenger.* On both occasions the diptych made for quick periodical filler. With "The Lightning-Rod Man," however, reprinting embedded Melville in new relation to his peers. The story appeared in William Evans Burton's *Cyclopedia of Wit and Humor,* published first in 1857 and several times subsequently right through to 1898. A former actor, Burton founded *Burton's Gentleman's Magazine* in 1837 and worked with Poe as his editor until their tempestuous relationship broke down in 1840; he sold the magazine a year later, at which point it became *Graham's Magazine.* The *Cyclopedia* anthologized humorous magazine and book sketches and stories from America, Ireland, Scotland, and England, and combined them with several steel and hundreds of wood engravings in a two-volume extravaganza of lighthearted reverie.

"The Lightning-Rod Man" appears in volume 2. Sixty pages earlier appeared "Our New Livery and Other Things," a section of *The Potiphar Papers* that Curtis published in *Putnam's Monthly* in April 1853. Burton even deemed Curtis important enough to include his engraved portrait. And Curtis was not the only fellow Putnamite in the *Cyclopedia.* Burton also included two contributions from Charles Frederick Briggs: "Elegant Tom Dillar" and "Clearing a Stage." Burton's book reads like a who's who of forgotten nineteenth-century American writers. Unspectacularly in their midst stands Melville and "The Lightning-Rod Man," complete with an illustration by the prolific caricaturist and humorist Henry Stephens.

The only other story that reappeared after *The Piazza Tales* was the one over which Curtis changed his mind so dramatically, "The Bell-Tower." Like "The Lightning-Rod Man," what marked out this slightly later Melville story for editors was its generic qualities. The Italian Renaissance setting added a layer of mystery and distance to the events of Bannadonna's demise. In 1875, Rossiter Johnson included "The Bell-Tower" in the third volume of what would become an eighteen-volume series of collected short stories and essays titled *Little Classics.* "Exile" and "Intellect" structured the first two volumes; Melville's story fell under the heading of "Tragedy." After Poe's "Murders in the Rue Morgue" and stories by J. W. DeForest and William Mudford, "The Bell-Tower" precedes Emily C. Judson and Henry Mackenzie before Thomas De Quincey's "The Vision of Sudden Death" rounds off the volume.

Johnson was a former newspaper editor who became a gatherer, filterer, and précisist of Anglophone life and culture. Notwithstanding "some feeling of embarrassment" at the "lack of any perfect test" for a classic, Johnson in his preface to the series claims "ours is the day of small things,—small as the diamond and the violet are small." While the novel is not yet done, he argued, brevity in literature possessed distinct advantages in the modern age: "The work of art which, embodying a sacred principle or a living idea, condenses its plot, its moral, and its effective climax into the limits of a single sitting must, in an age of crowding books and rushing readers, possess a decisive advantage over the unwieldy conventional novel, with its caravan of characters and its long bewilderment of detail."[7] In this preface one can here turning the gears of genre distinction out of which rolled the short story.

Johnson also worked as coeditor on various multi-volume projects, including the *American Cyclopaedia* with George Ripley and Charles Dana, before taking over as general editor of *Appletons' Cyclopaedia of American Biography*. In *Little Classics* Melville's name and work take their place once more besides his *Harper's* and *Putnam's* companions. The fourth volume of the series, "Life," featured a piece of fiction from the December 1853 issue of *Putnam's Monthly* in which the second installment of "Bartleby" appeared. But Johnson's choice was not "Bartleby." Instead, he selected "My Chateaux," one of Curtis's Titbottom pieces that appeared in book form as *Prue and I*. In the final volume of the series, Johnson provided pen portraits of each of the 150 authors whose work made up the previous seventeen volumes. In this volume Melville bumped along with Curtis, with William Douglas O'Connor, John Greenleaf Whittier, Henry David Thoreau, Arthur Clough, Thackeray, Bayard Taylor, Charles Reade, Donald Mitchell, James Russell Lowell, Longfellow, Edward Everett Hale, Dickens, William Cullen Bryant, and Joseph Addison. All these authors at one time or another shared the pages of the same magazines in which Melville appeared or were mentioned in the same breath as Melville. In Johnson's series Melville was embedded as just one among the many, and Curtis, not Melville, offered a more credible vision of "Life."

The final appearance of "The Bell-Tower" was similarly embedded in a voluminous publishing venture, Edmund C. Stedman and Ellen M. Hutchinson's *Library of American Literature from the Earliest Settlement to the Present Time* (1887–90). A forerunner of the Norton and Heath anthologies, this work followed in the tradition of Evert and George Duyckinck's *Cyclopaedia of American Literature* (1855), one aim of which was to make available to the public a digestible and modestly priced publication for the home library. In their preface, Stedman and Hutchinson write: "If our task shall be rightly executed, an important addition will be provided for the library of an American household. The work, as its name implies, will be a library in itself, whose contents are most attractive, offering precisely that of which the home-reader wishes to be informed."[8] Melville appeared in the seventh of eleven volumes. His presence was more substantial than in either the Burton or Johnson anthology. Three poems from *Battle-Pieces* appear immediately after "The Bell-Tower," and Melville's portrait, based on Joseph Eaton's 1870 oil painting, is one of fourteen engravings in the volume.

But even this accolade makes the inclusion of "The Bell-Tower" and three poems seem partial and slight. The anthology spends three volumes on the period 1835–1860. This is necessary, the authors argue, "for any representation of the genius of Poe, Emerson, Longfellow, Bancroft, Motley, Hawthorne, Lowell and other worthies of their prime."[9] As well as "Young Goodman Brown," extracts from *The Scarlet Letter, The Blithedale Romance, The House of the Seven Gables,* and *The Marble Faun* represent the range of Hawthorne's career. But there is nothing from *Typee* or *Moby-Dick* to suggest Melville had a career in novels. Arranged chronologically by the author's date of birth, the series included Curtis in volume 8. Together with an engraving there were two short poems and extracts from *The Potiphar Papers, Prue and I,* and a eulogy Curtis gave for Wendell Phillips. Melville and Curtis occupied precisely the same number of pages—fourteen—in this library of American literature. Curtis was no longer "Mr. Melville's younger brother in letters," as Fitz-James O'Brien once described him, but Melville's twin. Neither warranted a steel engraving conferring status. That honor in these three crucial volumes went to Hawthorne, Poe, James Russell Lowell, Oliver Wendell Holmes, Francis Parkman, and Bayard Taylor. Melville and Curtis, who together circulated through American homes in the covers of *Putnam's* and *Harper's,* now recirculated in a library compendium as the dark matter between American literature's true stars. In that position Curtis still hangs suspended; gravity eventually exerted enough pressure on Melville that he took his place in the night sky, but with no "Bartleby" and no "Benito Cereno," American literature looked a very different galaxy at the end of the nineteenth century.

The aim of this book has been to show that historical contingencies inspired the production of Melville's magazine writing but that contingency of this kind does not by itself account for their finished form. Melville's embedded authorship brought him into relation with the materials of his trade, lodged him in the genres of magazine writing that set the parameters for his work, and brought him into contact with actors in the publishing industry who judged his work. But these contexts do not by themselves account for why Melville produced writing so different from, say, Curtis's. When he is steering the *Pequod* in "The Try-Works" chapter of *Moby-Dick,* Ishmael observes his fellow whalers as they turn blubber into oil. In the intensity of his observation, he suddenly finds himself turned about, "fronting the ship's stern, with my back to her prow and the compass" (*MD* 424). In this moment Ishmael sees himself and those he observes in a new light. Melville found perspective by turning in a different direction to face the world in which he lived; this capacity is what shaped the magazine writing's form and saw him produce writing not expected or, in some instances, not wanted by his context. Curtis was never able to achieve this.

Not all of Melville's magazine work demonstrates these qualities. One story absent from this book until now is "Jimmy Rose," a story little written about during the last 160 years and for good reason. Of all the stories Melville published in *Harper's* and *Putnam's* it remains the most stubbornly prosaic. A sentimental sketch that blended seamlessly with the magazine content alongside which it appeared in *Harper's*, this story has been forgotten even by the anthologists. There are traces of techniques Melville used to better effect elsewhere in his magazine writing: the iterative diction of "The Paradise of Bachelors and the Tartarus of Maids" in the repetition of the word "fine"; Jimmy's rosy cheeks that reprise the maids' cheeks from that same story. But there are none of the signs that Melville was facing the world of downward mobility and migration from country to city he represents in the story with the cryptic perspective he adopted in his more memorable magazine work. Melville wrote "Jimmy Rose" in the summer of 1854 under the same conditions and in the same circumstances and contexts in which just a few months later he wrote "Benito Cereno." The first part of this later story appeared in *Putnam's* in the same month *Harper's* published "Jimmy Rose." Why Melville wrote such a conventional narrative in one story and such an innovative narrative in the other is a mystery that a specifically print-oriented approach cannot answer.

By the same token, my understanding of embedded authorship does not by itself sufficiently explain this distinction nor the longevity of some of Melville's stories. What each of the chapters in this book has shown is that embeddedness is only an occasion for innovation; oftentimes that occasion passes by unclaimed by writers. But not always. Melville lived in a papermaking district of Massachusetts and bought his paper from an industrialized paper mill. There was no guarantee this experience would end up as fiction nor in the form Melville created when he turned it into

"The Paradise of Bachelors and the Tartarus of Maids." Of all the ways Melville could have rewritten Delano's or Trumbull's narratives, many would not have achieved the effects he created in *Israel Potter* or "Benito Cereno." Concentrating on the embeddedness of his experience as a writer makes it possible to understand the conditions in which Melville wrote; showing what he did with these conditions makes it possible to appreciate the nature of his achievement. Whether one conceives of the author as a genius, as dead, or as a node in a matrix, the study of print is poorer when it underplays what occurs in authors' minds and hands as they turn experience into surprising, disorienting, or astounding literary form.

Our access to this form is one inescapably marked by the passage of time. Humor might be the sum of tragedy plus time, but what would be the sum of writing plus time? Taking texts out of their time capsules recognizes that they are not timeless but "time-full."[10] Melville was never in a position to take responsibility for the afterlife of his writing. The one thing for which he could take responsibility was the writing itself. In its shape he carved the qualities over which time would drag its judgments and form its impressions. As I noted in the introduction, Melville's prophetic qualities as a writer play a part in his reputation. By taking up "Bartleby," the Occupy movement would seem to bear this out. But there is no prophecy in "Bartleby." The story lasts because in it Melville responded to his embeddedness with defiance and innovation. A genre story rooted in the magazine and novel world of lawyers and clerks, and in a social milieu where young male urban workers increasingly consumed representations of themselves in magazines and books, "Bartleby" did more than reflect that world back to its original readers like so many other stories in this genre. The story can usefully help Occupy make sense of the madness of Wall Street and the economic system embodied there, but even the importance and significance of this setting cannot reduce the story to this context.

There is no well-developed critical vocabulary for explaining the time-travelling qualities of artworks, or at least not one that does not rely on transcendent timelessness. Wai-Chee Dimock offers the idea of "resonance." Rather than texts whose integrity withstands the passage of time, Dimock suggests we think of "semantically elastic" texts whose endurance is a result of their "persistent unraveling" and their "lack of insulation against the currents of semantic change."[11] Whether this elasticity and openness is inherent to the nature of textuality itself or only to certain texts is not clear. If the former, then it does not help answer why some texts endure more readily than others; it would seem to push the responsibility for that endurance back onto the institutions of critical canon building and taste making. But the selection of survivor texts need not be imitative or random; if one wants to make a crown one must first buy jewels.

The "Bartleby" industry is just as much a result of Melville's story as the readers or the context of their reading. The hundred-year gap between the story's original publication and its emergence into the American literary canon prompts pause for thought. Is it the case that only the new circumstances of the postwar period—where, perhaps, the corporatization of life cast new shadows over the status of the individual worker, or where American literary studies cast around for heroes in the time of its maturity—provided context enough for "Bartleby" to achieve meaningful visibility? Curtis admired "Bartleby" and other *Putnam's* readers did too, but few original readers, or later ones like Rossiter Johnson, thought this ordinary magazine story offered an insightful diagnosis of contemporary life. Yet even if it was the social and historical circumstances of the 1950s that electrified "Bartleby" into life, the meaningfulness of the story is generated by the story itself, not by the context of the 1950s. A story has first to make itself adaptable to a context before a context can find a way to adapt to a story. This quality is what makes a story last; such adaptability is an internal quality of "Bartleby, the Scrivener"—though not of "Jimmy Rose"—and not the result of external forces.

Treasures can remain hidden, like gems buried in the ground, or antiques abandoned in attics. When found, rather than setting them to work perhaps we might try to understand what it is about them that shines. In the "The Apple-Tree Table," the narrator sits "spellbound" and stands "becharmed" when the first bug emerges from the table he retrieves from the attic at the beginning of the story. Embedded for many decades in the wood used to make the table, the bug shines first like a glowworm and then "a sparkling object, . . . a real marvel" (*PT* 389). The second bug emerges and lights up the room "like a fiery opal"; it is a "jeweler's bug—a bug like a sparkle of a glorious sunset" (*PT* 395). At the end of the story the miraculous bugs are "embalmed in a silver vinaigrette" and sit on the table ready for the narrator's daughters to show them off to visitors (*PT* 397). As with the best of Melville's magazine writing, embeddedness is the occasion for the creation of gems. One should understand why apple-tree wood so successfully provides a home for bugs, just as one should understand why the Wall Street setting and the lawyer's office and its occupants provide material suitable for a *Putnam's* magazine story. But being spellbound or becharmed by sparkling and glorious objects is also an appropriate critical response to the beauty of buried treasure.

One also needs patience. As if in ratification of his own idea that "the greatest, grandest things are unpredicted," the longevity and ubiquity of "Bartleby" is the gem that eventually emerged from Melville's embeddedness in the contingencies of his reluctant magazine writing during the 1850s.[12] In "Hawthorne and His Mosses," Melville writes that truth reveals itself in literature "only by cunning glimpses . . . , covertly, and by snatches," but that when it does, the reader senses "those deep far-away things" that hint at "the very axis of reality" (*PT* 244). Generation after generation continue to find such glimpses in "Bartleby." Melville's stories endure in proportion to the imaginative dexterity with which he transforms his own embeddedness into his magazine writing.

Other writers achieved similar effects within magazine wrappers. In his long and successful career as a writer of fiction for annuals and magazines, Hawthorne wrote dozens of pieces in which he reimagined the events of New England's past and present; refining and adapting the formal and narrative expectations of this familiar territory meant he made important contributions to the larger story this book helps illuminate: the invention of the American short story. The emergence of this form in the nineteenth century has little concerned critics since the 1980s; when literature is culture and history, genre is only a subsidiary of ideas, politics, and ideology. But the short story is not only a genre or form. Born in the magazine, it is the matter of material culture. Embedded in the magazine's transformation at the start rather than the end of his fiction-writing career, however much Hawthorne wrote about American religion, history, and gender he did so by bringing his writerly imagination to bear repeatedly on the short prose form, making important contributions to the genre in new material circumstances.

Harriet Beecher Stowe may have written the novel that started the Civil War, but she did so in the pages of the magazine, not between the covers of a book. The success and publicity of *Uncle Tom's Cabin,* and the novel's subsequent critical standing, also overshadow the remainder of her magazine-writing and, albeit brief, magazine-editing career. Stowe was there from very near the beginning of the *Atlantic Monthly*'s reign as American premier literary periodical. The magazine serialized *The Minister's Wooing* between December 1858 and December 1859; *Agnes of Sorrento* ran from May 1861 through April 1862 and appeared at the same time in London's *Cornhill Magazine.* Many of her shorter sketches also appeared in the *Atlantic* and played their part in helping Stowe, like Hawthorne, imagine New England afresh. Stowe also clearly understood her value as a writer in the magazine economy; where Melville hoped with *Israel Potter, The Confidence-Man,* and *The Piazza Tales* to double up his earnings from a later printing, Stowe was an expert in turning not just *Uncle Tom's Cabin* but her New England sketches into future income when they were published and anthologized in other forms. Feminist literary critics recovered Stowe's reputation after it waned following the Second World War, but her embeddedness in the magazine world also suggests there is more to say about her contribution to the success of the *Atlantic* and of late nineteenth-century new regionalist writing, for which magazines were an important outlet.

Henry James was a prolific magazine writer. As William Dean Howells noted in 1888 in the pages of *Harper's Monthly*: "With 'The Aspern Papers' in *The Atlantic,* 'The Liar' in *The Century,* 'A London Life' in *Scribner's,* and 'Louisa Pallant' and 'Two Countries' in *Harper's,* pretty much all at once, the effect was like an artist's exhibition. One turned from one masterpiece to another, making his comparisons, and delighted to find that the stories helped rather than hurt one another, and that their accidental massing enhanced his pleasure in them."[13] James wrote with magazine audiences in mind, and in searching for wider appeal modified his shorter work later in his career to cater to broader audiences. He was certainly happy to publish in lower-ranking magazines more reliant on advertising than the quality literary monthlies if that meant being paid well. The sheer number of magazines in which James published makes studying his writing a very different proposition than the one faced here with Melville. But James's continual fascination with the art of fiction, when set against his desire to earn money, means that similar forces are working alongside one another in the magazine writing: from his embeddedness in the requirements of paid writing he must first imaginatively create what audiences read.

Melville, Hawthorne, Stowe, and James are all familiar literary figures with careers that withstand the burden of intense scrutiny. To date, the magazine plays a more important role in our understanding of Stowe and James than it does of Melville and Hawthorne. This book has tried to correct the record for Melville and to put his magazine writing career into focus in ways that would also benefit the broader study of writers and magazines in the nineteenth century and beyond. Melville's embeddedness took its own shape; for each writer different variables combine to give their experiences a unique fingerprint. But in all these cases, pressing familiar and obscure fictions back between the pages of the magazines in which they first appeared can be the occasion for watching with new eyes how writers turn their embedded experience of print production and circulation into literary form.

Notes

Abbreviations

DEC Dix, Edwards & Company Letters and Agreements (MS Am 800.13), Houghton Library, Harvard University. With item number.

GPP George Palmer Putnam Collection, Manuscripts Division, Department of Rare Books and Special Collections, Princeton University Library. With box and folder number.

GWCC George William Curtis Correspondence (MS Am 1124–1124.1), Houghton Library, Harvard University. With item number.

Introduction

1. Two letters from Catharine Maria Sedgwick to Harper Brothers, on September 8 and 25, 1856, bear the same "Carson's Dalton" stamp as Melville's letter to Duyckinck. Record ID 137550, Misc American Harper, Department of Literary and Historical Manuscripts, Morgan Library & Museum, New York.
2. One explanation for why Melville took what for him was an unusual step is that having the plates ready would speed up the publication of the novel and so pay him royalties more quickly.
3. Leah Price, *How to Do Things with Books in Victorian Britain* (Princeton: Princeton University Press, 2012), 19–38.
4. *Godey's Lady's Book,* January 1851, 72.
5. Heather A. Haveman, *Magazines and the Making of America: Modernization, Community, and Print Culture, 1741–1860* (Princeton: Princeton University Press, 2015), 27.
6. A draft of this letter is in box 11, GPP.
7. Meredith McGill, *American Literature and the Culture of Reprinting, 1834–1853* (Philadelphia: University of Pennsylvania Press, 2003), 4.
8. Both *Harper's* and *Putnam's* are freely available through Cornell University Library's Making of America Collection: http://ebooks.library.cornell.edu/m/moa/.

9. As long ago as the 1960s Barbara Welter based her understanding of the "cult of true womanhood" on the ideological tenor of magazines directed at female audiences; Nina Baym subsequently pioneered the recovery of women's reading more generally in the nineteenth century. Barbara Welter, "The Cult of True Womanhood: 1820–1860," *American Quarterly* 18.2 (1966): 151–74; and Nina Baym, *Novels, Readers, and Reviewers: Responses to Fiction in Antebellum America* (Ithaca: Cornell University Press, 1984). See also Ellen Gruber Garvey, *The Adman in the Parlor: Magazines and the Gendering of Consumer Culture, 1880s to 1910s* (New York: Oxford University Press, 1996); Aleta Feinsod Cane and Susan Alves, eds., *"The Only Efficient Instrument": American Women Writers and the Periodical, 1837–1916* (Iowa City: University of Iowa Press, 2001); Amy Aronson, *Taking Liberties: Early American Women's Magazines and Their Readers* (Westport, CT: Praeger, 2002); Patricia Cline Cohen, Timothy J. Gilfoyle, and Helen Lefkowitz Horowitz, *The Flash Press: Sporting Male Weeklies in 1840s New York* (Chicago: University of Chicago Press, 2008). For the intersection of gender and race, see Noliwe M. Rooks, *Ladies' Pages: African American Women's Magazines and the Culture That Made Them* (New Brunswick, NJ: Rutgers University Press, 2004). On magazines and the American middle class, see Heidi L. Nichols, *The Fashioning of Middle-Class America: "Sartain's Union Magazine of Literature and Art" and Antebellum Culture* (New York: Peter Lang, 2003); Cynthia Lee Patterson, *Art for the Middle Classes: America's Illustrated Magazines of the 1840s* (Jackson: University of Mississippi Press, 2010).
10. The story of the creation of a reading public and the nature of that public's reading demands and habits is told in Ronald J. Zboray, *A Fictive People: Antebellum Economic Development and the American Reading Public* (New York: Oxford University Press, 1993). For a more theoretical approach to readers and modes of reader response, see two books by James L. Machor: *Readers in History: Nineteenth-Century American Literature and the Contexts of Response* (Baltimore: Johns Hopkins University Press, 1993); and *Reading Fiction in Antebellum America: Informed Response and Reception Histories, 1820–1865* (Baltimore: Johns Hopkins University Press, 2011). Books that concentrate on specific reading groups and practices include Sarah Wadsworth, *In the Company of Books: Literature and Its "Classes" in Nineteenth-Century America* (Amherst: University of Massachusetts Press, 2006); Gillian D. Silverman, *Bodies and Books: Reading and the Fantasy of Communion in Nineteenth-Century America* (Philadelphia: University of Pennsylvania Press, 2012); and Maura D'Amore, *Suburban Plots: Men at Home in Nineteenth-Century American Print Culture* (Amherst: University of Massachusetts Press, 2014).
11. Putnam letter draft, box 11, GPP.
12. On Poe, see Kevin J. Hayes, *Poe and the Printed Word* (Cambridge: Cambridge University Press, 2000); Jonathan H. Hartmann, *The Marketing of Edgar Allan Poe* (New York: Routledge, 2008); J. Gerald Kennedy and Jerome McGann, eds., *Poe and the Remapping of Antebellum Print Culture* (Baton Rouge: Louisiana State University Press, 2012). On Stowe, see Claire Parfait, *The Publishing History of Uncle Tom's Cabin, 1852–2002* (Aldershot, UK: Ashgate, 2007); Mark Canada, *Literature and Journalism in Antebellum America: Thoreau, Stowe, and Their Contemporaries Respond to the Rise of the Commercial Press* (New York: Palgrave Macmillan, 2011). On James, see Michael Anesko, *"Friction with the Market": Henry James and the Profession of Authorship* (New York: Oxford University Press, 1986); Amy Tucker, *The Illustration*

of the Master: Henry James and the Magazine Revolution (Stanford: Stanford University Press, 2010). On popular women writers, see Susan Coultrap-McQuin, *Doing Literary Business: American Women Writers in the Nineteenth Century* (Chapel Hill: University of North Carolina Press, 1990); Melissa J. Homestead, *American Women Authors and Literary Property, 1822–1869* (Cambridge: Cambridge University Press, 2005); Melissa J. Homestead and Pamela T. Washington, eds., *E. D. E. N. Southworth: Recovering a Nineteenth-Century Popular Novelist* (Knoxville: University of Tennessee Press, 2012).

13. Lewis Mumford, *Herman Melville: A Study of His Life and Vision* (New York: Harcourt, Brace, 1929), 227; William V. Spanos, *Herman Melville and the American Calling: Fiction after Moby-Dick, 1851–1857* (Albany: State University of New York Press, 2008), 7; Nina Baym, "Melodramas of Beset Manhood: How Theories of American Fiction Exclude Women Authors," *American Quarterly* 33.2 (1981): 129; Samuel Otter, *Melville's Anatomies* (Berkeley: University of California Press, 1999), 4; Marvin Fisher, *Going Under: Melville's Short Fiction and the American 1850s* (Baton Rouge: Louisiana State University Press, 1977), xii; William B. Dillingham, *Melville's Short Fiction, 1853–1856* (Athens: University of Georgia Press, 1977), 11.
14. Fisher, *Going Under,* 1–12; Mumford, *Herman Melville,* 361; Spanos, *Herman Melville,* 11, 25.
15. Leon Jackson, *The Business of Letters: Authorial Economies in Antebellum America* (Stanford: Stanford University Press, 2008), 2, 3.
16. Francesca Sawaya, *The Difficult Art of Giving: Patronage, Philanthropy, and the American Literary Market* (Philadelphia: University of Pennsylvania Press, 2014).
17. Melville's lifetime earnings from *Moby-Dick* amounted to $1,260, of which just over $700 was received as an advance on royalties from his British publisher, Richard Bentley. See *MD* 689.
18. The reviewer in the *Albany (NY) Evening Journal* was sure Melville's reputation would help sell *The Confidence-Man* "even if its merits were much less than they are," while the *Boston Evening Transcript* thought Melville had "become so widely known, that any work from his pen is sure to find a host of readers." The *Cincinnati Enquirer,* on the other hand, considered the novel "one of the dullest and most dismally monotonous books we remember to have read," declaring in summation that Melville's "authorship is toward the nadir rather than the zenith, and he has been progressing in the form of an inverted climax." Brian Higgins and Hershel Parker, eds., *Herman Melville: The Contemporary Reviews* (Cambridge: Cambridge University Press, 1995), 487, 506.
19. Ibid., 545.
20. Trish Loughran, *The Republic of Print: Print Culture in the Age of U.S. Nation Building, 1770–1870* (New York: Columbia University Press, 2007), 3.
21. For more on the reappraisal of Melville's long writing career, see "Late Melvilles," a special issue of *Leviathan,* 18.3 (2016).
22. Hershel Parker, *Herman Melville: A Biography,* 2 vols. (Baltimore: Johns Hopkins University Press, 1996 and 2002), 2:921. According to Parker, a typesetter may have mistakenly added "Hiram" to Melville's surname to make good in a headline the omission of Melville's first name from Hillard's obituary. After recognizing the mistake, someone then chiseled away the metal type so that later editions of the newspaper appeared with an inky blur where the first name should be. The results

of this correction are evident in the digitized version of the *New York Times.* Before Hillard's tribute, the *New York Times* printed two short obituaries on September 29 and October 2, both of which referred to "Herman Melville." How "Hiram" became "Henry," as it did in Jay Leyda's *Log,* is not clear. Leyda, *The Melville Log: A Documentary Life of Herman Melville, 1819–1891,* 2 vols. (New York: Harcourt, Brace, 1951), 2:788. To complicate matters, the name "Harry Melville" appears in the digitized indexing of the *New York Times.*

23. *New York Times,* October 6, 1891.
24. Jackson, *The Business of Letters,* 2; McGill, *American Literature and the Culture of Reprinting,* 4; Jonathan Dollimore, foreword to *The Demonic: Literature and Experience,* by Ewan Fernie (New York: Routledge, 2013), xvi.
25. David Dowling, *Literary Partnerships and the Marketplace: Writers and Mentors in Nineteenth-Century America* (Baton Rouge: Louisiana State University Press, 2012), 5.
26. Attention to form and aesthetics refused to go away even in the historicist turn of the 1980s and 1990s. See Cindy Weinstein and Christopher Looby, eds., *American Literature's Aesthetic Dimensions* (New York: Columbia University Press, 2012), 2–3.
27. Rita Felski, *The Limits of Critique* (Chicago: Chicago University Press, 2015), 152, 12. See also Marjorie Levinson, "What Is the New Formalism?" *PMLA* 122.2 (2007): 558–69; Stephen Best and Sharon Marcus, "Surface Reading: An Introduction," *Representations* 108.1 (2009): 1–21; Graham Harman, "The Well-Wrought Broken Hammer: Object-Oriented Literary Criticism," *New Literary History* 43.2 (2012): 183–203.

1. The "Plain Facts" of Paper

1. The median survival rate for magazines increased from 0.4 years in the 1740s to 1.9 years in the 1840s and 1850s. The number of magazines lasting more than 25 years increased from 4.3 percent for those first published between 1801 and 1820 to 8.2 percent for those first published between 1821 and 1840, and 10.5 percent for magazines first published between 1841 and 1860. Heather A. Haveman, *Magazines and the Making of America: Modernization, Community, and Print Culture, 1741–1860* (Princeton: Princeton University Press, 2015), 29.
2. "Monthlies," *New York Times,* April 3, 1855.
3. Jacques Derrida, *Paper Machine,* trans. Rachel Bowlby (Stanford: Stanford University Press, 2005), 43.
4. This accounting is also taking place in several books on the history of paper published in recent years. See Ian Sansom, *Paper: An Elegy* (London: Fourth Estate, 2012); Nicholas A. Basbanes, *On Paper: The Everything of Its Two-Thousand-Year History* (New York: Knopf, 2013); Alexander Monro, *The Paper Trail: An Unexpected History of a Revolutionary Invention* (London: Allen Lane, 2014); Lothar Müller, *White Magic: The Age of Paper,* trans. Jessica Spengler (Cambridge, UK: Polity Press, 2014); Lisa Gitelman, *Paper Knowledge: Toward a Media History of Documents* (Durham, NC: Duke University Press, 2014); Mark Kurlansky, *Paper: Paging through History* (New York: Norton, 2016).
5. Elizabeth Renker, *Strike through the Mask: Herman Melville and the Scene of Writing* (Baltimore: Johns Hopkins University Press, 1996), xviii, 61.

6. Hershel Parker, *Herman Melville: A Biography,* 2 vols. (Baltimore: Johns Hopkins University Press, 1996 and 2002), 2:142.
7. Ibid., 139, 143.
8. Ibid., 143.
9. Ibid., 161, 163, 164.
10. "Our Young Authors—Melville," *Putnam's Monthly Magazine,* February 1853, 164.
11. Harrison Elliott, "A Century Ago: An Eminent Author Looked upon Paper and Papermaking," *Paper Maker* 21.2 (1952): 55–58; Judith A. McGaw, *Most Wonderful Machine: Mechanization and Social Change in Berkshire Paper Making, 1801–1885* (Princeton: Princeton University Press, 1987), 384.
12. Jay Leyda, *The Melville Log: A Documentary Life of Herman Melville, 1819–1891,* 2 vols. (New York: Harcourt, Brace, 1951), 1:403; Marvin Fisher, "Melville's 'Tartarus': The Deflowering of New England," *American Quarterly* 23.1 (1971): 79; Philip Young, "The Machine in Tartarus: Melville's Inferno," *American Literature* 63.2 (1991): 214; Parker, *Herman Melville,* 1:810.
13. McGaw, *Most Wonderful Machine,* 383.
14. A. J. Valente, *Rag Paper Manufacture in the United States, 1801–1900: A History, with Directories of Mills and Owners* (Jefferson, NC: McFarland, 2010), 35.
15. Quoted in Parker, *Herman Melville,* 1:801.
16. McGaw, *Most Wonderful Machine,* 10.
17. Christina Lupton, "The Theory of Paper: Skepticism, Common Sense, Poststructuralism," *Modern Language Quarterly* 71.4 (2010): 427.
18. Kevin McLaughlin, *Paperwork: Fiction and Mass Mediacy in the Paper Age* (Philadelphia: University of Pennsylvania Press, 2005), 27.
19. Valente, *Rag Paper Manufacture,* 35, 201; Daniel Pidgeon, *Old-World Questions and New-World Answers* (London: Kegan Paul, Trench, 1884), 107; *History of Berkshire County, Massachusetts,* 2 vols. (New York: J. B. Beers, 1885), 1:664.
20. McGaw, *Most Wonderful Machine,* 160–62; for differences in the machines, see 96–103. The authoritative guide to papermaking machines is R. H. Clapperton, *The Paper-Making Machine: Its Invention, Evolution and Development* (Oxford: Pergamon Press, 1967).
21. McGaw, *Most Wonderful Machine,* 183.
22. Ibid., 182. "Cleaned" and "dressed" in this context mean prepared for the vat where rags were turned to pulp.
23. Aaron Winter, "Seeds of Discontent: The Expanding Satiric Range of Melville's Transatlantic Diptychs," *Leviathan* 8.2 (2006): 29.
24. McGaw, *Most Wonderful Machine,* 182; Avi J. Cohen, "Technological Change as Historical Process: The Case of the U.S. Pulp and Paper Industry, 1915–1940," *Journal of Economic History* 44.3 (1984): 787.
25. Wayne E. Fuller, *The American Mail: Enlarger of the Common Life* (Chicago: University of Chicago Press, 1972), 66.
26. Maynard H. Benjamin, *The History of Envelopes, 1840–1900* (Alexandria, VA: Envelope Manufacturers Association, 2002), 29.
27. David M. Henkin, *The Postal Age: The Emergence of Modern Communications in Nineteenth-Century America* (Chicago: University of Chicago Press, 2006), 60, 95.
28. Leo L. Lincoln and Lee C. Drickamer, *Postal History of Berkshire County, Massachusetts, 1790–1981* (Williamstown, MA: Lee C. Drickamer, 1982), 1.

29. Valente, *Rag Paper Manufacture,* 9.
30. Benjamin Franklin, "Paper; a Poem," in Dard Hunter, *Papermaking: The History and Technique of an Ancient Craft* (1947; repr., New York: Dover Publications, 1978), 239–40.
31. Fuller, *American Mail,* 25.
32. Lincoln and Drickamer, *Postal History,* 54–55, 23.
33. Valente, *Rag Paper Manufacture,* 12.
34. Derrida, *Paper Machine,* 42, 44.
35. Leo Marx, "Melville's Parable of the Wall," *Sewanee Review* 61.4 (1953): 602.
36. The other examples are Helmstone, the narrator of "The Fiddler," and the narrator of "The 'Gees." Blandmour in "Poor Man's Pudding and Rich Man's Crumbs" is a poet although not the narrator of the piece.
37. For more on this, see Graham Thompson, "'Dead Letters! . . . Dead Men?': The Rhetoric of the Office in Melville's 'Bartleby, the Scrivener,'" *Journal of American Studies* 34.3 (2000): 395–411.
38. Marx, "Melville's Parable of the Wall," 627, 626.
39. All these pieces appeared in *Harper's New Monthly Magazine:* "The Railway Works at Crewe," August 1850, 408–11; "Novelty Iron Works; with Description of Marine Steam Engines, and Their Construction," May 1851, 721–34; "Weovil Biscuit Manufactory," September 1851, 487–88; "Galvanoplasty," November 1854, 811–14; "How Gunpowder Is Made: Visit to the Hounslow Mills," April 1852, 643–47.
40. McLaughlin, *Paperwork,* 116.
41. It is noticeable that the detailed understanding of the place of writers in the antebellum literary market is not matched by an understanding of the practicalities of writers writing. Other than the biographies, there are two exceptions in Melville's case: Elizabeth Renker, *Strike through the Mask*; and Michael Kearns, *Writing for the Street, Writing in the Garret: Melville, Dickinson, and Private Publication* (Columbus: Ohio State University Press, 2010), 84–119.
42. Derrida, *Paper Machine,* 65.
43. Michael Newbury, *Figuring Authorship in Antebellum America* (Stanford: Stanford University Press, 1997), 63; David Dowling, *Capital Letters: Authorship in the Antebellum Literary Market* (Iowa City: University of Iowa Press, 2009), 143.
44. Newbury, *Figuring Authorship,* 76.
45. Sylvia Jenkins Cook, *Working Women, Literary Ladies: The Industrial Revolution and Female Aspiration* (New York: Oxford University Press, 2008), 131.
46. Dowling, *Capital Letters,* 143.
47. Cindy Weinstein, *The Literature of Labor and the Labors of Literature: Allegory in Nineteenth-Century American Fiction* (Cambridge: Cambridge University Press, 1995), 6.
48. Lupton, "The Theory of Paper," 407.
49. Ibid., 408.
50. Dowling, *Capital Letters,* 18, 19.
51. Newbury, *Figuring Authorship,* 65.

2. "What Nots" and the Genres of Magazine Writing

1. *Putnam's Monthly Magazine,* June 1853, 704.

2. Philip H. Brown, January 23, 1855, box 4, folder 29, and Eve Wilder, October 19, 1854, box 9, folder 61, GPP.
3. Several other pieces in *Yankee Doodle* have been attributed to Melville: "The New Planet," July 24, 1847; "On the Sea Serpent," September 11, 1847; "A Short Patent Sermon. According to Blair, the Rhetorician," July 10, 1847; and "View of the Barnum Property," July 31, 1847. "On the Chinese Junk" was a series of thirteen pieces, which appeared between July 17 and September 18, 1847. Melville probably wrote some, but not all, of these short pieces of filler.
4. *Harper's* was organized enough to semi-automate the addressing of each subscription issue: "Subscribers who receive their copies through the mail directly from the Publishers will notice that the address is printed upon each copy. These are all set up in type, and printed on narrow slips of paper. . . . A little machine, hardly as large as an 'apple-parer,' turned by hand, cuts off every address from the long slip, and pastes it on the Magazine." The slip also included the issue number when one's subscription expired. "Making the Magazine," *Harper's New Monthly Magazine,* December 1865, 22.
5. Nathaniel Parker Willis, *Dashes at Life with a Free Pencil* (New York: J. S. Redfield, 1845), 5.
6. The popularity of their work, however, indicates the broader cultural function it served. Maura D'Amore argues that Donald Mitchell, Nathaniel Parker Willis, and Henry Ward Beecher, for instance, "cultivated a masculine domesticity of self-nurture" in their genteel magazine forms, whose purpose was to defend "the boundaries of personhood through domestic modes and activities that bespoke individual dreams and aspirations." Maura D'Amore, *Suburban Plots: Men at Home in Nineteenth-Century American Print Culture* (Amherst: University of Massachusetts Press, 2014), 3–4.
7. Eliza Leslie, *Pencil Sketches; or, Outlines of Character and Manners* (Philadelphia: Carey, Lea & Blanchard, 1833), 13.
8. Catharine Maria Sedgwick, *Tales and Sketches* (Philadelphia: Carey, Lea & Blanchard, 1835), 165, 170, 174, 179.
9. Susan Williams argues that "cacoethes scribendi" was a common discourse for discussing authorship in the nineteenth century, and that it "became a stock way to talk about amateur, unrestrained writing as opposed to professionalized authorship." Williams, *Reclaiming Authorship: Literary Women in America, 1850–1900* (Philadelphia: University of Pennsylvania Press, 2006), 21. In Sedgwick's story, Alice is the only female character to resist the urge to write, but the only one to make it into print. The inference is that having an "itch" is not enough to make one an author.
10. In an early judgment that would affect later critical treatments, Fred Pattee wrote off the 1850s as the undistinguished "Decade after Poe," when the development of the short story stalls during "an orgy of feminine sentimentalism and emotionalism, a half-savage rioting in color and superlatives and fantastic fancies." Fred Lewis Pattee, *The Development of the American Short Story* (New York: Harper & Bros, 1923), 152. It is also worth noting Susan Williams's argument that many women writers were eager to distinguish themselves from their "scribbling" companions. Williams, *Reclaiming Authorship,* 24–29.

11. For more on Child's challenges to time-honored institutions of race and gender, see Carolyn L. Karcher, *The First Woman in the Republic: A Cultural Biography of Lydia Maria Child* (Durham, NC: Duke University Press, 1994).
12. Lydia Maria Child, *Fact and Fiction: A Collection of Stories* (New York: C. S. Francis, 1846), 147.
13. For more on New York's intellectual culture during the 1840s and 1850s, see the classic account in Perry Miller, *The Raven and the Whale: The War of Words and Wits in the Era of Poe* (New York: Harcourt, Brace, 1956); and Edward L. Widmer, *Young America: The Flowering of Democracy in New York City* (New York: Oxford University Press, 1999).
14. Michael Slater, *Charles Dickens: A Life Defined by Writing* (New Haven: Yale University Press, 2009), 474.
15. Eugene Exman, *The Brothers Harper: A Unique Partnership and Its Impact on the Cultural Life of America from 1817–1853* (New York: Harper & Row, 1965), 309.
16. David Marvin Stone, February 6, 1854, box 6, folder 52, and Dr. Theodore Johnson and Dr. Francis Johnson, October 18, 1854, box 2, folder 46, GPP.
17. Kristie Hamilton, *America's Sketchbook: The Cultural Life of a Nineteenth-Century Literary Genre* (Athens: Ohio University Press, 1998), 15.
18. Marvin Fisher, *Going Under: Melville's Short Fiction and the American 1850s* (Baton Rouge: Louisiana State University Press, 1977). A more recent example of this tendency is evident in Timothy Helwig, "Melville's Liminal Bachelor and the Making of Middle-Class Manhood in *Harper's New Monthly Magazine*," *American Periodicals* 24.1 (2014): 1–20. Helwig assumes that *Harper's* was oblivious to Melville's ideological critique of the bachelor persona.
19. For examples from the year Melville first published in *Harper's*, see "Storm and Rest," July 1854, 229–32; "Drunkard's Bible," August 1854, 385–90; "Father and Son," September 1854, 525–31; "Faithful Margaret," October 1854, 659–64.
20. See, respectively, Egbert S. Oliver, "'Cock-a-Doodle-Doo!' and Transcendental Hocus-Pocus," *New England Quarterly* 21.2 (1948): 204–16; William B. Dillingham, *Melville's Short Fiction, 1853–1856* (Athens: University of Georgia Press, 1977), 57–61; Sheila Post-Lauria, *Correspondent Colorings: Melville in the Marketplace* (Amherst: University of Massachusetts Press, 1996), 170.
21. Quoted in Hershel Parker, *Herman Melville: A Biography,* 2 vols. (Baltimore: Johns Hopkins University Press, 1996 and 2002), 2:188.
22. "Blind Man's Wreath," *Harper's New Monthly Magazine,* May 1854, 767.
23. "Better than Diamonds," *Harper's New Monthly Magazine,* March 1853, 501.
24. "The Virginian Canaan," *Harper's New Monthly Magazine,* December 1853, 32–33.
25. "A Word at the Start," *Harper's New Monthly Magazine,* June 1850, 1–2.
26. Melville possibly took his inspiration for the bipartite stories from a book he read on diptych paintings in 1848 and from viewing pictures of this sort during a visit to London in 1849. See Andrew Delbanco, *Melville: His World and His Work* (New York: Knopf, 2005), 224. *Godey's Lady's Book,* to which Melville subscribed, also published stories in this mode. See Post-Lauria, *Correspondent Colorings,* 172–73.
27. Amanpal Garcha, *From Sketch to Novel: The Development of Victorian Fiction* (Cambridge: Cambridge University Press, 2009), 49.
28. James Fenimore Cooper, "Old Ironsides," *Putnam's Monthly Magazine,* May 1853, 473.

29. Francis H. Underwood, March 7, 1853, box 6, folder 70, GPP.
30. Jared Gardner, *The Rise and Fall of Early American Magazine Culture* (Urbana: University of Illinois Press, 2012), 161.
31. *Harper's* printed author details above contributions from its better-known authors. In both *Putnam's* and *Harper's* editorial responsibility remained anonymous. *Harper's* gave original publication details for reprinted material during its first year; thereafter it dropped the credits. Looking back at the change in an August 1877 editorial column, George William Curtis observed: "The attraction of a magazine to the general reader is greater if the contents have the air of being—what, in fact, they really are for him—then and there first published." See John Dowgray, "A History of Harper's Literary Magazines, 1850–1900" (PhD diss., University of Wisconsin, 1956), 69.
32. One caveat: as with "Bartleby," anonymous publication was no guarantee of anonymity. Newspaper gossip, at least for those who read it, revealed Melville as the author of "The Encantadas" in the *New York Evening Post* of February 14. William Cullen Bryant tipped off readers that Melville was awake from the nightmare of *Pierre* and that *Putnam's* was to publish what he described as "a reminiscence of life among a group of islands on the equator." For the attribution of this note to Bryant, see Parker, *Herman Melville,* 2:211. If Bryant, however, was only just noticing that Melville was awake after *Pierre,* then Melville's authorship of "Bartleby" was obviously not widely known following the leaking of his authorship of that story by *The Literary World.*
33. Fisher, *Going Under,* 29.
34. Several interpretations exist of the name Salvator R. Tarnmoor. Salvator R. is understood to refer to Salvator Rosa, the seventeenth-century Italian painter; Tarnmoor is a portmanteau word that condenses Gothic and racial blackness in various ways by juxtaposing "tar," "tarn," and "moor." See Parker, *Herman Melville,* 2:211; Fisher, *Going Under,* 29–30; Denise Tanyol, "The Alternative Taxonomies of Melville's 'The Encantadas,'" *New England Quarterly* 80.2 (2007): 255–56.
35. *The Living Age,* January 10, 1846, 71.
36. "Monthly Record of Current Events," *Harper's New Monthly Magazine,* September 1852, 546.
37. "The Whale Fishery, and American Commerce in the Pacific Ocean," *Friends' Review; A Religious, Literary and Miscellaneous Journal,* September 4, 1852, 807.
38. "A Trip to the Galapagos Islands," *The Pioneer; or, California Monthly Magazine,* February 1854, 97–103; "Facts and Wonders of the Tortoise Family," *The Eclectic Magazine of Foreign Literature,* December 1850, 505–14.
39. Tanyol, "Alternative Taxonomies," 244–45. As Tanyol notes (266–67), whether Melville read Darwin's *Voyage* is a matter of guesswork: the frigate *United States,* on which Melville sailed during 1842–43, held a copy of the book, and Melville bought a copy along with a large number of other books in 1847.
40. Charles Darwin, *Journal of Researches into the Natural History and Geology of the Countries Visited during the Voyage of H.M.S. Beagle Round the World, under the Command of Capt. Fitz Roy, R.N.,* 2nd ed. (London: John Murray, 1845), 505.
41. Hester Blum, *The View from the Masthead: Maritime Imagination and Antebellum American Sea Narratives* (Chapel Hill: University of North Carolina Press, 2008), 155, 157.

42. George William Curtis to J. A. Dix, April 19, 1855, item 42, DEC.
43. Garcha, *From Sketch to Novel,* 35.
44. Washington Irving, *The Sketch-Book of Geoffrey Crayon, Gent.* (Oxford: Oxford University Press, 2009), 292.
45. John Bryant, *Melville and Repose: The Rhetoric of Humor in the American Renaissance* (New York: Oxford University Press, 1993), 69.
46. For more on colonialism in "The Encantadas," see Christopher Freeburg, *Melville and the Idea of Blackness: Race and Imperialism in Nineteenth-Century America* (New York: Cambridge University Press, 2012), 132–64.
47. See Merton M. Sealts Jr., "Did Melville Write 'The Fiddler'?" *Harvard Library Bulletin* 26.1 (1978): 77–80.
48. For examples of this kind of approach, see Fisher, *Going Under,* 146–55; Michael James Collins, "'The Master-Key of Our Theme': Master Betty and the Politics of Theatricality in Herman Melville's 'The Fiddler,'" *Journal of American Studies* 47.3 (2013): 759–76.
49. James A. Maitland, *The Lawyer's Story; or, The Orphan's Wrongs* (New York: H. Long & Brother, 1853), 7.
50. The *Tribune* and the *Times* published the first chapter in the form of a long advertisement for the *Sunday Dispatch,* which serialized the novel every week until May 29, 1853. The story appeared in book form later that year. See Johannes Dietrich Bergmann, "'Bartleby' and *The Lawyer's Story,*" *American Literature* 47.3 (1975): 432–36.
51. *Putnam's Monthly Magazine,* February 1853, 160.
52. *Putnam's Monthly Magazine,* April 1853, 353.
53. See Brian P. Lusky, *On the Make: Clerks and the Quest for Capital in Nineteenth-Century America* (New York: New York University Press, 2010).
54. *Putnam's Monthly Magazine,* January 1853, 1.
55. Ibid., 2.
56. Brian Higgins and Hershel Parker, eds., *Herman Melville: The Contemporary Reviews* (Cambridge: Cambridge University Press, 1995), 473, 472, 479, 483.

3. "Passing Muster" at *Putnam's*

1. George William Curtis to J. A. Dix, June 18, 1855, item 58, DEC; George William Curtis to George Curtis, March 15, 1851, item 25, GWCC; George William Curtis to J. A. Dix, June 19, 1855, item 59, DEC.
2. George William Curtis to J. A. Dix, June 18, 1855, item 58, DEC.
3. Arnold Tew has shown conclusively that "Mr. Law" was Dana and not Frederick Law Olmsted, who invested $5,500 in the magazine in March 1855 when Putnam sold to Dix and Edwards. Arnold G. Tew, "Putnam's Magazine: Its Men and Their Literary and Social Policies" (PhD diss., Case Western Reserve University, 1969), 77–80. Tew's is the most detailed account of the history of *Putnam's Monthly.*
4. George William Curtis to J. A. Dix, June 19, 1855, item 59, DEC. There is no evidence to suggest that Curtis's poems made their way into the pages of *Putnam's.*
5. The circulation of *Harper's* fluctuated, but Frank Luther Mott suggests that after early print runs of 7,500 copies, the magazine was soon up to 50,000 and reached 200,000 just before the Civil War. Mott, *A History of American Magazines,* 5 vols.

(Cambridge: Harvard University Press, 1930–1968), 2:391. For the *Putnam's* figures, see Ezra Greenspan, *George Palmer Putnam: Representative American Publisher* (University Park: Pennsylvania State University Press, 2000), 318, 321.

6. *Putnam's Monthly Magazine,* March 1857, 296.
7. Putnam to Harper & Brothers, December 14, 1853, box 2, folder 17, GPP.
8. George William Curtis to Charles Eliot Norton, May 28, 1853, item 67, GWCC.
9. *Putnam's* was not entirely averse to promoting books and authors from the Putnam stable. In its very first issue, in January 1853, it carried a long review essay of *Homes of American Authors* (23–30), recently published by G. P. Putnam & Co.
10. Sheila Post-Lauria, *Correspondent Colorings: Melville in the Marketplace* (Amherst: University of Massachusetts Press, 1996), 151–209.
11. Greenspan, *George Palmer Putnam,* 295; Meredith McGill, *American Literature and the Culture of Reprinting, 1834–1853* (Philadelphia: University of Pennsylvania Press, 2003), 271.
12. Quoted in Gordon Milne, *George William Curtis and the Genteel Tradition* (Bloomington: Indiana University Press, 1956), 75.
13. J. Henry Harper, *The House of Harper: A Century of Publishing in Franklin Square* (New York: Harper & Brothers, 1912), 101.
14. Mott, *A History of American Magazines,* 2:389.
15. "Our Young Authors," *Putnam's Monthly Magazine,* January 1853, 74–75, 77.
16. *Harper's New Monthly Magazine,* 281.
17. O'Brien's articles and stories for *Harper's* include "A Dead Secret," November 1853, 806–15; "The Bohemian," July 1855, 233–42; "Bird Gossip," November 1855, 820–25; "A Trip to Newfoundland," December 1855, 45–57; "The Dragon-Fang Possessed by the Conjuror Piou-Lu," March 1856, 519–26; "How to Keep Well," December 1856, 56–61; "The Crystal Bell," December 1856, 88–91; and "A Paper of All Sorts," March 1858, 507–15. O'Brien also wrote "The Man about Town" series for *Harper's Weekly.*
18. George William Curtis to Putnam, August 26, 1854, box 1, folder 62, GPP. According to Tew, "The Editor at Large" column was written by Briggs; Wayne Kime suggests the author was O'Brien. See Tew, "Putnam's Magazine," 58; Wayne R. Kime, ed., *Fitz-James O'Brien: Selected Literary Journalism, 1852–1860* (Selinsgrove, PA: Susquehanna University Press, 2003), 126–38.
19. Quoted in Milne, *George William Curtis,* 57.
20. George William Curtis to William Douglas O'Connor, March 9, 1855, item 85, GWCC.
21. George William Curtis to William Douglas O'Connor, March 19 and April 2, 1855, items 87 and 89, GWCC.
22. George William Curtis to William Douglas O'Connor, September 7, 1855, item 99, GWCC.
23. "Making the Magazine," *Harper's New Monthly Magazine,* December 1865, 21.
24. George William Curtis to William Douglas O'Connor, January 15, 1856, item 107, GWCC.
25. Quoted in Beryl Rowland, "Grace Church and Melville's Story of 'The Two Temples,'" *Nineteenth-Century Fiction* 28.3 (1973): 339–46. Melville climbed Trinity's church steeple with his brother-in-law Lemuel Shaw Jr. on January 18, 1848. See *PT* 701.
26. "New-York Church Architecture," *Putnam's Monthly Magazine,* September 1853, 234.

27. Perry Miller, *The Raven and the Whale: The War of Words and Wits in the Era of Poe* (New York: Harcourt, Brace, 1956), 53.
28. *Broadway Journal,* March 8, 1845, 153.
29. Quoted in Betty Weidman, "Charles Frederick Briggs: A Critical Biography" (PhD diss., Columbia University, 1968), 109.
30. Quoted ibid., 212.
31. Charles Frederick Briggs, *The Trippings of Tom Pepper* (New York: Burgess, Stringer & Co., 1847), 71.
32. Charles Frederick Briggs, *Bankrupt Stories, Edited by Harry Franco* (New York: John Allen, 1843), 61. *The Haunted Merchant,* parts of which originally appeared in the *Knickerbocker,* was the first volume in an envisaged series of "Bankrupt Stories." No other volumes followed.
33. James T. Fields to George Palmer Putnam, November 7, 1853, box 1, folder 87, GPP.
34. James Russell Lowell, *The Poetical Works of James R. Lowell: Volume II* (Boston: Ticknor & Fields, 1863), 70.
35. John Dowgray, "A History of Harper's Literary Magazines, 1850–1900" (PhD diss., University of Wisconsin, 1956), 24.
36. "Advertisement," *Harper's New Monthly Magazine,* vol. II, December 1850–May 1851, ii.
37. Jennifer Phegley, "Literary Piracy, Nationalism, and Women Readers in *Harper's New Monthly Magazine,* 1850–1855," *American Periodicals* 14.1 (2004): 66.
38. Thomas Lilly, "The National Archive: Harper's New Monthly Magazine and the Civic Responsibilities of a Commercial Literary Periodical, 1850–1853," *American Periodicals* 15.2 (2005): 149.
39. *Harper's New Monthly Magazine,* September 1859, 519–37. Fletcher Harper rejected Horace Greely's offer to respond: "We published Senator Douglas's article because it was an exposition of an important phase of the political history of the country, prepared by a statesman whose experience of territorial jurisprudence has been large, and whose leadership of an influential political party is undoubted. Should the recognized leaders of the Republican or the Southern Parties think fit to prepare similar expositions of the same historical question, from their respective points of view, we should probably be willing to publish them in the periodical which contained the article of Senator Douglas." Quoted in Harper, *House of Harper,* 136.
40. "Making the Magazine," *Harper's New Monthly Magazine,* December 1865, 21, 22. The dedication to simultaneity was such, Guernsey writes, that "where several customers reside in the same city special care is taken that the supplies for all shall go by the same conveyance, so that no one shall have any advantage over another" (22).
41. "New-York Daguerreotyped," *Putnam's Monthly Magazine,* February 1853, 121. The first two articles on "Business-Streets, Mercantile Blocks, Stores, and Banks" appeared in *Putnam's* in February 1853, 121–37, and April 1853, 353–69. Others in the series were "Benevolent Institutions of New York," June 1853, 673–91; "Educational Institutions of New York," July 1853, 1–17; "New-York Church Architecture," September 1853, 233–49; and "Private Residences," March 1854, 233–48.
42. Dennis Berthold, "Class Acts: The Astor Place Riots and Melville's 'The Two Temples,'" *American Literature* 71.3 (1999): 441, 446.
43. Miller, *The Raven and the Whale,* 316.

44. This decision caused some editorial disagreement. Curtis wrote to Charles Eliot Norton that "Briggs was opposed, not because it was not good, but he thought it rather pointless for a magazine article. Godwin & I liked it very much, & differed with the good B. We, of course, carried the day." George William Curtis to Charles Eliot Norton, April 20, 1853, item 65, GWCC.
45. Partnership Documents, March 1 and April 2, 1855, item 206, DEC.
46. Partnership Documents, May 1, 1856, item 206, DEC.
47. George William Curtis to J. A. Dix, April 17, 19, and 20, 1855, and July 31, 1855, items 41–43 and 79, DEC.
48. George William Curtis to J. A. Dix, January 2, 1856, and September 7, 1855, items 97 and 89, DEC.
49. Russ Castronovo, "Radical Configurations of History in the Era of American Slavery," *American Literature* 65.3 (1993): 525, 538, 540. Ivy G. Wilson also argues that Melville's allusions to slavery "ultimately divulge how racialized slavery could not but permeate his consciousness" and that in the story "ante-bellum America surfaces in the tale as a concomitant critique of the vicissitudes of U.S. nationalism." Wilson, "'No Soul Above': Labor and the 'Law in Art' in Melville's 'The Bell-Tower,'" *Arizona Quarterly* 63.1 (2007): 30.
50. Nathaniel Hawthorne, *The Blithedale Romance and Fanshawe*, ed. William Charvat and others, vol. 3 of *The Centenary Edition of the Works of Nathaniel Hawthorne* (Columbus: Ohio State University Press, 1964), 3.
51. George William Curtis to William Douglas O'Connor, January 16, 1856, item 107, GWCC.
52. "Sea from Shore," *Putnam's Monthly Magazine,* July 1854, 47.
53. George Santayana, "The Genteel Tradition in American Philosophy" (1911), in *Essential Santayana: Selected Writings,* ed. Martin A. Coleman (Bloomington: Indiana University Press, 2009), 527.
54. Wilfred M. McClay, "Two Versions of the Genteel Tradition: Santayana and Brooks," *New England Quarterly* 55.3 (1982): 368. It should be noted that Curtis did manage to outrage his father's tastes with his portraits of Syrian women.
55. F. O. Matthiessen, *American Renaissance: Art and Expression in the Age of Emerson and Whitman* (1941; repr., London: Oxford University Press, 1968), 485.
56. "Our Authors and Authorship: Melville and Curtis," *Putnam's Monthly Magazine,* April 1857, 384, 389–90, 392, 393.
57. Godwin's key essays for *Putnam's* included "Our New President," September 1853, 301–11; "Our Party and Politics," September 1854, 233–47; "What Impression Do We and Should We Make Abroad," October 1853, 345–54; "American Despotisms," December 1854, 624–32; "Secret Societies—The Know Nothings," January 1855, 88–97; "The Kansas Question," October 1855, 425–36; "The Real Question," April 1856, 428–35; and "The Political Aspect," July 1856, 85–95. For more on the political nature of *Putnam's* during this period see Tew, "Putnam's Magazine," 255–73.
58. Milne, *George William Curtis,* 104–5.
59. "Our Authors and Authorship," 393.
60. George William Curtis, *The Duty of the American Scholar to Politics and the Times: An Oration, Delivered on Tuesday, August 5, 1856, before the Literary Societies of Wesleyan University, Middletown, Conn.* (New York: Dix & Edwards, 1856), 7, 8, 45, 17, 20.
61. George William Curtis to J. A. Dix, July 31, 1855, item 79, DEC.

62. Maurice S. Lee, "Melville's Subversive Political Philosophy: 'Benito Cereno' and the Fate of Speech," *American Literature* 72.3 (2000): 500.
63. For more on Brockden Brown and the picturesque, see Dennis Berthold, "Charles Brockden Brown, *Edgar Huntly,* and the Origins of the American Picturesque," *William and Mary Quarterly* 41.1 (1984): 62–84.
64. See Angela Miller, *The Empire of the Eye: Landscape Representation and American Cultural Politics, 1825–1875* (Ithaca: Cornell University Press, 1993). Samuel Otter argues that the depiction of Saddle Meadows in *Pierre* shows how "the antebellum ideology of the imperative landscape compelled and incarcerated." Otter, *Melville's Anatomies* (Berkeley: University of California Press, 1999), 177. Larry Kutchen argues that *Pierre* is a "stunning deconstruction . . . of the picturesque as imperialist aesthetic that concealed the dark legacies of revolutionary violence." Kutchen, "The 'Vulgar Thread of the Canvas': Revolution and the Picturesque in Ann Eliza Bleecker, Crèvecoeur, and Charles Brockden Brown," *Early American Literature* 36.3 (2001): 420.
65. Castronovo, "Radical Configurations of History," 541.
66. "Our Young Authors—Melville," *Putnam's Monthly Magazine,* February 1853, 163, 164. For more on Browne's influence on Melville's work from *Mardi* onward, see Brian Foley, "Herman Melville and the Example of Sir Thomas Browne," *Modern Philology* 81.3 (1984): 265–77.
67. Wayne R. Kime, "'The Bell-Tower': Melville's Reply to a Review," *ESQ: A Journal of the American Renaissance* 22.1 (1976): 28–38.
68. Ibid., 37.
69. See, for instance, in *Harper's,* "The Return of Pope Pius IX to Rome," June 1850, 90–95; "Clara Corsini—A Tale of Naples," December 1851, 68–75; "The Italian Sisters," January 1854, 148–55; "Studies for a Picture of Venice," July 1854, 186–96; "Visits to the Dead in the Catacombs of Rome," April 1855, 577–600; "A Reminiscence of Rome," November 1857, 740–45. *Putnam's* published several poems with Italian settings, including "Ode to Southern Italy," July 1853, 23–25; "Songs of Venice," January 1853, 22–23; "Galgano," May 1853, 512–17.
70. George William Curtis, *Nile Notes of a Howadji* (New York: Harper & Brothers, 1852), 15.
71. Ida Rothschild, "Reframing Melville's 'Manifesto': 'Hawthorne and His Mosses' and the Culture of Reprinting," *Cambridge Quarterly* 41.3 (2012): 318–44.
72. "Authors and Authorship," 384.
73. Castronovo, "Radical Configurations of History," 525.

4. The "Unbounded Treasures" of Magazine Paratexts

1. Gérard Genette, *Paratexts: Thresholds of Interpretation,* trans. Jane E. Lewin (Cambridge: Cambridge University Press, 1997), 1.
2. Gérard Genette, *Palimpsests: Literature in the Second Degree,* trans. Channa Newman and Claude Doubinsky (Lincoln: University of Nebraska Press 1997), 4.
3. *Putnam's Monthly Magazine,* March 1854, 318.
4. Ryan Cordell, "'Taken Possession of': The Reprinting and Reauthorship of Hawthorne's 'Celestial Railroad' in the Antebellum Religious Press," *Digital Humanities Quarterly* 7.1 (2013), www.digitalhumanities.org.

5. It is worth noting that for Genette, paratexuality and intertextuality are both subcategories of a larger process of transtextuality, which is "all that sets the text in a relationship, whether obvious or concealed, with other texts." Genette, *Palimpsests,* 1.
6. *Harper's New Monthly Magazine,* June 1850, 1.
7. When the novel was published in book form, Melville changed the title to *Israel Potter: His Fifty Years of Exile.* The change from "; or," to ": His" appears small, but by weakening the integration of title and subtitle Melville changes the reader's perspective. Thus in the magazine title the fifty years of exile are another way of revealing what happens to Israel and less a subtitle than an indication of theme and Israel's own perspective; the colon and the "His" of the book title put Israel at one remove and indicate a third-person, authorial perspective on those years. The magazine version also has a further subtitle indicating theme: "A Fourth of July Story." This is missing entirely from the book version. For more on the function of titles and subtitles, see Genette, *Paratexts,* 55–103.
8. Hershel Parker, *Herman Melville: A Biography,* 2 vols. (Baltimore: Johns Hopkins University Press, 1996 and 2002), 2:216.
9. Thomas Mayo Brewer to George Palmer Putnam; December 27, 1852, box 7, folder 27, GPP.
10. "The American Association for the Advancement of Science," *Putnam's Monthly Magazine,* September 1853, 321–22.
11. Theodore Ledyard Cuyler, *Recollections of a Long Life: An Autobiography* (New York: Baker & Taylor, 1902), 10. For more on Henry's teaching of Melville, see Meredith Farmer, "Herman Melville and Joseph Henry at the Albany Academy; or Melville's Education in Mathematics and Science," *Leviathan* 18.2 (2016): 4–28
12. Joshua Matthews, "Peddlers of the Rod: Melville's 'The Lightning-Rod Man' and the Antebellum Periodical Market," *Leviathan* 12.3 (2010): 58.
13. Allan Moore Emery, "Melville on Science: 'The Lightning-Rod Man,'" *New England Quarterly* 56.4 (1983): 567.
14. For more on the rise of spiritualism in this period, and the reasons behind it, see Bret E. Carrol, *Spiritualism in Antebellum America* (Bloomington: Indiana University Press, 1997); Molly McGarry, *Ghosts of Futures Past: Spiritualism and the Cultural Politics of Nineteenth-Century America* (Berkeley: University of California Press, 2008).
15. Genette, *Paratexts,* 2.
16. Jay Leyda, "Notes," in *The Complete Stories of Herman Melville* (New York: Random House, 1949), xxvi–xxvii; Michael T. Gilmore, *The Middle Way: Puritanism and Ideology in American Romantic Fiction* (New Brunswick, NJ: Rutgers University Press, 1977), 9; William Dillingham, *Melville's Short Fiction, 1853–1856* (Athens: University of Georgia Press, 1977), 177.
17. "Spiritual Materialism," *Putnam's Monthly Magazine,* August 1854, 158, 160, 159, 164.
18. *The Literary World,* March 16, 1850, 276.
19. "Spiritual Materialism," 163.
20. Cathy Gutierrez, *Plato's Ghost: Spiritualism in the American Renaissance* (New York: Oxford University Press, 2009), 45–75.
21. Ethnology attracted Melville's attention before "The 'Gees." Samuel Otter shows how *Moby-Dick* takes up ethnology's fascination with the examination and classification of the human body. In contrast to the ethnological primal scene of visual penetration, according to Otter, Melville "suggests an epistemology of the body

based on . . . contact between individuals." Otter, *Melville's Anatomies* (Berkeley: University of California Press, 1999), 101.

22. Parker, *Herman Melville,* 1:354–55.
23. "Is Man One or Many?" *Putnam's Monthly Magazine,* July 1854, 1–14.
24. Carolyn L. Karcher, "Melville's 'The 'Gees': A Forgotten Satire on Scientific Racism," *American Quarterly* 27.4 (1975): 425.
25. Ibid., 439–40.
26. *Putnam's Monthly Magazine,* March 1853, 338.
27. "Is Man One or Many?" 5, 14.
28. Frederick Douglass, *The Claims of the Negro Ethnologically Considered* (Rochester, NY: Lee, Mann & Co., 1854), 28, 16.
29. "Are All Men Descended from Adam?" *Putnam's Monthly Magazine,* January 1855, 87.
30. For more on the relationship between science and religion at this moment, see G. Blair Nelson, "'Men Before Adam': American Debates over the Ubiquity and Antiquity of Humanity," in *When Science and Christianity Meet,* ed. David C. Lindberg and Ronald L. Numbers (Chicago: University of Chicago Press, 2003), 161–82.
31. "Editor's Table," *Harper's New Monthly Magazine,* September 1854, 548, 549.
32. "Editor's Table," *Harper's New Monthly Magazine,* October 1854, 687, 688, 690.
33. T. Addison Richards, "The Juniata," *Harper's New Monthly Magazine,* March 1856, 440.
34. "Commodore Perry's Expedition to Japan," *Harper's New Monthly Magazine,* March 1856, 450.
35. "Passages of Eastern Travel," *Harper's New Monthly Magazine,* March 1856, 485.
36. These articles include, for example, "Tunnel of the Alps," June 1850, 77; "Greenwich Weather-Wisdom," July 1850, 265–69; "Borax Lagoons of Tuscany," August 1850, 397–400; "The Railway Works at Crewe," August 1850, 408–11; "Steam-Bridge of the Atlantic," August 1850, 411–14; "The Crystal Palace," April 1851, 584–88; Jacob Abbott, "The Novelty Works," May 1851, 721–34; "How Gunpowder Is Made," April 1852, 643–47; "Galvanoplasty," November 1854, 811–14; Elias Loomis, "Astronomical Observatories in the United States," June 1856, 25–52.
37. "Editor's Table," September 1854, 549.
38. Brian Higgins and Hershel Parker, eds., *Herman Melville: The Contemporary Reviews* (Cambridge: Cambridge University Press, 1995), 472.
39. Peter Coviello describes this as a "sentimental logic of equivalence" and argues that "Benito Cereno" has a "withering regard for such a vision of harmonious mutual legibility." Coviello, "The American in Charity: 'Benito Cereno' and Gothic Anti-Sentimentality," *Studies in American Fiction* 30.2 (2002): 165.

5. Melville's "Pilfering Disposition"

1. Washington Irving, *The Sketch-Book of Geoffrey Crayon, Gent.* (Oxford: Oxford University Press, 2009), 69, 70, 71.
2. David S. Reynolds, *Beneath the American Renaissance: The Subversive Imagination in the Age of Emerson and Melville* (New York: Alfred A. Knopf, 1988), 7, 9.
3. Mary K. Bercaw Edwards, *Melville's Sources* (Evanston, IL: Northwestern University Press, 1987), 27.

4. John Bryant, *Melville Unfolding: Sexuality, Politics, and the Versions of "Typee"* (Ann Arbor: University of Michigan Press, 2008), 221, 222.
5. For more on the problem of determining the composition of *Moby-Dick,* see *MD* 648–59; Edwards, *Melville's Sources,* 24–27.
6. *Israel Potter* is something of a hybrid. For the sections involving John Paul Jones, Melville relied on Robert C. Sands's *Life and Correspondence of John Paul Jones* (1830) and John Henry Sherburne's *Life and Character of the Chevalier John Paul Jones* (1825), while chapters 22 and 23 draw on Ethan Allen's autobiographical *A Narrative of Colonel Ethan Allen's Captivity,* first published in 1779 and reprinted several times in the nineteenth century.
7. Robert Macfarlane, *Original Copy: Plagiarism and Originality in Nineteenth-Century Literature* (Oxford: Oxford University Press, 2007), 8.
8. For the biographical impact on Melville of a literary culture where borrowing and appropriation are endemic, see Ellen Weinauer, "Plagiarism and the Proprietary Self: Policing the Boundaries of Authorship in Herman Melville's 'Hawthorne and his Mosses,'" *American Literature* 69.4 (1997): 697–717.
9. Bryant, *Melville Unfolding,* 228.
10. For a defense of the position that plagiarism has always been a transhistorical literary crime, see Christopher Ricks, *Allusion to the Poets* (Oxford: Oxford University Press, 2002).
11. Nina Baym, "Melville's Quarrel with Fiction," *PMLA* 94.5 (1979): 910, 920.
12. Meredith L. McGill, *American Literature and the Culture of Reprinting, 1834–1853* (Philadelphia: University of Pennsylvania Press, 2003), 5. For McGill, *Wheaton v. Peters* was significant because it established "going-into-print as the moment when individual rights give way to the demands of the social" and defined "the private ownership of a printed text as the temporary alienation of public property" (45–46). Rather than hastening the arrival of a modern understanding of authorship in which literary property rights belong to the individual, *Wheaton v. Peters* subordinated individual rights to the interests of the public and the state. Ryan Cordell takes McGill's argument about authors and texts one step further to imagine the virtual figure of the "network author," who "accounts for the ways in which meaning and authority accrued to acts of circulation and aggregation across antebellum newspapers." Cordell, "Reprinting, Circulation, and the Network Author in Antebellum Newspapers," *American Literary History* 27.3 (2015): 418.
13. Irving, *Sketch-Book,* 72.
14. For more on the prehistory, success, and decline of the magazine novel, see Jared Gardner, "Serial Fiction and the Novel," in *The American Novel, 1870–1940,* ed. Priscilla Wald and Michael A. Elliott (New York: Oxford University Press, 2014), 289–303. Patricia Okker examines how the production and consumption of magazine serials helped shape communal identity in *Social Stories: The Magazine Novel in Nineteenth-Century America* (Charlottesville: University of Virginia Press, 2003); while Michael Lund provides a full, although not complete, list of novels published in serial form in *America's Continuing Story: An Introduction to Serial Fiction, 1850–1900* (Detroit: Wayne State University Press, 1993).
15. For interpretations of *Israel Potter* that emphasize its ideologically progressive or subversive terms, see Gale Temple, "*Israel Potter:* Sketch Patriotism," *Leviathan* 11.1 (2009): 3–18; Joshua Tendler, "A Monument Upon a Hill: Antebellum

Commemoration Culture, the Here-and-Now, and Democratic Citizenship in Melville's Israel Potter," *Studies in American Fiction* 42.1 (2015): 29–50.

16. David Chacko and Alexander Kulcsar, "Israel Potter: Genesis of a Legend," *William and Mary Quarterly* 41.3 (1984): 367. Chacko and Kulcsar reconstruct the real life of Israel Potter in *Beggarman, Spy: The Secret Life and Times of Israel Potter* (Cedarburg, WI: Foremost Press, 2010). They have also fictionalized Potter's life in *Gone Over* (Cedarburg, WI: Foremost Press, 2009) and *The Brimstone Papers* (Cedarburg, WI: Foremost Press, 2010).
17. *Putnam's Monthly Magazine,* May 1855, 548.
18. George William Curtis to William Douglas O'Connor, March 19, 1855, item 87, GWCC.
19. Robert S. Levine, "The Revolutionary Aesthetics of *Israel Potter,*" in *Melville and Aesthetics,* ed. Samuel Otter and Geoffrey Sanborn (New York: Palgrave Macmillan, 2011), 167.
20. Ibid., 170.
21. Henry Trumbull, *Life and Remarkable Adventures of Israel R. Potter* (Providence, RI: Henry Trumbull, 1824), 15.
22. Hershel Parker, *Herman Melville: A Biography,* 2 vols. (Baltimore: Johns Hopkins University Press, 1996 and 2002), 2:243.
23. Levine, "Revolutionary Aesthetics," 160.
24. John Thomas Smith, *The Cries of London: Exhibiting Several of the Itinerant Traders of Antient and Modern Times* (London: J. B. Nichols & Son, 1839), 53.
25. Tzvetan Todorov, "The Typology of Detective Fiction," in *The Poetics of Prose,* trans. Richard Howard (Oxford: Blackwell, 1977), 47.
26. Robert S. Levine, *Conspiracy and Romance: Studies in Brockden Brown, Cooper, Hawthorne, and Melville* (Cambridge: Cambridge University Press, 1989), 198.
27. See Barbara Foley, "From Wall Street to Astor Place: Historicizing Melville's 'Bartleby,'" *American Literature* 72.1 (2000): 87–116; and Dennis Berthold, "Class Acts: The Astor Pace Riots and Melville's 'The Two Temples,'" *American Literature* 71.3 (1999): 429–61.
28. Levine, *Conspiracy and Romance,* 191, 197.
29. Amasa Delano, *A Narrative of Voyages and Travels in the Northern and Southern Hemispheres: Comprising Three Voyages Round the World; Together with a Voyage of Survey and Discovery, in the Pacific Ocean and Oriental Islands* (Boston: E. G. House, 1817), 318, 320.
30. Ibid., 320, 321–322.
31. Todorov, "Typology of Detective Fiction," 47.
32. Trish Loughran, "Reading in the Present Tense: *Benito Cereno* and the Time of Reading," in *American Literature's Aesthetic Dimensions,* ed. Cindy Weinstein and Christopher Looby (New York: Columbia University Press, 2012), 230, 230–31. Loughran repeats a mistake that Alma MacDougall corrected almost thirty years before: George William Curtis did not warn Joshua Dix "away from publishing *Benito Cereno* as a freestanding novel" (ibid., 228) when he wrote to him advising that he "decline any novel from Melville that is not extremely good." The book about which Dix consulted him was *The Confidence-Man.* See Alma A. MacDougall, "The Chronology of *The Confidence-Man* and 'Benito Cereno': Redating Two 1855 Curtis and Melville Letters," *Melville Society Extracts,* no. 53 (February 1983): 3–6.

33. Charles Swann, "Whodunnit? Or, Who Did What? *Benito Cereno* and the Politics of Narrative Structure," in *American Studies in Transition,* ed. David E. Nye and Christen Kold Thomsen (Odense: Odense University Press, 1985), 210.
34. George William Curtis to J. A. Dix, April 19, 1855, item 43, DEC.
35. Catherine Toal, "'Some Things Which Could Never Have Happened': Fiction, Identification, and 'Benito Cereno,'" *Nineteenth-Century Literature* 61.1 (2006): 33.

Conclusion

1. Dan McCall, *The Silence of Bartleby* (Ithaca: Cornell University Press, 1989), x.
2. For full details of known reprintings of Hawthorne's stories, see George Monteiro, "Fugitive Periodical Printings of Nathaniel Hawthorne," *Nathaniel Hawthorne Review* 37.1 (2011): 143–55.
3. George William Curtis to J. A. Dix, June 29, 1855, item 35, DEC. For confirmation of the date of this letter see Alma A. MacDougall, "The Chronology of *The Confidence-Man* and 'Benito Cereno': Redating Two 1855 Curtis and Melville Letters," *Melville Society Extracts,* no. 53 (February 1983): 3–6.
4. Frederick L. Olmsted to J. A. Dix, September 4, 1856, item 184, DEC.
5. Quoted in Arnold G. Tew, "Putnam's Magazine: Its Men and Their Literary and Social Policies" (PhD diss., Case Western Reserve University, 1969), 117. The published works included S. C. Smith, *Chile Con Carne*; Frederic Townsend, *Glimpses of Nineveh* (excerpts of which appeared in *Putnam's*); T. H. Gladstone, *The Englishman in Kansas*; and M. Field, *Rural Architecture.*
6. Tew, "Putnam's Magazine," 118.
7. Rossiter Johnson, ed., *Little Classics* (Boston: James R. Osgood and Co., 1875), iii, iv.
8. Edmund C. Stedman and Ellen Hutchinson, eds., *A Library of American Literature from the Earliest Settlement to the Present Time, Volume 1* (New York: Charles L. Webster & Co., 1887), v.
9. Ibid., viii.
10. Rita Felski, *The Limits of Critique* (Chicago: Chicago University Press, 2015), 161.
11. Wai-Chee Dimock, "A Theory of Resonance," *PMLA* 112.5 (1997): 1062.
12. From Melville's marginalia on his copy of John Milton's *Paradise Regained,* quoted in Hershel Parker, *Herman Melville: A Biography,* 2 vols. (Baltimore: Johns Hopkins University Press, 1996 and 2002), 2:162.
13. "Editor's Study," *Harper's Monthly Magazine,* October 1888, 800.

Index